Recollections

of

Rear Admiral Henry L. Miller,
U. S. Navy (Retired)

Volume I

U. S. Naval Institute
Annapolis, Maryland
1973.

Preface

Volume one of the recollections of Rear Admiral Henry L. Miller, USN (Retired), covers four interviews beginning in March 1971. They were obtained by John T. Mason, Jr., Director of Oral History for the U. S. Naval Institute. They encompass the Admiral's active Naval career from the date of his graduation in 1934 to the assumption of duties on the staff of CINCPAC in 1962. The researcher is advised that they incorporate a wealth of material on Naval Aviation, ranging from the Admiral's early assignment to train the B-17 pilots chosen to take off from the deck of the USS *Hornet* for the raid on Tokyo (1942), to his command of CARDIV 15 -- the anti-submarine Hunter-Killer Task Group in the Pacific (1961).

The second volume of recollections will follow shortly and will include in the appendix certain documents of interest to the student of Naval Aviation.

Admiral Miller has corrected the transcript taken from the tapes and it has been re-typed. A comprehensive subject index is added for the benefit of the user.

REAR ADMIRAL HENRY LOUIS MILLER, UNITED STATES NAVY, RETIRED

A native of Fairbanks, Alaska, our 49th state, Admiral Miller entered the U. S. Naval Academy on appointment from Alaska in July 1930. He was graduated with the Class of 1934, was designated Naval Aviator at the Naval Air Station, Pensacola, in June 1938, and subsequently completed the Bombardiers' Course at Sandia Base and the All Weather Flight Course at Corpus Christi, Texas.

His early service included three years' duty at sea in the battleship TEXAS and engineering and gunnery duties in Fighting Squadron 3, based on the aircraft carrier SARATOGA. From November 1940 until October 1942 he was a Flight Instructor and Personnel Officer at the Naval Air Station, Ellyson Field, Florida, and while there during the early period of World War II, trained General Jimmy Doolittle's "Tokyo Raiders" in carrier take-offs, then accompanied them to within 700 miles of their destination, on board the USS HORNET in April 1942.

From November 1942 to May 1944 he commanded Air Group 23, based on the USS PRINCETON, and during the remainder of the war had command of Air Group 6, based on the USS HANCOCK. He was "recalled" from an air strike on Tokyo when hostilities ceased in August 1945. For World War II service he holds the Legion of Merit with Combat "V"; the Distinguished Flying Cross with four Gold Stars in lieu of additional awards; the Air Medal with five Gold Stars; the Army Commendation Ribbon; and the Navy Unit Commendation Ribbon (USS HANCOCK).

He had duty in the Navy Department during the period December 1945 until July 1948, first assigned to writing Air Operations Instructions, later serving as Executive Officer, Air Branch, Office of Naval Research. For two years he served as Public Information Officer on the Staff of Commander in Chief, Atlantic Fleet, and from June 1950 to August 1952 served successively as Executive Officer of Composite Squadron 7, and of the USS LEYTE (CV-32).

After graduation from the Industrial College of the Armed Forces in July 1953, he returned to the Office of the Chief of Naval Operations for a tour of duty in the Strategic Plans Division. In August 1955 he assumed command of the U. S. Naval Station, Sangley Point, Luzon, P. I., and on September 1, that year, became Commander Fleet Air, Philippines, and Commander Naval Air Bases, Philippines. Relieved of this "3 hat" job in May 1957, he became Assistant Director, later Director, of the Progress Analysis Group, Office of the Chief of Naval Operations. In January 1959 he assumed command of the USS HANCOCK.

Selected for Rear Admiral, July 22, 1959, he reported on March 3, 1960 as Chief of Staff and Aide to the Commander Naval Air Force, Pacific. He commanded Carrier Division FIFTEEN, an Anti-Submarine Hunter-Killer Task Group, from May 1961 to June 1962. He served as Assistant

R. Adm. H. L. Miller, USN, Ret.

Chief of Staff for Plans, Joint Staff, Commander in Chief, Pacific, during the time when the situation in S. E. Asia began to escalate. In September 1964 he assumed command of Carrier Division THREE, a Heavy Attack Carrier Task Group, and at the same time took command of Task Force, 77, the Carrier Striking Force of the SEVENTH Fleet.

In February 1965, as CTF 77 he launched the first of a succession of aircraft carrier strikes on North Vietnam from the decks of the USSs RANGER, CORAL SEA and HANCOCK. He was awarded a Gold Star in lieu of the Second Legion of Merit "for exceptionally meritorious conduct...as Commander Attack Carrier Striking Force SEVENTH Fleet (CTF-77) for the period from September 24, 1964 to March 17, 1965..." In October of 1965, he took the nuclear powered Task Group, the USS ENTERPRISE and USS BAINBRIDGE from Norfolk, Virginia to Subic Bay, P. I., and subsequently on December 2, 1965, he engaged the first nuclear powered Task Force in combat with the enemy in Vietnam.

On April 13, 1966 he became Chief of Information, Navy Department and "for exceptionally meritorious conduct..." in that capacity was awarded a Gold Star in lieu of the Third Legion of Merit. In October 1968 he reported as Commander Naval Air Test Center, Patuxent River, Maryland, with additional duty as Commander Fleet Air, Patuxent River and Naval Air Systems Command Test and Evaluation Coordinator. Again awarded the Legion of Merit (Gold Star in lieu of the Fourth), he was cited for "...his coordination of resources among testing activities, (as a result of which) over 100 aircraft previously assigned for other purposes were returned to the fleet or retired from service..." He served as such until relieved of active duty pending his retirement, effective September 1, 1971.

5 January 1972

REAR ADMIRAL HENRY LOUIS MILLER, UNITED STATES NAVY, RETIRED

PERSONAL DATA:

Born: Fairbanks, Alaska; July 18, 1912
Mother: Mrs. Mary Miller
Wife: Lucille Dean of Opp, Alabama
Children: Henry Louis Miller, Jr. and Richard Brian Miller
Official Address: Fairbanks, Alaska
Education: Drews Preparatory School, San Francisco, California; U. S. Naval Academy (BS, 1934); Naval Air Station, Pensacola, Florida (NA, 1938); Bombardiers' Course, Sandia Base; All Weather Flight Course, Corpus Christi, Texas; Industrial College of the Armed Forces (1952-1953)

PROMOTIONS:

Commissioned Ensign, May 31, 1934
Lieutenant (jg), 1937
Lieutenant, 1940
Lieutenant Commander, 1943
Commander, 1944
Captain to date from July 1, 1953
Rear Admiral to date from July 1, 1960

DECORATIONS AND MEDALS:

Legion of Merit, with Combat "V" and three Gold Stars
Distinguished Flying Cross, with four Gold Stars
Bronze Star Medal With Combat "V"
Air Medal, with five Gold Stars
Army Commendation Ribbon
Navy Unit Commendation (USS HANCOCK)
American Defense Service Medal
American Campaign Medal
Asiatic-Pacific Campaign Medal, with nine battle stars
World War II Victory Medal
Navy Occupation Service Medal, Asia Clasp
National Defense Service Medal with bronze star
Vietnam Service Medal with three stars
Republic of Vietnam Campaign Medal with Device
National Order of Vietnam Fourth Class with Rosette
Republic of Vietnam Cross of Gallantry Army Level with Bronze Palm

CITATIONS:

Legion of Merit: "For exceptionally meritorious conduct...in connection with the bombing of Tokyo by American forces, April 1942. Assigned the distinctive task of training pilots in special technique for

R. Adm. H. L. Miller, USN, Ret.

this daring and hazardous flight, Lieutenant Miller fulfilled his important mission with tireless energy, remarkable initiative and a high standard of achievement..."

Gold Star in lieu of the Second Legion of Merit: "For exceptionally meritorious conduct...as Commander Attack Carrier Striking Force SEVENTH Fleet (CTF-77) for the period from September 24, 1964 to March 17, 1965. In his capacity as Task Force Commander, Rear Admiral Miller has been personally responsible for the activities of SEVENTH Fleet attack carriers...Rear Admiral Miller, through his exceptional leadership, personal aggressiveness and professional knowledge, has drawn together all the myriad of details associated with conducting complex attack carrier operations...He developed highly effective procedures which contributed in large measure to the successful strikes (in Southeast Asia). He has responded to commitments that were accomplished by an organization inspired by superb leadership. The highly successful air strikes of February 7 and 11, 1965, in North Vietnam were the culmination of many months of difficult operations, training and constantly maintained readiness. The reprisal strikes against Dong Hoi staging area ordered by the President were delivered within twelve hours of the initial attacks against U. S. forces in South Vietnam. The successful response to the challenge was made possible by the exemplary planning, coordination, dedication and professional skill of Rear Admiral Miller. The capability of the forces under Rear Admiral Miller to change plans rapidly with minimal notification and with no apparent degradation of effectiveness is praiseworthy and indicative of the superlative state of training and readiness which existed throughout his command..."

Gold Star in lieu of the Third Legion of Merit: "For exceptionally meritorious conduct...as Chief of Information from April 1966 to October 1968. Rear Admiral Miller brought to this assignment an exceptional awareness of the importance of improving the Navy's public image in connection with combat operations in Southeast Asia. As the tempo of operations in Vietnam increased, coupled with incidents of international significance elsewhere in the world, he gave his personal attention to strengthening and maintaining constant liaison and coordination between his office and other agencies of the Department of Defense and the civilian community resulting in enhanced cooperation which has been of great mutual benefit (He) has been aggressive in promoting the positive approach in all areas leading to an increased understanding of the vital role of Naval Forces not only within the Department of Defense but more importantly by the American people. Additionally, he conceived and initiated a daily summary of Vietnam news appearing in the national press which is provided to all units deployed to Western Pacific. This has proved to be a significant morale incentive. (He) has displayed outstanding skill, perseverance, and extraordinary devotion to duty in promoting the Navy's image. The effectiveness of the above and other programs which he has initiated is already apparent and their continuance will result in many benefits as yet unforeseen..."

R. Adm. H. L. Miller, USN, Ret.

Bronze Star Medal: "For meritorious service from October 21, 1965 through February 16, 1966 as Commander Attack Carrier Striking Group SEVENTY-SEVEN POINT SEVEN of the SEVENTH Fleet. During this period, Rear Admiral Miller introduced the first nuclear-powered surface ships into combat operations and for extended periods was the officer in tactical command of air-strike and support operations conducted in North and South Vietnam by SEVENTH Fleet attack carriers. His dynamic leadership, initiative and resourcefulness produced a smoothly coordinated and effective air-strike effort against the enemy. The complex operations for which he was responsible included aerial reconnaissance, air interdiction of enemy lines of communications, close and direct air support of friendly troops in ground action and air strikes against important fixed targets in North Vietnam. Through his outstanding planning and execution of these operations, Rear Admiral Miller produced exceptionally successful results, typical of which was the highly effective coordinated attack on the vital enemy thermal power plant at Uong Bi, North Vietnam on December 22, 1965. His personal enthusiasm and tireless efforts to acquaint the public with the contributions that nuclear-powered surface ships can make to a modern navy have assisted materially in creating an increased understanding and awareness of the use of nuclear power..."

Distinguished Flying Cross: "For heroism and extraordinary achievement in aerial flight as Commanding Officer of Fighting Squadron TWENTY THREE, attached to the USS PRINCETON, during action against enemy Japanese forces in the Solomon Islands and Bismark Archipelago from November 1 to 11, 1943. Flying escort for bomber planes on strikes against enemy installations and shipping, (then) Lieutenant Commander Miller contributed materially to the success of his section in subsequent strafing runs, assisting in beaching a medium-sized cargo vessel, firing two motor torpedo boats and two small cargo vessels and silencing four enemy antiaircraft positions..."

Gold Star in lieu of Second Distinguished Flying Cross: "For heroism and extraordinary achievement in aerial flight as Pilot, and Commanding Officer of Fighting Plane Squadron TWENTY THREE, during operations against enemy Japanese forces at the Marshall Islands, from February 2, 10, 12, and 16, and against the Palau Islands on March 30 and 31, 1944...On March 30, while leading a flight of twenty-four planes engaged in an air strike, he pressed home a determined attack against four enemy fighters, destroying one and damaging another. Despite considerable antiaircraft fire, he also executed strafing runs which destroyed a plane, damaged two others and scored hits on buildings and a cargo vessel. Encountering an enemy fighter plane while escorting torpedo bombers on March 31, 1944, he shot it down and braved heavy antiaircraft fire to carry out aggressive strafing runs which damaged enemy buildings and shops..."

R. Adm. H. L. Miller, USN, Ret.

Gold Star in lieu of Third Distinguished Flying Cross: "For heroism and extraordinary achievement in aerial flight as Pilot of a Plane, attached to the USS HANCOCK, in action against enemy Japanese forces in the vicinity of Kyushu, Honshu, Shikoku, Wake Island, Hokkaido and the Nansei Shoto from March 18 to July 15, 1945. Completing his twentieth mission during this period, Commander Miller inflicted extensive damage on enemy shipping, airfields and installations..."

Gold Star in lieu of Fourth Distinguished Flying Cross: "For heroism and extraordinary achievement in aerial flight as Air Group Commander and Pilot of a Fighting Plane in Air Group SIX, attached to the USS HANCOCK, during operations against enemy Japanese forces in Kure Harbor, Japan, on July 24, 1945. Skillfully leading fourteen air groups in a bombing attack on major units of the Japanese Fleet, Commander Miller enabled his flight to obtain hits on all assigned targets and to inflict severe damage to two battleships, two heavy cruisers, two carriers, two light cruisers and one carrier hull..."

Gold Star in lieu of Fifth Distinguished Flying Cross: "...during operations against enemy Japanese forces in Kure Harbor, Japan, on July 28, 1945...(He) personally scored a direct hit on a battleship-carrier despite intense enemy antiaircraft fire from shore installations and from major units of the enemy fleet, and aided directly in the sinking of that vessel. In addition, by his courageous leadership, he contributed materially to the sinking of a cruiser and a 45,000-ton aircraft carrier..."

Gold Star in lieu of the Fourth Legion of Merit: "For exceptionally meritorious service as Commander Naval Air Test Center, Patuxent River, Maryland; and as Naval Air Systems Command Test and Evaluation Coordinator, from September 1968 through August 1971. During this period, (he) was responsible for the test and evaluation of naval aircraft weapon systems and for the coordination of test resources allocated among the various field activities engaged in such testing. Through his interest and involvement in special management programs, identifiable cost savings of over $12 million were realized over a two-year period. As a result of his coordination of resources among testing activities, over 100 aircraft previously assigned for other purposes were returned to the fleet or retired from service. Rear Admiral Miller was responsible for the development of the prototype Antisubmarine Warfare Tactical Support Center, a major improvement in antisubmarine warfare capability for fleet commanders, which formed the basis for similar systems installed at operational bases and aboard aircraft carriers. He achieved a degree of coordination and cooperation among field activities of the Naval Air Systems Command which will significantly enhance the development of aircraft weapon systems for years to come..."

R. Adm. H. L. Miller, USN, Ret.

His Air Medal and Gold Stars in lieu of five additional Air Medals were awarded for meritorious achievement while in command of Fighting Squadron TWENTY-THREE attached to the USS PRINCETON, in the Marshall and Caroline Islands, and as pilot of a plane from the HANCOCK in the vicinity of Kyushu, Honshu, Shikoku and the Nansei Shoto areas in 1944 and 1945, respectively.

Letter of Commendation (Army), with Ribbon: "...for superior work and cooperation in the training of all pilot personnel for the recent successful bombing missions against the territory of the Japanese Nation for the period of 1 March 1942 to 30 April 1942..."

CHRONOLOGICAL TRANSCRIPT OF NAVAL SERVICE:

Jul 1934 - Jun 1937	USS TEXAS (Junior Division Officer in Engineering, Communications and Gunnery)
Jul 1937 - Jun 1938	Naval Air Station, Pensacola (Instruction)
Aug 1938 - Oct 1940	VF-3, USS SARATOGA (Personnel, Asst. Engineering, Asst. Gunnery Officer)
Nov 1940 - Oct 1942	NAS, Ellyson Field, Pensacola (Instructor and Personnel Officer)
Nov 1942 - May 1944	Air Group 23, USS PRINCETON (Commanding Officer)
Jun 1944 - Nov 1945	Air Group 6, USS HANCOCK (CO)
Dec 1945 - Dec 1946	Office of Chief of Naval Operations, Navy Department (Writing Air Ops. Instructions)
Dec 1946 - Jul 1948	Air Branch Office of Naval Research (Executive Officer)
Jul 1948 - Jun 1950	Staff, Commander in Chief, Atlantic Fleet (Public Information Officer)
Jun 1950 - Aug 1951	Composite Squadron 7 (Executive Officer)
Aug 1951 - Aug 1952	USS LEYTE (Executive Officer)
Aug 1952 - Jul 1953	Industrial College of the Armed Forces (Instruction)
Jul 1953 - Jun 1954	Office of CNO (Strategic Plans Division)
Aug 1955 -	U. S. Naval Station, Sangley Pt., Luzon, P. I (CO)
Sep 1955 - May 1957	Commander Fleet Air, Philippines, and Commander Naval Air Bases, P. I.
Aug 1957 - Jan 1959	Office of the Chief of Naval Operations, Navy Dept. (Asst. Director, later Director Progress Analysis Group)
Feb 1959 - Mar 1960	USS HANCOCK (CO)
Mar 1960 - Apr 1961	Chief of Staff and Aide to Commander Naval Air Force, Pacific Fleet
May 1961 - Jun 1962	Commander Carrier Division 15
Jun 1962 - Aug 1964	Assistant Chief of Staff for Plans, Joint Staff Commander in Chief, Pacific
Sep 1964 - Feb 1966	Commander Carrier Division 3
Apr 1966 - Oct 1968	Chief of Information, Navy Department

R. Adm. H. L. Miller, USN, Ret.

Oct 1968 - Sep 1971   Commander Naval Air Test Center, Patuxent River, land, with additional duty as Commander Fleet Patuxent River and Naval Air Systems Command T Evaluation Coordinator

1 Sep 1971   Transferred to the Retired List of the U. S. Navy

Navy Office of Information
Internal Relations Division (OI-430)
5 January 1972

DECLARATION OF TRUST

The undersigned does hereby appoint and designate as his (her) Trustee herein, the Secretary-Treasurer and Publisher of the United States Naval Institute to perform and discharge the following duties, powers, and privileges in connection with the possession and use of a certain taped interview between the undersigned and the Oral History Department of the United States Naval Institute.

1. Classification of Transcript.

   (X)a. If classified OPEN, the transcript(s) may be read or the recording(s) audited by the qualified personnel upon presentation of proper credentials, as determined by the Secretary-Treasurer of the U. S. Naval Institute.

   ( )b. If classified PERMISSION REQUIRED TO CITE OR QUOTE, the user will be required to obtain permission in writing from the interviewee prior to quoting or citing from either the transcript(s) or the recording(s).

   ( )c. If classified PERMISSION REQUIRED, permission must be obtained in writing from the interviewee before the transcribed interview(s) can be examined or the tape recording(s) audited.

   ( )d. If classified CLOSED, the transcribed interview(s) and the tape recording(s) will be sealed until a time specified by the interviewee. This may be until the death of the interviewee or for any specified number of years.

2. It is expressly understood that in giving this authorization, I am in no way precluded from placing such restrictions as I may desire upon use of the interview at any time during my lifetime, nor does this authorization in any way affect my rights to the copyright of my literary expressions that may be contained in the interview.

Witness my hand and seal this 23rd day of May 1973.

Henry L. Miller

I hereby accept and consent to the foregoing Declaration of Trust and the powers therein conferred upon me as Trustee:

H. L. Miller #1 - 1

Interview No. 1 with Rear Admiral Henry L. Miller, U. S. Navy

Place: Naval Air Test Center, Patuxent, Maryland

Date: Wednesday morning, 24 March 1971

Subject: Biography

By: John T. Mason, Jr.

Q: Admiral, I'm delighted that you've decided to do an oral biography. You've had an exciting career, which continues, as a matter of fact, and I think it's very useful to have this as a record, not only at the Naval Institute, but, I trust, at the Naval History Office as well.

A proper biography begins, of course, with the date and place of your birth, and some details about your family background and that sort of thing.

Admiral M.: Well, Mr. Mason, I was born in Fairbanks, Alaska, July the 18th 1912. I spent the first 17 years of my life in Fairbanks and around that area. I went to grade school and high school in Fairbanks, graduated from high school in 1929, and many times during the summer I worked in various areas there on farms, in hydraulic mining--that's mining for gold and . . .

Q: What kinds of farms do they have in that area?

Adm. M.: They're very good farms.

Q: Raising cattle?

Adm. M.: No. Vegetables, some cattle, some hogs and chickens,

H. L. Miller #1 - 2

but up there there is a good soil, and during the summertime the reason that everything grows so fast is that we have almost 24 hours of sunshine.

Q: It has to grow fast in order to mature, doesn't it?

Adm. M.: That's right. The vegetables are all very good, grow fast, very tasty. There are, of course, other industries up there, too. It was predominantly mining, though, when I was growing up. Everybody was looking for a short way to get rich in the gold-mining business, but I saw very few rich gold-miners. My father was in the gold-mining business. At one time, he operated two hydraulic mines. I worked at one of them between my junior and senior year of high school. As a matter of fact, the summer of 1928, I spent 111 days at one mine and I received $5 a day, plus my room and board and clothes, everything. I got a check for $555 and I felt as though I was a pretty rich young man going back to my senior year of high school.

Q: Just as a footnote, Sir, would you tell me what a hydraulic mine is?

Adm. M.: A gold mine that we label as a hydraulic mine uses water from, say, an accumulation at a dam. It's hauled to the site in a ditch that's been carved out of the mountainside, and then the water coming down to the immediate site comes though a pipeline, straight down the mountainside, or the hillside, to nozzles that they call "giants." You open the valve that lets the water out and you direct that water at gravel that holds the gold, and you push that gravel up against big boards that are

H. L. Miller #1 - 3

funneled into a sluice box--a box that all the gravel has to run through. At the bottom of that sluice box are short pieces of railroad rail put athwartships. The gold falls to the bottom of the sluice box. It's the heaviest of the minerals--so it has to fall. The rock goes out the end of the sluice box, and there, another nozzle at the end of the sluice box pushes all that dirt that accumulates up on a high pile that they call tailing piles. And the water rushes on down the stream.

Q: The pile, then, is something like the strip-mining for coal?

Adm. M.: That's right.

Q: It mars the countryside, doesn't it?

Adm. M.: Yes, it mars the countryside, but over the years the gravel that accumulates is covered with dirt and later vegetation starts to grow again. When I left Alaska in 1929 to go to prep school in San Francisco prior to going to the Naval Academy, the price of gold was about $16 an ounce, and I remember when people said, oh, if the price went up a little bit more, everybody would really get rich. But, later on, when President Roosevelt raised the price of gold to $32 an ounce, they still didn't get very rich. Many of the old-timers that were there in Alaska and mined for gold in the initial strikes really did strike some pretty rich ground, but their mining methods were not very refined or precise.

Q: It was kind of primitive, was it?

H. L. Miller #1 - 4

Company, which was a branch of the Guggenheims, brought five dredges up to the interior of Alaska and they went over all the old ground with those dredges and took out an awful lot of money, an awful lot of gold, that was still there.

Of course, when I was growing up, I saw a great deal of the interior of Alaska. There was wonderful hunting and fishing, lots of opportunity to walk around and observe nature.

Q: This you did in the summertime?

Adm. M.: That's correct, and in the wintertime we went hunting, along with skiing, ice-skating and tobogganing. Of course, when it got cold, we devoted our energies to sports that could be done indoors, like wrestling and basketball. Alaska is a very exciting country. It's a beautiful country. There's an awful lot going on and you might say, as far as the United States is concerned, it's America's last frontier. I normally get up there once or twice a year. I still have family in Fairbanks and we do own property up there.

Q: Tell me, Admiral, the fact that you observed all these people trying to get rich quick and the fact that they didn't get rich so quick, did this have any effect on your thinking?

Adm. M.: Yes, it did. As a matter of fact, the gold-mining business is a very exciting business. Once you get the bug, you're almost doomed to continue gold-mining until you reach the end of your days. I saw a great deal of it, all the time that I was growing up, and I saw where you couldn't make a million every year, so I made up my mind that I was going to devote my energies to some other activity. You might say, well, how come you picked out the Naval Academy? It so happened that we had a couple of boys from Fairbanks who had gone to the Naval Academy and one of them had gone with my oldest sister. So, from time to time, he would write and tell her all about it, and with that I checked up on the Naval Academy through <u>The Book of Knowledge</u>. I read all about it and I said, that's what I want to do. I want to go to the Naval Academy. I said that when I was in the eighth grade of school and, believe it or not, at that time the delegate from Alaska was approached and he said, sure, I'll hold an appointment for him.

Q: Who was that, Mr. Diamond?

Adm. M.: No, that was, Judge Wickersham, but then Tony Diamond got it and he held it for me. So that's the way I made up my mind and I stuck to that decision right straight on through high school.

Q: Did this please your parents?

Adm. M.: Oh, yes. As a matter of fact, my oldest brother had an appointment. He could have had appointments either at Annapolis or West Point. He didn't take it. My next youngest brother had his appointment to Annapolis and West Point, and he didn't take it. My youngest brother wanted to go to the Naval Academy, went to the same prep school in San Francisco that I went to, and while there he took a physical exam and found that he had one bad eye, and at that time, you couldn't wear glasses, so he went to Stanford instead and he's now with the United States

H. L. Miller #1 - 6

Information Agency at the Embassy in London. But I wanted to go to the Naval Academy, I stuck to it, and to brush up on a couple of subjects I went to Drews Prep School in San Francisco in 1929 and 1930.

Q: How was the general preparation in Fairbanks?

Adm. M.: The high school at Fairbanks was a very good high school, but I wanted to be sure that I would pass all the exams, so I went to prep school in San Francisco at Drews. It was a very fine prep school, highly recommended, and I did make the grade. It is still operating at California and Broderick street in San Francisco.

Q: How long did you spend at Drews?

Admiral M.: I spent about eight months at Drews. I entered the Naval Academy in 1930 with the Naval Academy class of 1934. That was during the Depression, a very trying period, but since we were so busily engaged at the Naval Academy, the Depression really didn't mean much to us. We saw it, but it didn't sink in, since we weren't exposed to all the trials and tribulations that the rest of America was going through at that time.

Q: Did you get any repercussions from your father? Was he affected greatly by the Depression?

Adm. M.: No, as a matter of fact, Alaska really didn't know what the Depression was all about. There had never been a Depression in Alaska. There was always lots of work. Anybody that wants to work can make a living in Alaska.

H. L. Miller #1 - 7

Q: Why is that, because it is a frontier area?

Adm. M.: It's a frontier area. There's plenty of work to do.

Q: An expanding economy.

Adm. M.: It's not a rapidly expanding economy. It's very slow. There's lots of work to do for the people who are there, and I never did know of a poor family in the Fairbanks area. If there were any, they were automatically taken care of by somebody. I never did see it. So, as far as the Depression was concerned, I really didn't know too much about it.

Q: Didn't you get some repercussions from some of the older midshipmen who were at the point of graduating and of not getting commissions?

Adm. M.: At that time, the class of 1931 and the class of 1932 received their commissions, all those who were eligible. But with the Depression continuing, the class of 1933, only half of them received commissions. I remember also at that time the Navy wasn't playing the Army in football, but in the year of, I think, 1930 they did play the Army-Navy football game in New York stadium to raise funds for charity, and then that series of football games resumed.

Q: The fact that the boys of the class of 1933 were not all being commissioned, did this put a damper on the enthusiasm of the class of 1934?

Adm. M.: Not too much. As a matter of fact, at that time, I

H. L. Miller #1 - 8

remember I stood in the lower half of the class, so my last year I studied a little bit harder and got myself elevated into the upper part of the class so I could take my choice of whether or not I wanted to stay in the Navy or try civilian life. I liked the Navy and I certainly enjoyed my four years at the Naval Academy. I was on the boxing team, and really enjoyed that. My No. 1 coach at that time was the great Spike Webb. We had a good time at the Naval Academy.

Q: Tell me about the courses of study and all that.

Adm. M.: Well, at that time we didn't have the great number of courses and the choices that the Naval Academy offers today.

Q: There were really no electives, were there, except of language?

Adm. M.: No, the only electives were in the languages, and it was a predominantly, 100 percent almost, engineering course. Some of those courses were of very little use in our naval careers. So I'm delighted to see the Naval Academy changed to what they have today. I think it's tremendous. But at that time there weren't many changes in the country. Everybody was trying to hold the status quo, trying to survive during a very bad depression. So there weren't any changes in schools, very little in government or in state and local governments. They all stayed just about as is.

Q: Tell me about your summer cruises. Were you deprived of them as a result of the Depression?

H. L. Miller #1 - 9

Adm. M: The first summer cruise was in 1931. We had the full cruise, three months' cruise to Copenhagen; Greenock, Scotland; Gibraltar; then Norfolk, Virginia; and up to Annapolis. From Copenhagen, we took a tour to Berlin. We were in Berlin for three days and three nights. We saw everything and, as you can well imagine, as a bunch of midshipmen we got very little sleep.

Q: That was the beginning, the very beginning, of the Nazi period, wasn't it?

Adm. M.: No, that was a little bit before. When we made that trip to Berlin in June 1931, President Hoover had just declared a moratorium on German war debts, so the German people just thought we were the greatest nation on earth. We were just a wonderful bunch of people. So we were given just about everything in Berlin. We had a great time. We rode the very funny little compartmented trains to Berlin and back to Copenhagen. Of course, we loved Copenhagen, too. It's a great city. I remember on the 4th of July, the day after we left Copenhagen, we were out at sea, and we put on the boxing matches and the regular 4th of July celebrations.

Q: You were on a battle ship, were you?

Adm. M.: I was on the battleship <u>Arkansas</u>. That was quite an oldtimer, and we did the regular work of the sailors. The sailors and the upperclassmen, the class of 1932, supervised us. We had a great time on that cruise. We saw a lot of Scotland and all the bargains in Gibraltar, prior to coming back to Norfolk,

H. L. Miller #1 - 10

then Annapolis, and going on September leave. At that time, we didn't have the airplane transportation, so with only 30 days' leave I couldn't go back home to Alaska. There wasn't enough time.

Q: What did you do with your leave period, then?

Adm. M.: I went to Chicago. I had a sister in Chicago. I had a good time spending my September leave in Chicago and in the Washington and Baltimore area.

Q: You never did get home, then, during . . .?

Adm. M.: Oh, yes, because following that cruise, the next year was our second-class summer and we saw that they were cutting down on the cruises, so that last year they gave us two months' leave and a two-month cruise. I was one of the first groups to go on leave, so I went home to Alaska. Drove across country with some of the midshipmen, then took the boat from Seattle to Valdez, Alaska, and went over the highway from Valdez to Fairbanks. That was the best summer vacation I think I've ever had because I had a wonderful trip up on the boat. . .

Q: It's a pretty spectacular trip, isn't it?

Adm. M.: Oh, it's beautiful. I had a wonderful trip on the boat and over the highway. The highway goes through hundreds of miles of scenic beauty.

Q: Is that the Alcan Highway?

Adm. M.: It's part of it now. Before I left I also visited the

H. L. Miller #1 - 11

mining town of Livengood. I went over to see one of my brothers because I hadn't seen him up there--and I was leaving the next day. So I went to Livengood. I hired this plane and a pilot, and Livengood was just like one of the mining towns you see in the moving pictures of the days of '98. It was a rip-roaring little mining town, and I certainly did enjoy every part of it. There was a catch. It just so happened that the night we took off, going back to Fairbanks, after a very big party in Livengood, that included the girls from the red-light district and everybody else, we encountered some difficulty.

Q: That's 1898!

Adm. M.: That's the days of 1898! We had a great time.

Q: Was there any shooting?

Adm. M.: No, no shooting. But I recall that when we took off and I woke up again, we were landing back in Livengood, and I asked the pilot, who was later killed in an accident, why, and he said he couldn't get in to Fairbanks because it was zero-zero from the forest fires. The next day was fine and I still had a chance to make my connections to get back to the Naval Academy, but it so happened that there was an appendicitis case and I was to make the decision whether they take me or the appendicitis case. Naturally, I said, take the patient. Well, that knocked me out of the transportation that I had all planned, so by the time I got back to the Naval Academy it all cost me about $500 extra. But I still said, when I arrived in Washington, D. C., that it was worth ten times $500.

H. L. Miller #1 - 12

Q: Just to have stopped in that mining town!

Adm. M.: That's right. I got off the train in Washington, D. C. and my roommate from Connecticut met me, and I asked him, "How did you know that I was going to be on this train?" He said, "I guessed it." I said, "How much money do you have?" He said, none. So, he asked me how much I had and I said $25. Of course, we were starting the cruise the next day, so we called up my girl in Baltimore and went out on the town with that $25.

Our cruise that summer was aboard the Wyoming, the battleship Wyoming.

Q: Was it a coastal cruise?

Adm. M.: No, the cruise went to the Maderia Islands; Norfolk, Virginia; Newport, Rhode Island; and then back to Annapolis.

Q: Why was Maderia selected as your destination?

Adm. M.: Probably because the Wyoming didn't have that allowance of oil that we had before when times were a lot more properous. They couldn't go far. Everything was cut in the Navy, and after graduation I think we made about $135 a month and we took a ten percent pay cut. And at that time, we still thought the Navy was paying us too much.

Q: Admiral, you were talking about the various cruises that you went on while you were at the Academy. Cruises are an opportunity, I believe, to put into practice some of the theory you learned in your classes. Did this have any bearing on the attitude of

H. L. Miller #1 - 13

result of their cruise experience, or did they become more eager than ever to become sailors?

Adm. M.: In the main, I think most all the midshipmen thoroughly enjoyed those midshipmen cruises. We had a great time. We saw a great many places. We enjoyed the camaraderie amongst ourselves and with the sailors and the upperclassmen aboard ship. I think, all in all, that the cruises sort of cemented our desire to stay in the Navy. It was again, join the Navy and see the world, and it was all very exciting. And when you compare, at that time, our cruises and the places that we visited with the very little it cost us in comparison to what we saw in the Depression in the United States, it makes a difference.

Q: You were saying that it really locked most of you into a naval career. Did you, while you were at the Naval Academy, have any actual experience in naval aviation?

Adm. M.: The only experience we had at the Naval Academy in naval aviation was getting a couple of rides in the seaplanes that the aviation detachment had at the Naval Academy to give us this aviation indoctrination.

Q: This was what was called "aviation summer," was it?

Adm. M.: Yes, it was our second-class summer, and part of it was aviation summer. But it really didn't do much of a job in selling us naval aviation. We rode along and sort of saw what the aviators did, and that was just about it.

Q: By that time, had you determined on a career in aviation?

H. L. Miller #1 - 14

Adm. M.: Oh, no. As a matter of fact, I had no desire to go into naval aviation. Maybe this would be a good time to tell how I got there.

Q: Right.

Adm. M.: When I graduated from the Naval Academy, I went aboard the battleship Texas, a wonderful ship. It was the flagship for one of the battleship divisions, the New York, Texas, and Oklahoma. In the Texas, I received the normal tour, six months in engineering, six months in gunnery, six months in communications, and they brought me back to gunnery again. At that time when the oldsters who belonged to the gun club in the Navy took charge of you, you were pretty much in. Lieutenant Commander Keliher kept track of me, assigned me to gunnery duties when I was through with engineering and communications.

Q: Was this because you showed a special aptitude for gunnery?

Adm. M.: Yes, Sir, I was sent to two gunnery schools in the summer of 1935 and in the summer of 1936, Secondary Battery Gunnery Schools. I excelled in spotting. As a matter of fact, at the first gunnery school I was high spotter in night firing. I liked gunnery. It was a lot of fun. But I used to go riding with the aviators. Get in the back seat of that plane and be shot off the catapult. I'd always leave my stomach right back on the catapult, but I enjoyed it. Every year I would take a physical exam, the naval aviation physical exam, just to see whether or not I could pass it, not because I wanted to go in for naval aviation.

H. L. Miller #1 - 15

Well, in 1937 I went over to the battleship <u>West Virginia</u> where they had a navy flight surgeon. I took the physical exam, passed it, and, as I came out of the flight surgeon's office, I ran into Lieutenant Commander Keliher who was then a commander and assigned to the staff of the commander of battleships, battle force, and he said, "What are you doing over here?" I said, "I came to take an aviation physical." He said, "Are you going to put in for aviation?" And I said, "Oh, no, Sir. I do this every year." He said, "Better stick to gunnery." "Yes, Sir."

A couple of months later I received a set of orders to aviation. This was when we were on a cruise to Hawaii, and it just so happened that the Bureau of Medicine and Surgery sent a copy of my flight physical to the Bureau of Navigation, and, since I was a likely prospect, they gave me a set of orders to Pensacola to learn aviation. At the time, the skipper of the ship asked me if I wanted to go, and I said, "Well, I think I'll go and give it a try."

After that cruise when we got back to San Francisco there was a big reception there, and I ran into Lcdr. Keliher. He said, "I see you've joined the Air Force!" And I said, "No, as a matter of fact I never did put in for it," and I told him the story. He said, "O.K., Hank, if you don't like it send me a note and we'll take you back."

That's how I got into naval aviation.

Q: But it was perfectly acceptable to the line officer, then, wasn't it?"

Adm. M.: Yes, Sir. The aviators at that time in the Navy really weren't too popular. They were still trying to pioneer the whole aviation effort in the Navy, and there were a great many regular line officers who just didn't believe in aviation.

Q: There was a great deal more respect for them, however, than there was ten years before, wasn't there?

Adm. M.: Oh, definitely. But, of course, I enjoyed my three years in the battleship Texas. I was in gunnery most of the time. I coached the boxing team, I coached the basketball team, and I helped out in a great many other things. So I was pretty busy and enjoyed the officers and the men that were on that ship. I certainly enjoyed Pensacola. When I finished there after a year . . .

Q: Would you tell me a little about the training course there and some of your experiences?

Adm. M.: Pensacola, to my mind, was pretty easy because I had spent quite a few hours every day aboard the battleship Texas doing something, and when I went to Pensacola just learning to fly, I just didn't have enough to do. The ground school was easy, and the flying wasn't too difficult.

Q: So you had an aptitude there, too, a natural aptitude?

Adm. M.: Well, one of the instructors who had been an aviator on the Texas asked me if I would help him out in football, in managing a football team. I told him I'd be delighted to do that since I had time on my hands, and about two weeks later he was placed as officer in charge of night flying, so I had

H. L. Miller #1 - 17

the football team. I bought the equipment, I carried the water buckets, I got the uniforms, made out the schedule, collected the money. I spent about 16 hours a day on football and two hours on flying. But I enjoyed it, and the coach at that time was now-deceased Rear Admiral "Jumping Joe" Clifton, who was one of the most famous naval aviators we've ever had in this Navy, and quite a wonderful naval officer.

Pensacola was pretty easy, the flying end of it. We had a different course than they have now. We started out in pontoon seaplanes, we had regular land-based trainers, and we had the big boats and seaplanes, and we had, at that time, the fighter aircraft. So we had a very comprehensive course.

Q: Did you, by any chance, have anything to do with gliders?

Adm. M.: No, Sir, not at that time. We didn't have gliders at Pensacola. The first time I flew gliders was right here at Patuxent last year. We have two Sweitzer gliders that we use in the test pilot school curriculum here.

Q: I know that Ralph Barnaby was at Pensacola, but I think it was prior to your time, and had introduced gliders as a preliminary to instruction and also to eliminate certain men who were not-- didn't have the aptitude.

Adm. M.: I've heard about Barnaby and the glider business for many, many years, but we did not have the gliders at Pensacola at that time. However, we had quite a number of types of airplanes that we checked out in and we flew, and we received instruction in. We did have day and night flying, we had the basic seaplane, we

H. L. Miller #1 - 18

had the torpedo planes, we had the big boats, the fighters, basic land-plane training. It was a good solid year of flying, and we enjoyed it.

Q: What was the student body at that time? How many men were in training?

Adm. M.: To tell you the truth, I forgot the numbers of flyers that were going through each class. There was a class that started every six months, and I think there were probably about 40 in each class. We received a good comprehensive course. From there, we had our choice of going to seaplanes or fighters or torpedo planes or bombers. I put in for a fighting squadron 3 aboard the USS Saratoga.

Q: First, may I ask, do you have any idea of what it cost to train a man at Pensacola in those days?

Adm. M.: No, Sir, I don't, but I know it was probably one-fiftieth of what it costs today.

Q: I think Admiral Strean told us that last year it cost half a million or something like that.

Adm. M.: I don't think it's half a million, but it's a good bit over $100,000, and that's a lot of money for training anybody.

Q: Were there many casualties among the students?

Adm. M.: No, Sir. It was pretty safe. As a matter of fact, no student of our class was killed. There were very few casualties there during the time I went through, and we did the day and night

H. L. Miller #1 - 19

flying, just like they always had.

Q: Maybe this is a good time to ask you a question since you did night flying. Why was it that when we got into World War II, we didn't go in very much for night flying from carriers?

Adm. M.: Well, we didn't know too much about night flying because we would check out in it and, you might say, qualify again during this period of time to go aboard ship and fly off at night and land back aboard. We didn't do much of it, and we didn't because there was no absolute necessity to have a lot of night time under our belts. When the war came, it was a horse of a different color. We knew that we were going to have to have a night-flying capability, but it's a tremendous training problem, and at that time we just had so many things to do in training the great number of aviators that we had to get out to the fleet that there wasn't time to do everything. So the time was spent in making a basic aviator out of a man and giving him the daytime flying. I was there at the start of the war, I was there at the finish of World War II, so I saw it from the very beginning to the bitter end.

Q: You say that it's quite a problem to train a man thoroughly in night flying. What are the factors involved in training him in that way?

Adm. M.: Well, during day flying you learn the basics of flying. You have all the visual points to alert you to any dangers in flying. You can see. At night, you have to put an awful lot of faith in those instruments that are on the dashboard in front of you. And, at that time, prior to World War II, and during

H. L. Miller #1 - 20

World War II, we didn't have the instrumentation on that board in front of us that they have today. So, we did have to go back to the fundamentals, and we did not have the instruments to help us in doing this night flying and taking care of some of the daylight vision for us.

Q: I see. Well, now, we were focusing at that time upon the Japanese as a potential enemy in the Pacific, were we not, and we did have knowledge that they were training in night flying. Did this not alert us to the need for it?

Adm. M.: Yes, but then, we had a limited amount of night flying experience, too. At that time, I had no idea to what extent the Japanese had gone into it, because basically the war in the Pacific was fought, as far as aviation was concerned, from carriers, mostly in daylight hours. Sure enough, you took off in the pitch-black darkness of the morning, but when you got to that target the sun was up and you could see, and that was why you could identify your target, attack it, and get out. Now, there wasn't, as far as the carrier Navy was concerned, much flying at night, and the reason is because we couldn't identify, pinpoint, specific targets at night. We had to save our big punch for the daylight hours. This was one of the reasons we stuck mainly to daylight hours.

We did have specialized night fighter detachments of 4 planes on each carrier to go up after Jap reconnaissance planes that were tracking the Task Force or against Jap night bombers who were more harrassment than real.

Q: Admiral Gallery was telling me the other day about training men on a jeep carrier in the Atlantic, antisubmarine warfare, insisting on night flying as a technique, and that very quickly was adopted by the other jeep carriers as well.

Adm. M.: They had a different problem. They had to keep planes in the air 24 hours around the clock hunting those submarines. We had a different problem in the Pacific in attacking Japanese fighters or Japanese land-based or ship targets.

Q: You said you elected to go with the Saratoga.

Adm. M.: Yes, Sir. As a matter of fact, before I left Pensacola I had this set of orders to go to the Saratoga. I'd put in for Fighter Squadron 3 of the USS Saratoga--and one of the officer's wives asked me if I was going hom after Pensacola, and I said, no, it was too far up to Alaska for just 30 days' leave. She said, "Why don't you put in for two months' leave?" So I did, and I got two months' leave and seven days' travel time. So that gave me 67 days, and I went to Alaska. I reported into Fighter Squadron 3 on August the 13th 1938. It was a Saturday morning and everybody was lined up in front of the door of the squadron office wanting to shake the hand of the first naval officer they ever knew that got 67 days' leave!

Q: Quite an accomplishment! Were you married at that point?

Adm. M.: No, Sir, that was 1938. I was married in 1939. At that time, Lieutenant Commander Artie Doyle was the skipper of Fighting-3. Artie just died last year in the rank of admiral,

H. L. Miller #1 - 22

United States Navy.

The day I reported in, August 13th 1938, since I was the last aviator reporting to the Fighting-3 from that batch, the skipper, Artie Doyle, had a party that night. He invited the squadron commanders and quite a few other officers from the Saratoga air group and he served a concoction of mint juleps, great big mint julep punch. Well, I had been exposed to mint juleps at Pensacola, so I was very careful about how much of that solution I was going to absorb, especially when I saw him pouring bottle after bottle of straight whiskey over the ice. That evening Artie Doyle had reserved a table at the officers' club for the new pilot, Lieutenant Miller, and Artie's wife, Jamie, the air group commander and his wife, and a few others. But since the mint julep party lasted long and loud, there were only three people who showed up for that dinner--Artie Doyle, Jamie Doyle, and one Hank Miller. All the rest were either home in bed or on their way home. It was a riotous success.

Also at that time, Captain A. C. Read--Putty Read--was the skipper of the Saratoga. He was the one that made the NC-4 flight across the Atlantic, and after we went aboard for a week's training cruise, the air group commander and the squadron commanders had a party for the captain, the executive officer, and the heads of departments of the Saratoga on Saturday night before we sailed. Since I was a bachelor, I was invited to fill in to dance with the ladies, and after dinner, the music began. I picked out this nice-looking woman as a partner. When we were dancing I told her who I was and asked her name. She replied that she was Mrs. Read. Then I said, "Who do you belong to?" And she said, "Oh, I'm Captain Read's wife." And I said, "Now, don't kid me. You're not married to that little old man." But I found out she certainly was! Well, for ever and ever after, Mrs. Read was one of my best friends.

Q: Tell me a little about Captain Read--Admiral Read.

Adm. M.: Admiral Read was a very quiet individual. He was sharp. He knew what he wanted to do. He really, in naval aviation, was one of the greatest that we had. He made history, an almost impossible flight going across the Atlantic. He did a lot of other things in naval aviation after that, being skipper of the Saratoga. He was also in command at the naval air station at Pensacola. He started a tremendous program that they initiated prior to and during World War II. They had to turn out the pilots, and he was the commanding officer who got that whole program going. He was a man of very few words. He knew what he wanted, and he would always back you up in anything you did--and his wife was a very gracious woman.

Q: Tell me about the Saratoga and your tour there.

Adm. M.: Well, the Saratoga was great. We had short training cruises aboard the Saratoga. However, normally each year there was one big fleet cruise, and in 1939, it just so happened that the Saratoga was sent up to the Navy Yard for an overhaul, so we took Fighting-2's place in the USS Lexington. Fighting-2 was getting new airplanes. Admiral Ernie King flew his flag in the Lexington. He was in charge of Aircraft, Battle Forces. He went south from the West Coast, though the Panama Canal, to the East Coast. Down south, around Guantanamo, we joined up with the new carriers the Yorktown and the Enterprise. We had the Ranger with us, and we did quite a few training exercises there with that force. We got to Norfolk, Virginia, and were going up to New York. I had already made plans for the past six or eight months for my girl to come up from Alabama, meet me in New York City, and we were going to get married at St. Patrick's Cathedral. Mind you, I'd taken one ribbing after another that whole cruise on, "So you're going to get married, huh?" The first day as I was getting ready to go ashore at Norfolk to call the future wife to tell her everything was all set, one of the champion ribbers on the ship sat on my doorstep while I was shaving and said, "I see you're not going to get married in New York after all!" I was so caloused to all that stuff that I didn't even listen to him. I got dressed, and as I was walking through the wardroom to catch the boat, everybody said, "Well, I see you're not going to get married in New York, after all." And I said, "What's the trouble? What happened?" "Haven't you seen the dispatches?" Then, I knew that they were kidding! Except, here was the dispatch that said they were going to turn the fleet around and send it back to the West Coast, because they didn't want to sort of flaunt the fleet in front of Hitler's eyes. Hitler was raising cain over there in Europe. So I went ashore and told my bride--my would-be bride--that I would meet her in the not-too-distant future in Coronado, California, where we would be married. And with that, we turned around and came back to the West Coast.

H. L. Miller #1 - 25

Q: Was that actually the reason for reversing. . . ?

Adm. M.: Yes, Sir! The reason was they didn't want to, you might say, wave the flag in Hitler's face.

Q: That was the day of Chamberlain, wasn't it?

Adm. M.: Yes. So they sent us back to the West Coast, and we finally got married in Coronado, California, on May the 17th 1939. But we enjoyed that cruise on the Lexington. We broke the world's records in carrier landings, time getting aboard, and carrier take-offs. We were a pretty hot crew.

Q: Did you affect an attack on the canal, or did you . . . ?

Adm. M.: Oh, we always did that as sort of an exercise. The skipper of the Lexington at that time was Captain John Hoover. . .

Q: "Genial John?"

Adm. M.: Yes. He was a pretty tough man, but he was fair and square with us, except that he did borrow my white dinner jacket, got red wine all over it and didn't clean it!

Q: He was a charming man in his later days. I got to know him fairly well. So, you got routed to the Pacific Fleet, instead?

Adm. M.: Later, on the 1940 cruise, we went with the fleet to Hawaii, and were sitting there in Hawaii when they decided to send the Saratoga back to the West Coast for some sort of interim fixing, and we were the only ones that came back--the only carrier. The other deployed in and out of Hawaii. At that time in Coronado,

California, it was so deserted that you had your pick of almost any house in the town at a very, very reasonable rent. Probably the only time in Coronado's history that there was ever a situation like that.

Then in the fall of 1940 I received orders to Pensacola as an instructor.

Q: Is this something you wanted?

Adm. M.: No. We had a wonderful fighter squadron. Fighting Squadron - 3 was one of the top fighter squadrons in the Navy. At that time, our chief competition was right across North Island, Fighting Squadron-4, which was then commanded by Lieutenant Commander Windy Switzer. He and Artie were great friends. In the competition between fighter squadrons the most coveted prize is being the No. 1 fixed gunner in the Navy. Well, at that time, Fighting Squadron-4 had Lieutenant "Jumping Joe" Clifton, who was the former football coach at Pensacola, in their squadron, and Joe was one of these guys who was never born to lose. He was a winner all the way through. And when it came time for the fixed gunnery shoot, Joe was high gunner of Fighting Squadron-4 with 62 hits out of 144 shots. He used to come over to BOQ and wake me up every morning and say, "How are you people doing in fixed gunnery?", because I was assistant gunnery officer. I kept telling him that we were improving slowly, and he said, "If anybody beats me, who do you think it will be?" And I said, "Joe, it's going to be either Artie or me." He said, "You!" I said, "Yes, I've really been hitting lately."

Well, Saturday morning came and this was our record firing

practice. Joe was there. He stayed there all day with the official party marking the targets. Artie and I went out on the first flight, and we had the advantage. It was nice and calm in the morning. Artie had red bullets and I had blue bullets. We came back. Joe was there marking the targets. They marked it three times, and I hit 63 out of 144 shots, which was one more than Joe. Well, he stayed there all day long marking targets. Finally, when it was all over at the end of the day, with a heart that was just broken in two, he said, "I sure would have felt bad had it been anyone but you or Artie." Here he was, almost crushed. Joe was a great one, though, and later on we hooked up in the war, and he was a great one to work with.

Q: What kind of planes were you using?

Adm. M.: At that time, we were flying the Grumman biplane, the F-3-F-1. Following that we got the first fighter monoplanes in the Navy, the Brewster F-2A-1. That was a fun plane to fly, but as a combat plane it wasn't too much good. After the F-2A-1, we had the improved version of the Brewster monoplane fighter, the F-2A-2, and then the Navy started getting the Grumman F-4F-4s.

Q: New types were coming out, weren't they?

Adm. M.: The Grumman F-4F-4 was the Navy's Wild Cat that started in World War II. It was replaced by the later Grumman model F-6F, which was a wonderful fighter plane, and the Chance-Vought F-4U fighter, and I flew both of those airplanes in World War II.

Q: Was progress being made with arresting gear on carriers, at that time?

Adm. M.: Yes, at that time catapults - both catapults and arresting gear got better and better. They had to, in order to launch the heavy airplanes with faster speeds and also to recover heavier airplanes at faster speeds. The Bureau of Aeronautics kept up with it all. I think they did a marvelous job in the catapult and arresting gear business. We had really no trouble with catapults and arresting gear at that time, and we launched thousands and thousands of airplanes.

Q: Had we learned anything from the experience of the British in those areas?

Adm. M.: Oh, yes, Sir. The British, you might say, gave us the steam catapult after World War II. Prior to World War II, we had the hydraulic catapults. The steam catapult launches a plane heavier and faster. Additionally, the British gave us the angled deck on the aircraft carriers, and it saved us millions of dollars in airplanes and lives, since this did land the planes away from the parked areas aboard ship. Additionally, too, the British gave us a visual landing device with lights that we could follow. When the light was green, fine, we could keep on coming right on down to the carrier, we were on the right glide slope, right speed, doing fine. The red light showed that we were too low. We had to come up. The yellow light, too high. So, the British really gave us a lot and saved us an awful lot of money, even though they had much less experience in the aircraft carrier business. I might mention that when I went back to Pensacola from Fighter Squadron-3 and I became an instructor - that was in 1940, about November of 1940. In 1941 the war started - and in February of 1942, I was assigned to train General Jimmy Doolittle's Tokoyo raiders to take off from an aircraft carrier.

Q: You were still on the staff at Pensacola?

Adm. M.: Yes. I was still an instructor there at Ellyson Field, Pensacola.

Q: When you went to Pensacola, did you notice any change in techniques or anything of the sort in the few short years since you'd been there?

Adm. M.: Not much. There were still the same fundamentals of instruction in flying. They still had the same types of airplanes, getting a little bit more modern, but not much. They did have a tremendous number of students to train and turn out.

Q: It was a speed-up program?

Adm. M.: It was a speed-up program. There was a great hump of students, and at one time we were flying seven days a week. We didn't mind, though. We knew that it had to be done and everybody turned to and did it. There were no gripes or growls, even though it was seven days a week and a couple of nights of night flying, too. Everybody turned to and did the job. In addition, the basic training centers in the country were so jammed that they gave us 500 civilians that we had to train to be sailors, teach them the basic fundamentals of marching, carrying a gun, and everything else. We didn't mind it. It was a lot of fun.

H. L. Miller #1 - 30

After the war started, the first thing that I did was to sign up for a cross-country flight to Philadelphia to get some some trainer planes down, and I dropped into Washington and asked for a fighter squadron to go to war. They told me that we were frozen, as far as the Navy was concerned, because they had to have instructors to get the students out. So in February when I received a set of orders to go to Eglin Field and train the Doolittle fliers, I was . . .

Q: Did your orders reveal what you were going to do?

Adm. M.: No, but let me get a copy of them. The orders were 28 February 1942 from the Commandant (this was Captain A. C. Read at that time) to Lieutenant Henry L. Miller.

Subject: Temporary additional duty

1. In accordance with authority contained in reference A. you will proceed without delay on 28 February 1942 to the place or places in the order given indicated below for temporary duty. This is in addition to your present duties and upon the completion thereof, you will return to your station via naval aircraft.

To Eglin Field, Florida, via naval aircraft reporting to the commanding officer for temporary duty.

2. It is anticipated that the duty at Eglin Field, Florida, will exceed 72 hours (and the way orders were written in those days, 72 hours sort of dictated that you were not supposed to be away from your command more than 15 days).

3. You will be allowed a per diem of $6.00 in lieu of actual and necessary travel expenses during your absence from your station,

H. L. Miller #1 - 31

in the performance of this duty while in an air travel status.

(Signed) A. C. Read, Commandant

Well, in the first place, the Navy gave me an old SBU plane that they pulled out of the boondocks at Ellyson Field that had been in the sand, and said, here's your airplane, you go down to Eglin Field, which is about a 30-minute ride . . .

Q: You'd almost think they didn't value your life!

Adm. M.: That's right. I went down on a Sunday. I reported to the colonel in charge of the base, and I read him my orders and I said, "Do you know what I'm down here for?", and he said, "no." So I explained to him that I was an instructor at Pensacola, I was a carrier pilot before I came back there as instructor, and I was supposed to come down and teach the Army Air Force pilots flying, how to take off from a carrier. He still said he didn't have any idea of why I came down there, so I was just getting up to say, well, it must have been a mistake, when I asked him if he knew anything about Lieutenant Colonel Doolittle's detachment there. With that, he closed the doors, he practically asked me to talk in a whisper . . .

Q: Why did you raise that? How did you know?

Adm. M.: I had talked to Lieutenant Commander Switzer, the assistant training officer at Pensacola, and he said that it had something to do with Lieutenant Colonel Doolittle, and I said, "Is that the great Jimmy Doolittle?", and he said yes. Well, with that, the colonel at Eglin Field put me in his car and took me over

H. L. Miller #1 - 32

to the place that I was staying, and then after I got my gear squared away, he took me down to a building set aside for Lieutenant Colonel Doolittle's B-25 detachment. Jimmy Doolittle wasn't there, neither was his executive officer, Jack Hilger - Major Jack Hilger. So I talked to a Captain York, and Lieutenant Davey Jones, and Lieutenant Ross Greening. I told them who I was and what I was supposed to do - teach them carrier take-offs. They said, "Have you ever flown a B-25?", and I said no, I'd never even seen one. So, with that, we went down the line, we climbed into a B-25, we went over to - I was the co-pilot with Davey Jones - the field that was set aside for this work. It was assigned to us exclusively. I told them that this was the way you made a carrier takeoff: number one, you held both feet on the brakes, for this plane we'll try one-half flaps. I asked them how much manifold pressure we could hold on for, say, 30 extra seconds, and put the stabilizer back about three-fourths, and with engine full bore, I told them to release the brakes, start coming back on that yoke, watch the air speed, and just keep coming on back until the airplane took off.

Q: You had time to study the B-25?

Adm. M.: I hadn't had time to even look at it, except I had a feel for it and they told me the take-off speeds that they'd been using. They were taking off at 110 miles an hour. So the first take-off, they observed the air speed and it showed 65-67 miles an hour, and they said it's impossible, you can't do that. Well, the B-25 that we flew that day was light loaded. I said, O.K., come on back and we'll land and try it again. So the second

H. L. Miller #1 - 33

take-off the same way indicated an air speed of 70 miles an hour when we were in the air, and they were convinced that a B-25 could take off at that slow speed.

For the second run, you might say, over Japan, the B-25 was going to be at 31,000 pounds, that was 2,000 pounds over the maximum designed load. To start out with at this field that was set aside at Eglin Field, I checked out all the pilots for light loads, then intermediate loads, then, finally, the maximum load that they would take on the raid. Everybody did pretty well. We had extra crews. I took data on each one of the pilots and marked off the field. We had observers. I borrowed pilots to act as observers. We got a portable anemometer to find out how much wind they had. We measured the distance for each plane that got off. I recorded all that data. Also, in the cockpit I observed techniques, because you get a feel for who's a good pilot and who isn't, no matter what his take-off distance is. A funny thing happened just before then, just before we finished up that first day. I was over at this room that they gave me, getting my flight jacket because it was chilly, and I thought, gee whizz, here I am a lieutenant in the Navy and this Army Air Force gives me a dirty, junky room like this! No carpet on the deck, just cold concrete, and look at that crummy bed! So, with that I put on my jacket, and wondered who else was staying in this little group of rooms, this little cell block. I went out to see the name of this place and it said, "VIP Quarters." And I said, they must be kidding. So I went up to the next room and I looked at the name plate and it was Lieutenant Colonel Doolittle's name. I went up to the next one, and here was Mr. Kettering, you know, of General Motors. I went over to this other one and I saw, Major Johnson. So, I said, my gosh, this is pretty fast company I'm in, I'd better not complain about this horrible room that they've put me in, because evidently these guys have the same kind of horrible rooms. But that's the way the Army lived at that time. That's the way they lived all over the United States, only in some places like Sacramento it was worse.

Q: By that time, did you know the destination of this mission?

Adm. M.: I found out where they were going. My contact, and only contact as far as the Navy was concerned, at that time was Captain Wu Duncan, who was, a special assistant to Admiral Ernie King, who was Chief of Naval Operations. I took my orders from Lieutenant Colonel Doolittle and Captain Duncan. During this training period at Eglin Field - I was supposed to be there for 15 days, get through with the training, and go back to Pensacola. However, we did have some foggy days and, actually, it was going to take longer. But it didn't create any problem because Jimmy Doolittle, on his trips to Washington, would keep Captain Duncan informed, and Captain Duncan, in turn, would give me permission to stay as long as I wanted down there on this set of orders.

As we went along and everything appeared to be going on schedule, we came to the last day, and in the next day, or two, or three, the planes were going to shove off for the West Coast.

Q: How many planes were involved?

Adm. M.: There were 16 planes involved, and I'll get to that. But, the last day came, I checked out all the crews, except the

H. L. Miller #1 - 35

last, which was a pilot by the name of Lieutenant Bates. He finished his but I wasn't satisfied because Bates was letting the plane fly him, so I said, OK, all observers get out, and I said, "Bates, you have to try it again. You fly this plane smoothly. You fly the plane. Don't let it fly you. Once more around." Well, we took off. He took off in a skid, he pushed into a harder skid, however, and he didn't push the throttles to the floorboard, and the plane settled right back down on the runway on its belly. We came to an abrupt stop. It didn't catch fire. We were lucky, because we had gasoline all over that airplane. All the pilots were there watching it. Fortunately, I had a fire truck there for the first time in days, and it came out OK.

The next day, Jimmy Doolittle came back from Washington and he said, "I hear you had an accident." I said, "Yes, Sir, but there's nothing wrong with the technique or anything else of the airplane. What was wrong was Bates. He just wasn't flying the airplane. The airplane was flying him." So, Jimmy Doolittle said, "OK. You know, I'm going to the West Coast today, and we're going to pick up another instructor out there to give us some more of this." I said, "Well, you know, Colonel, it's a matter of professional pride with me. I don't want anybody on the West Coast telling you, "No, let's start all over again with this technique." If it's possible I'd like to go with you, if we're going to have time to do more of this practice out there." And with that, he said, OK, "if it's all right with Washington, you can fly out with me this afternoon." So I called up Pensacola and had some laundry flown down and they picked up my airplane and anemometer and junk and took it back, and I flew out to the West Coast, to Sacramento, with Jimmy Doolittle.

We put the planes in the depot there at Sacramento to get a recheck, get them all set to go aboard the carrier, and as one plane would come out of that sort of interim overhaul period, I'd take it up with the crew to Willows, California, to a field there and give them take-offs at Willows. Then, the last day, Jimmy Doolittle said, "Well, we'll finish up at Willows then we're going to fly down to Alameda and go aboard. How do you think everybody's doing?" I said, "Oh, I think it's no strain at all. I think everybody's doing great." We were taking extra crews and he said, "Would you list the crews in order of take-off expertise, 1, 2, 3, 4, 5, 6, 7." They were going to take 15 airplanes and we really had, I think, 18 or 19 crews.

Q: And you were preparing to go aboard the Hornet?

Adm. M.: Yes, Sir. So I listed the people in order of what I thought was their ability, and General Doolittle and Major Hilger and a couple of others were looking over this list. Major Hilger said he thought Bates should be one of the crews that went and why did I object. I said, "Why, I'll tell you." I explained the accident and said, "After we crashed, they both were going to jump out of the windows, right into those whirling props, and I grabbed both of them, and said, "Sit down and wait until those props stop, and turn off all your switches." The switches were still on. I reached back to get my pencil, paper, notebook, came on back, the props had stopped, they had jumped out. I looked and they had turned off all the switches and turned them all on again. So I said, "You know, when you get on over enemy territory and you have some of those Japs chasing you, you've got to be really sharp and you've got to be thinking all the time. If you panic, you're lost." "I wouldn't take Bates." And they didn't take Bates. Bates, I guess, is mad at me to this day, but I wouldn't have taken him.

So, just before going aboard, Jimmy Doolittle asked me what I thought of the crews. I said I didn't think there'd be any trouble at all. I said, "You know, Colonel if you want proof, I've had less time in the B-25 than anybody. You can take an extra one along - a sixteenth airplane - and when we get 100 miles out of San Francisco, I'll take it off, I'll deliver it back to Columbia, South Carolina, back to the Army, and go back to Pensacola." He didn't say yea or nay. So I finished the day up at Willows checking out everybody I could and got in the last plane going to Alameda. When I landed at Alameda, Jimmy Doolittle came over to me and said he'd just been aboard ship, he saw some old Navy friends there, Captain Pete Mitscher, the skipper of the Hornet, Commander George Henderson, who was the executive officer, and Commander Apollo Soucek, who was the air officer, and Marcel Gwinn, who was the assistant air officer, and he said, "You know, I talked to them about your idea of taking an extra plane along and they go along with it, so we'll take sixteen and launch you 100 miles out." I said, "Gee, that's great."

So, the big day arrived. We sailed and just before lunch, I was up on the flight deck, and there was Jimmy Doolittle. We had parked the airplanes. We had about 495 feet for take off.

H. L. Miller #1 - 38

Jimmy Doolittle said, "Well, Hank, how does it look to you?" I sid, "Oh, gee, this is a breeze." He said, "Let's get up in that airplane and look." So he got in the cockpit and I was in the co-pilot's seat. He said, "Gee, this looks like a short distance," and I said, "You see where that tool kit is way up the deck by that island structure?" He said, "Yes." I said, "That's where I used to take off in fighters on the Saratoga and the Lexington." And he said, "Henry, what name do they use in the Navy for bull shit?"

With that, we went down to chow and just before finishing my dessert, they said, "Lieutenant Miller, report to the bridge." I got up on the bridge and Pete Mitscher said, "Well, Miller, I don't think I'll be able to give you 40 knots of wind over the deck." I said, "Captain, I don't need that anyway, because we have 495 feet. I taught these guys how to take off from an aircraft carrier with 40 knots of wind and 250 feet. We have lots of room." And I told him the story about talking to Jimmy Doolittle just before lunch. With that, Captain Mitscher said to me, "Well, Miller, do you have an extra pair of pants with you?" I said, "Oh, yes, Sir. I brought all my baggage with me because I'm going to fly nonstop to Columbia, South Carolina." And he said, "We'll take that extra plane." I replied, "Captain, will you drop me off at the next mail buoy, please. By the time I finish this trip I will have travelled half way around the world on a telephone call and I'll be an Ensign when I get back."

I told Pete Mitscher that I was tickled to death, too, because from the very beginning when I heard there was going to be a raid on Tokyo I wanted to go to the take-off spot, so

H. L. Miller #1 - 39

I was delighted with that.

Q: Did he send a dispatch to clear you?

Adm. M.: I don't really know what he did, because when we got back to Pearl Harbor, Captain Mitscher sent me over to see Admiral Halsey and get a set of orders reporting back to Washington to tell Admiral King about the raid, and then for me to report back to Pensacola after that.

It worked out very nicely that way. I got to Washington, D. C. after a very hectic ride across the Pacific in one of the Pan American clipper amphibious planes. I didn't know at the time when we crashed at Eglin Field that I had hurt my back, but it showed up and took me quite a while to get the soreness out of that back of mine from that crash.

Q: Would you revert back to the Hornet and tell me something about the morale of the pilots who were going off on this expedition?

Adm. M.: Oh, everyday the pilots aboard the Hornet would get an intelligence briefing plus going over all the equipment in the airplanes, plus getting in a sizable amount of poker-playing. They roomed with Navy fliers and Navy ship's officers. They were a great bunch of people, and you can imagine - of course, all of them being volunteers for this and they knew that it was going to be pretty difficult, because after they got through bombing Japan they were supposed to fly down the coast, then cut in - and I think they were supposed to go in at the 38th parallel, fly to this one field that was going to be held by

Chinese guerrillas, land, take on enough gasoline from hand pumps out of drums to fly on from there to Chungking, turn the planes over to Chiang Kai-shek and his people, then come out of China and back to the States. They were going to take off just before dark. Jimmy Doolittle was going to be off first. He was going to carry fire bombs and drop them on his targets in the Tokyo area just at dusk. The other planes would be coming in, say, a half to an hour afterwards and they would be bombing targets in the Tokyo area from the light of the fires that were caused by Doolittle's bombs.

Well, the big day arrived and everybody was supposed to stay in the ready rooms all day long. Lunch would be served and other food and everything else, because the task force was going to be at general quarters. They had to be on the alert. All planes were spotted for take-off tied down. It was a wet, windy, rough, miserable morning, and just at daylight the task force picked up a couple of Jap fishing boats. The cruisers started firing at the fishing boats. They did a horrible job of hitting them and we had some Enterprise planes in the air. They were dive-bombing and strafing the fishing boats. They had just as hard a time trying to hit them, and since Admiral Halsey, who was in charge, was afraid that the boats would get off a radio message to Tokyo, he sent a message over to the Hornet which said, "Launch Army pilots." And when I got up on deck and told Colonel Doolittle, he said, "Would you help get the pilots in the airplanes?" So, this I did. We launched the first one, I think, at 8:20 that morning. . .

H. L. Miller #1 - 41

Q: That was Doolittle himself?

Adm. M.: Oh, yes. Jimmy Doolittle was the first one off, and he did a fine job. He's a great aviator. He did it just like the book says.

Q: How far off the coast were you?

Adm. M.: We were over 600 miles, so we knew that the pilots really didn't have a Chinaman's chance of getting to China with those airplanes. It was just too far a trip. Additionally, they were hitting much stronger head winds than was anticipated going into Tokyo.

Q: You knew and they knew, too.

Adm. M.: That's right. The position of the <u>Hornet</u> at eight o'clock in the morning of the 18th of April was "at 0800 Inuboe Saki Light bears 27 degrees distance, 642 miles. Surface winds from 300 degrees. Force 26 knots."

Q: And the planned distance had been what?

Adm. M.: The planned distance was about 200 miles, and since that put them much farther out that we ever anticipated, we knew it was going to be a tough struggle getting in there.

Q: As it turned out, were Japanese fishing boats of that kind equipped with radio communications?

Adm.: Yes. All the Japanese fishing boats were equipped with radio. This was part of their reconnaissance safety force, you might say, off the coast of Japan.

H. L. Miller #1 - 42

Well, the planes went in. We estimated that they would be over the Tokyo area about five or ten minutes after one o'clock that day. At ten minutes after one, aboard the <u>Hornet</u>, listening in, Tokyo radio came on the air and said, "Enemy bombers dropped bombs in the area." They were all excited, and then bang, they went off the air. We knew that the planes were in and the raid successful.

Q: No message had been sent, then, from the fishing trawlers?

Adm. M.: I didn't know at that time. I know that here we have a picture of the Japanese fishing boats we saw there which was sunk. But I do not know right now whether or not they did get a message off. I know that's recorded some place.

Q: If so, it wasn't effective enough to prevent the raid, anyway.

Adm. M.: That's right.

Q: What was the real purpose? Was it purely psychological?

Adm. M.: The real purpose was to do some damage and to show the Japanese people that we could reach them, and additionally a tremendous shot in the arm to the American public.

Q: Which we needed then!

Adm. M.: Which we needed. That's right. I'll tell you an amusing story. At that time, Jimmy Doolittle and Roscoe Turner - Roscoe died last year - were probably two of the best aviators in the United States. Jimmy had been called back in by General "Hap" Arnold to help get their war move started. He was in uniform. During the time when he was assembling and getting all this stuff together, he ran across Roscoe in Cleveland, and Roscoe said, "Say, Jimmy, I've got an idea. You and I are probably two of the best aviators in the country. Why don't we get some of these kids organized on a bombing raid to bomb Tokyo?" Jimmy said, "Gee, that's a great idea, but I'll see you again, Roscoe. Hap brought me back in the Air Force and I haven't had time to do anything, except just work." About a month later, he ran across Roscoe again, and Roscoe said, "Hey, Jimmy, what about that idea of mine?" And he said, "What are you talking about?" "That bombing raid," and Jimmy said, "Oh, I'll talk to you again about that." A short time afterwards, big headlines in the papers said, "Doolittle Dooed it," and with that, Roscoe went into a Western Union office, picked up a message, and he sent it to Jimmy Doolittle. It said, "Dear Jimmy, you son of a bitch."

Q: That good idea which I thought of!

Adm. M.: They were a great gang, all the Army Air Force, enlisted and officers. They got along beautifully with sailors and officers. We helped them maintain the airplanes. We even took one engine out, took it to pieces, and put it back together. It clicked one hundred percent.

Q: You were proud of your handiwork, your accomplishment?

H. L. Miller #1 - 44

Adm. M.: Oh, yes. I should say so, because they all got off safely. One of the pilots, Travis Hoover, the second one off, pulled that nose up just like a fighter and I thought he was going to spin in, but he just pushed it over and away he went. They all did a great job. I think without a doubt every officer and man aboard the <u>Hornet</u> would have pinned every medal in the world on those people who went off that deck in those airplanes. They really had what it took, and when you look back at everything that happened subsequent to that, it was a big shot in the arm to the great American public. They saw we could do something. And it shocked the Japanese people. It was hard for them to believe that we'd get through like that, and it helped to pull a lot of their forces back around the country to protect that little old country called Japan. So, the raid had a great many things going for it, but at that time the biggest thing was morale for the American people.

Every year, we have a reunion of the Doolittle Tokyo Raiders, and this year, 1971, it's going to be 15, 16, 17 April in San Antonio, Texas. There are about 53 of the gang of 80 still living, and there'll probably be about 42 or 43 there with their wives, and some with the whole family. It's a very close group.

Q: On the actual raid, my memory fails me, were there any lost?

Adm. M.: Yes, Sir. After the raid, there was one airplane, Captain York and his crew, that landed in Russia. They were interned for a year, then escaped through Iran. Lieutenant Farrow and his crew were captured. Later on, after the trial, they shot Lieutenant Farrow.

Q: They were captured by the . . .

Adm. M.: By the Japanese. They landed in China. I must add that after the raid, all the raiders got a favorable tail wind out of Japan, so it looked as though they were going to make the Chinese coast.

Q: The rendezvous?

Adm. M.: Yes, it looked like it, but they ran into a terrible storm on the Chinese coast, so they all either had to jump or crashland, except the one plane that landed in Russia. There was one crew, Lieutenant Ted Lawson, who wrote Thirty Seconds Over Tokyo - he crashed-landed on the beach and, subsequently they had to cut off his leg. That was crew No. 5. Then crew No. 6, Dean Hallmark, they were captured, and Hallmark was shot by the Japanese after a so-called trial. His co-pilot, Lieutenant Meador, died of a heart attack in prison camp. He sort of gave up. He was in bad shape. In Lieutenant Farrow's crew, Corporal Jacob de Shazer, swore that if he got out of it alive, he was going to go back and be a missionary, and he is a missionary in Japan today.

Q: Really! Kind of conversion experience.

Adm. M.: Yes, that's right. The last plane that went, flown

by Lieutenant Don Smith, had the flight surgeon in it, Doc White, who was a lieutenant at that time. They were behind everybody till he eventually caught up to Ted Lawson who had really injured his leg, cut it severely, in his crash-landing, and it was Doc White who made the decision that the leg had to come off. There was one of the crew who was drowned in jumping, in one of the lakes that they have over there in China. Another one never did get out of the airplane. Either something happened or he elected to stay with the airplane, but we couldn't figure out why. He was killed, of course, when the plane crashed. None of the airplanes survived in one piece. Jimmy Doolittle told this story about his crash and jumping. They all jumped, and the next morning - it rained all night - they started walking toward a central position, and he ran into Bremer, who was one of his crewmen. They were captured and they were trying to tell the Chinese that they had bombed Tokyo, but it wasn't getting through till they got to this village and it looked as though the villagers were going to string them them up. And Bremer said, "We Americans, Americans." One little kid knew some English, went up to him and said, "Chiang kai-shek, he great man. Roosevelt, he great man." and the kid rescued them, told everybody who these guys were.

Q: Was there any concern for the instruments on the planes, that they might be taken over by the enemy?

Adm. M.: In what way?

Q: Special instruments.

H. L. Miller #1 - 47

Adm. M.: Oh, the bomb sight, yes, there was.

Q: That kind of thing.

Adm. M.: They had taken the Norden bomb sights out of the airplanes at Sacramento, and they used a little 20 cent sight that Major Ross Greening invented to do the bombing.

That's about most of it, right there, for the Doolittle gang.

Q: In your own personal story, Admiral, you said that when you got back to the States, it was a crash-landing.

Adm. M.: Well, no. That last take-off, the last crew at Eglin Field, we crashed. When I got back to the States, I reported in to Admiral King in Washington, D. C., and told him about the raid, I again went to the detail officer and asked for a squadron and they told me to go home again. Finally, I went back to Pensacola. About two months later, I got a call at Ellyson Field from one of the detail officers in Washington, D. C., and he said, "Are you the Henry Miller of Shangri-la?" "Yes, Sir. Is this Commander MacMahon?" He said, "Yes, Sir, it is. OK, can you get up to Washington on Wednesday?" I said, "I sure will," and he said, "Well, tell the Commandant to give you a set of orders" - and me being a lowly lieutenant! I said, "Yes, Sir." So I went to see my boss, Commander Dudley, and I told him about this and he said, "I'll give you an airplane." I said, "No, I don't want to take a chance on that. I've got to be up there on Wednesday, and I want to be sure, so I'll go over and get a set of orders from the main station and go up commercial."

So I thought, Oh, Boy, this is just great, another deal like the Doolittle raid, and I was glad to get out of the instructing business at Pensacola and go to war again. With that, I turned over my job in the squadron, all the communications business, and I told my wife I didn't know when I'd be back. I went up to Washington, and as I changed planes at Jacksonville, I looked across the aisle - it was at night - and I thought I recognized Bremer, who was one of Doolittle's crewmen, but I didn't know, so when we arrived at Washington National Airport in the morning, it was just getting light, and, sure enough, there was Bremer, so I said, "Let's talk." He'd just got back from the raid. And, with that, we went over to Jimmy Doolittle's office, but he wasn't there. I left word with his secretary. I said, "I'll be back, but I have to go over and check in with the Navy." Then I walked into Commander MacMahon's office and I said, "Commander, I am here, ready to go again." He said, "Did you bring your white uniform up?" I said, "Yes, Sir." And he said, "Didn't anybody tell you what you're supposed to come up here for?" I said, "No." He said, "You're going to a dinner party. You and Jimmy Doolittle are supposed to tell the Secretary of the Army and the Secretary of the Navy about the Doolittle raid from the Army and the Navy standpoint."

Well, I was disappointed because I sure didn't want to leave all that just for a dinner party. However, I did go to the detail officer again and say, how about that fighter squadron? I guess the guy was getting tired of me coming in there and asking because when I did get back to Pensacola, I received a set of orders to a fighter squadron.

H. L. Miller #1 - 49

Q: Will you tell me, first, about your relating the story to Admiral King, and then about the dinner party where you had to talk to the Secretaries? How did Admiral King receive the news?

Adm. M.: Admiral King was a very good listener, I made it short, and sweet, and told him all pertinent points. I knew he was a busy man, and he had an awful lot of information at his finger tips from that raid. He got the weather reports, and certain information from China that we didn't know about. But I told him about the cooperation and the wonderful association of the Army and the Navy aboard ship, the help that we gave them, and the friendships that were built up, all about the take-offs, the operations of the task group, and he seemed to be very pleased with the way the Army and the Navy got along and the whole operation.

Q: Was Duncan there with him?

Adm. M.: Yes, Sir. As a matter of fact, I didn't make a move without checking with Captain Duncan. He, you might say, kept me in a cage until he lined up somebody else for me to tell the story to, and I was there for about two days, then he let me go back to Pensacola.

Q: Were you thrown to the newspaper reporters?

Adm. M.: Oh, no, Sir, this was super-super-secret. Very few knew about this.

H. L. Miller #1 - 50

Q: Although it had gotten in the press from the . . .

Adm. M.: Oh, yes, from the raid, but all the details were not known. It's very interesting, but your friend Commander Artie Doyle and, of course, my former skipper - Artie was there on duty in the Navy Department, and when he saw me he said, "I know where you've been." And I said, "No, you don't." He said, "Oh, yes, I do. The young lieutenant that handles all the briefings in the morning told me that you were over there with Jimmy Doolittle." So Artie had his intelligence channels all worked out.

Q: These people get around! Tell me about the two secretaries and the dinner.

Adm. M.: The Secretary of the Army . . .

Q: This was Henry Stimson?

Adm. M.: We had the Secretary of the Army, the Secretary of the Navy, and the Assistant Secretary of War, at that time, for Air, Robert Lovett. Bob Lovett, if I recall correctly, was a former naval aviator of World War I fame.

Q: The same as Liv Ireland.

Adm. M.: Yes, Sir. What we did, we went over to the Mayflower Hotel, a dining room was set aside for the secretaries, the assistant secretary, Jimmy Doolittle, and myself. We had some drinks and dinner and lots of conversation on every aspect of the raid, and the secretaries seemed to be very appreciative

H. L. Miller #1 - 51

of getting all the details from the Army side, Jimmy Doolittle, everything that happened to him in China, and from the Navy side as far as the training of the people was concerned plus life aboard the Hornet right to the take-off spot. I enjoyed it. We had lots of conversation, questions. I think we told them just about everything that happened.

Q: You sort of got your spurs, then, as a PR man, did you?

Adm. M.: Oh, no. But, of course, when I came back to Pensacola I started in the instructing business once again, then I got my orders to commission a fighting squadron at Willow Grove, Pennsylvania, in November of 1942, and I was pretty happy with that set of orders.

Q: I imagine instructing at Pensacola was rather dull after that one episode!

Adm. M.: That's right. You asked about, were you afraid of giving any of your instruments away, well, the Army flyers used a 20-cent bomb sight in that Tokyo raid, and Ross Greening was the individual who invented this bomb sight that they took along, so there was quite a bit of publicity on that. We left the beautiful Norden bomb sight at Sacramento because we just didn't want it to fall into enemy hands.

Q: Was there any special preparation of pilots in case they were - in case they did fall into the hands of the enemy? Was there any special preparation as to how they should conduct themselves?

Adm. M.: The only information, as I recall, was name, rank, and serial number. They knew, I think it was generally known, that they were going to take a beating if they were caught. Everybody had heard about the people captured, you know, in the Philippines, and some of the torture, so everybody figured that it was going to be pretty tough if they were caught by the Japanese. They were prepared for it. There was one pilot who was captured, Bobby Hite, who I roomed with at the reunion in Miami, and I asked Bobby, "How come you look so good and Meador died of a heart attack? You were both in the same prison compound." And Bobby said, "Well, I'll tell you. Meador was always wondering whether or not the folks back home were worrying about him and all this. I didn't worry. I figured I was going to come out of this alive. I did. I just didn't worry. I made up my mind I wasn't going to worry." Of that crew, Lieutenant Farrow was the plane commander and he was shot. Bobby Hite - and Bobby Hite bought his way into that crew, as co-pilot, (he was really a plane commander of one of the extra crews.) The navigator, Lieutenant George Barr, was in poor physical shape from then on for years and years. De Shazer, as I told you, is a missionary. He had a good attitude. It all depended on the way you were thinking.

Q: Did you observe that elsewhere in World War II, that the success of a man engaged in battle or facing battle depended somewhat on his ability to forget, for the moment, family ties and concentrate on the thing at hand?

Adm. M.: That's right. There were people that went to war and said, well, I don't expect to come back alive, and they didn't. Others said I'm going to come through this OK, they're not going to get me. It was an attitude that I found all over the Pacific. A classmate of mine when we both went out the second time with air groups, said to me, "I don't think this is very good. You go out here so many times and one of those bullets is going to get you." Well, he was killed in the first raid that they went into on Tokyo with this new outfit. I just didn't have that attitude. I figured that I was going out there and give it the old college try, and I was going to come back with all my skin. After the Doolittle raid, I went out with two additional outfits, right through the end of the war. Just carrying that on a little bit farther, you sort of had a feeling for all this. You more or less seemed to know some of the outstanding ones that were in the war who you just knew weren't going to get killed, and they never seemed to fall in that category. They came through without a wound. And others that were always worrying about it, quite a number of those never did come back. On one strike, we went in to Kagashima Bay, and made attacks there with the air group. I had one of my pilots shot down. He was in Kagashima Bay. I called up the combat air patrol that I had up above and I said, "Call the force and tell them to send a seaplane in to pick up this pilot that's in a rubber boat in the bay. We'll stay here and watch on guard." Believe it or not, the word got back to the ship that I was down, and that word got back to the States. There was an air group commander who, just

H. L. Miller #1 - 54

before leaving the States and coming on out, had been with me on the Princeton during the war and all over the Pacific. He heard about it and said, "I'm just writing you this letter because they told me you were shot down, and I said, no, I'm going to write Hank right now, because I know the Japanese are never going to get that son of a bitch." And he wrote me two big long, typewritten pages. That's what he thought about me, you see. Incidentally, the seaplane picked up my pilot Slim Summerville in Kagashima Bay!

After Pensacola, I commissioned this fighter squadron at Willow Grove, Pennsylvania, and if you ever did that in today's Navy, you'd probably get court-martialed. I was a lieutenant and they sent me fighter pilots who were trained in the old training plane, the SNJ, and I was supposed to make fighter pilots out of them and go to war in about three months. The air field wasn't finished. They had to send to Youngstown, Ohio, to get the hangar doors. It was miserable. So, we weren't making much headway in getting airplanes together and holding ground school. It was raining and snowing, and then freezing. We just couldn't do anything.

The exec called me up from the ship - the ship was being built, the USS Princeton, one of those CVL carriers, over in the New York Shipbuilding yard over in Camden - and he said, "Say, Marine Corps station at Parris Island is open, nobody on it. The whole field is serviced by Marines. The Marines have moved out of there to Cherry Point, North Carolina. Go down there and see if you can get it." So I flew down to Parris Island

H. L. Miller #1 - 55

in my fighter that afternoon. The officer in command of the field was Major Pruitt, who was a Marine who used to be in my squad at the Naval Academy. So Benny Pruitt said, "What do you want?" I said, "I want the field for the air group." He said, "Well, it's wide open. I have Marines here to service it and do everything. Your sailors won't even have to work on security or anything else." I said, "What are the problems?" and he said, "The General!" With that, I called up Martha Spiers, who was Colonel Smith's daughter. Her husband, Jack Spiers, had been in Fighting-3. The war came along and they gave him a dive-bomber squadron and he killed himself dive-bombing in practice, so she was home with her mother and father. Colonel Smith was in charge of basic training. I called Martha and I said, "I'm here." She said, "What are you doing?" and I said, "I want Parris Island," so she said, "I'll come right down and get you." When we got up there, we convinced Mama, Mrs. Smith, on how we were going to go about this. When Colonel Smith came home, we gave him the story, and he said, "The general just doesn't like aviators," so, with that, we went next door to the chief of staff. We made a plan out on how to sell the general the next day, and in 15 minutes, he was sold. I called up Washington and I said, "Move us."

Q: Did you have any problem with Washington?

Adm. M.: No, I didn't. That was the 19th of December, and on the 4th of January we flew down to Parris Island. The next day we started flying. It was a wonderful place. Weather, targets, everything. It was beautiful.

Q: What happened to Willow Grove? Was it completed?

Adm. M.: Oh, yes. Willow Grove is still operating today. It's in good shape. It's a good station. But there was just too much rain and snow and no facility, so it was a poor place to go to war from. And we got in wonderful training at Parris Island. We went aboard the Princeton for a shake-down cruise in late May in the Chesapeake Bay. We went to the Gulf of Paria in Trinidad to get the rest of the shake-down, for day and night landings, qualifications, and all that, away from the submarine threat.

Q: That was a protected harbor, wasn't it?

Adm. M.: Yes, very well protected. We got back just before the 4th of July and they flew us off to Willow Grove, Pennsylvania. At that time, the station was complete and a very pretty station. We switched planes from the F4-F4 to the F6-F right there at Willow Grove and over that period got about a week's leave. I had taken two F6-Fs on the shake-down cruise and checked out all the pilots in those two F6-Fs aboard the carrier, so we did an awful lot of work there. Then, in July, we set sail aboard the Princeton for the Pacific.

Q: Who was the skipper?

Adm. M.: The first skipper of the Princeton was Captain George Henderson, who had been the executive officer of the Hornet for

H. L. Miller #1 - 57

the Tokyo raid. So we had quite a gang on there and a tremendous crew. The Princeton did a real outstanding job in World War II.

When we left the East Coast in the Princeton on 22 July, we went with another CVL carrier, the Belleau Wood. We joined up also with the USS Lexington down around Panama.

Q: While the Princeton was fitting out, did you have any voice in any of the special installations?

Adm. M.: No, Sir. As far as installations aboard ship were concerned, they were all more or less standard, set up by the Bureau of Aeronautics and Bureau of Ships, so that we had very little to say about it or do about it, except to ensure that the spare parts and the equipment that we needed to fight those airplanes were aboard and in sufficient quantity.

Q: Was that a difficult task, to amass those spare parts?

Adm. M.: At times, it got to be quite a game in who could steal the most for his particular ship. Spare parts were at a premium wherever you want, but we managed to keep our supply up in order to keep those planes going. This was pretty much the necessity of looking after yourself.

Q: A little bit of foresight in that regard was terribly important, wasn't it?

Adm. M.: That's right. But we managed to do pretty well. We

H. L. Miller #1 - 58

participated in exercises with the Belleau Wood, destroyers, and the Lexington from Panama all the way across to Pearl Harbor, and, on our arrival on 9 August of 1943 in Pearl, we had the biggest concentration and the largest number of carriers at Pearl Harbor that were known up to that time. The Yorktown had arrived in July, and the Essex and the Independence in June. The Saratoga and the Enterprise were also in the Pacific, and the British carrier HMS Victorious. All of a sudden, from a couple of carriers in the previous few months, now we had a sufficient number to go in there and start hitting the Japs.

Q: Did the arrival of all these carriers occasion a visit from Admiral Nimitz?

Adm. M.: Oh, yes, Sir. Every carrier that went in to Pearl, the skipper would go over and call on Admiral Nimitz and some of his staff. And Admiral Nimitz always took time out with all those visitors, and, gee, there were hundreds, to talk to them, to explain his part in the war, and what he expected of them. He was quite a gentleman, and quite a leader.

Q: Meanwhile, he was building up his little black book of potential officers for this service or that job!

Adm. M.: That's right, and he had . . .

Q: It gave him a chance to look you over.

Adm. M.: . . . he had Army, Navy, Marines, Britishers, everybody

H. L. Miller #1 - 59

working for him. He had quite a staff, quite a nice bunch of people, too. They worked hard, and they did their darndest to provide you with as much in the way of services as they possibly could.

Q: Who was on his staff for air at that point?

Adm. M.: To tell you the truth, I forget, but he had a very competent staff and they did a good job.

After Pearl, we took on a new boot admiral on his first combat operation. We left Pearl the 25th of August 1943 for our first war mission. This was to support the occupation of Baker Island out there in the Pacific. It was about 700 miles east of Tarawa, in that Gilbert group of islands.

Q: Were you part of the Third Fleet, at this point?

Adm. M.: We didn't call it a fleet at that time. This was August 1943 and the Third Fleet and the Fifth Fleet really hadn't built up to what they were later on. But that new boot admiral that we broke in on that mission was Admiral Radford. He was riding the Princeton. He was quite a guy. He learned very fast. He knew how to run that Task group. We were operating with the Belleau Wood, another CVL carrier there on that operation. We supported the occupation of Baker Island, shot down a few Jap airplanes, built an airstrip on Baker Island, then in September we sailed north and joined the USS Lexington and some cruisers and destroyers to make the first raid on Tarawa and Makin. On the 17th and 18th of September 1943, in the morning and afternoon we made

H. L. Miller #1 - 60

the strikes on Tarawa and Makin and left that area to go back to Pearl Harbor.

Q: What sort of opposition did you meet?

Adm. M.: Well, we only shot down one twin-engine bomber, or Betty, and the first two Emily Seaplanes in WWII. We destroyed planes and AA guns on the ground at Tarawa and Makin. We got four of those flying boats on the water at Makin.

Q: So it was a surprise raid?

Adm. M.: It was, and it was a well-timed, well-planned raid on those two islands. For that raid, Admiral Pownall was in command of the over-all force. Admiral Radford, was sort of breaking in, at that time. Then, after we came back into Pearl, not too long after, that on the 10th of October, we got a sudden set or orders to proceed down to the South Pacific to Espiritu Santo and join up with the Saratoga there. The Saratoga had already been there. After joining up with the Saratoga, we made a few practice raids together and then left there on the last of October and proceeded up the Solomons and made strikes on Buka and Bonis in the Solomon Islands. This was to support the Bougainville operation. We hit those places pretty hard, and then we heard that the Japanese had sent a big cruiser and destroyer force that was sitting at Rabaul and they were going to wipe out our forces that were landing in Empress Augusta Bay in the Solomons. So we were ordered to go up and hit Rabaul - that was the Saratoga and the Princeton - and Admiral Halsey told us later that he didn't expect to get the Saratoga and the Princeton back after these raids. He expected to lose us in that raid.

Q: How near to Rabaul did you go?

Adm. M.: We went to about 150 miles away and launched aircraft. It was a beautiful clear day. For 50 miles we could see, Japanese fighters taking off from all the fields around Rabaul to intercept us. It was quite a battle.

Q: And the high command really felt that the two carriers were expendable in terms of what was to be gained by this raid?

Adm. M.: Well, we had to save that Empress Augusta Bay operation, and I think they made a very wise decision because we went in that day and got a lot of Jap planes, we hit the cruisers and the destroyers, and the Japs had to send that force back to Japan and to Truk to get fixed. So it pulled the whole force out of the attack on Empress Augusta Bay.

Q: How many planes did we have involved from the two carriers in this operation? How big a raid was it?

Adm. M.: We had about 75 planes involved in the operation, and everybody did a marvelous job. They really carried the attacks home. Our own group - we lost several pilots - but we really did a darned good job. We got the hits and we shot down 17 Jap planes from our little squadron.

H. L. Miller #1 - 62

Q: Did the enemy achieve any hits on the carriers?

Adm. M.: No, the Japs didn't come close to us. They didn't find us.

Q: That was rather remarkable. What screen did you have with you?

Adm. M.: We had destroyers with us and we had two cruisers. Two cruisers and six destroyers. But even though they knew we were coming and we were fifty miles away, we sort of caught them by surprise. They really weren't counting on those attacks, so we hit the jackpot that day. It was one of the heaviest of our strikes.

Q: How do you account for that? Was it too daring - more than they expected?

Adm. M.: I think that was it. They just didn't believe that we would do it.

Q: Whose strategy was this? Was it Halsey, or was it Nimitz?

Adm. M.: I think it was Halsey and Nimitz. It was, you might say, another one of those shots heard around the world because we hit the jackpot, and we got by with very, very few losses.

Q: Did you personally have any exciting experiences in that raid?

Adm. M.: Yes, I got my first Jap fighter..

H. L. Miller #1 - 63

Q: Tell me about it.

Adm. M.: It was pretty easy. The date of 5 November 1943. And you know they always considered me the old man in the fighter squadron. I and a whole bunch of young kids. I think at that time I was about 31 years old, but I was the old guy, you know, couldn't see. But you know, when we got into combat, if there was anything in the air I was the first to see it. When we got in to Rabaul, we were the top cover and I saw four Jap Zero airplanes coming toward us and to the left. I assumed that everybody saw them, so I swung right around behind them with my division of four and I started in shooting. One airplane blew up right in front of me. I pulled up to the right to get at the other one and start shooting at him, and my three other planes literally in that division were all shook up because they hadn't even seen anything yet. They got quite a ribbing when they got back. But we did get quite a few planes that day. As I say, we hit the jackpot as far as the enemy was concerned. The Japs will never forget that strike on Rabaul, because it set them back badly in their contemplated go at all the operations in the South Pacific. We got that toehold at Empress Augusta Bay and we kept it, and there wasn't a darned thing they could do about it afterwards.

After that we came back to the Central Pacific to help out in the landings on Tarawa, but on the way we made three strikes on the island of Nauru. This was a lot of fun because we caught them by surprise and we got quite a few planes

H. L. Miller #1 - 64

on the ground, a few in the air, but we completed three strikes and left that area by two o'clock in the afternoon.

Q: What was the value of Nauru to the Japs?

Adm. M.: Not much, except for fertilizer and - I forget what comes out of there . . .

Q: It's largely fertilizer, isn't it?

Adm. M.: I think so.

Q: But as a strategic bastion in the South Pacific it wasn't that important, was it?

Adm. M.: No, it really wasn't. What we did was hit them, destroy some of their installations, some of their airplanes, and sort of give them a smacking blow as we went by. Following that, we went back to Pearl Harbor, after a few days on the line at Tarawa.

Q: That was a pretty bloody landing, wasn't it? From your vantage point can you tell me about it?

Adm. M.: They were too optimistic. For instance - maybe I should say from the aviation point of view, not from the Marine point of view, but from the aviator's point of view, they thought that they had just beaten the place to death, that there was probably very few living Japs there, they were just going to walk ashore and take over, because they'd really pounded it with airplanes, bombs, strafing, and those battleships and cruisers pounding away. The Japs had done a beautiful job in building solid fortifications in that bit of sand and dirt there on Tarawa.

Q: Pill boxes!

Adm. M.: That's right, and the Marines found it pretty tough going.

Q: Was not that our first actual contact with such fortification?

Adm. M.: Yes, that was the first time that the United States had really run into the tough fortifications that the Japs set up in a great many places in the Pacific. They found this out at Tarawa and they found out later that there were many other installations in the Pacific that were set up the same way.

Q: Aerial reconnaissance didn't reveal the fact that the fortifications were still intact?

Adm. M.: That's right. We didn't have the aerial reconnissance in those days that we have today, or that we had at the end of the war. We had some pretty good camera equipment at the end of the war, but not at that stage of the game. We thought we were pretty doggone good with our bombs and our bullets, but it didn't turn out that way.

Q: When you made a raid on shore fortifications like that, how low did you come in over them?

Adm. M.: Pilots used to come as low as they possibly could, depending on the bomb load that they had. Normally, they'd pull out around a thousand feet, and that's to give them greater accuracy in putting the bomb on the target, to be sure that it got there. It's the same as in war right today over in Vietnam, Laos, Cambodia, there are a lot of bombs that are wasted, a lot of bombs that don't do all that blasting that they're supposed to do.

Q: You mean just missing the target, or is it a faulty bit of ordnance?

Adm. M.: No, some are misses, some are faulty bits or ordnance. In a great many instances, bombs don't do the job that you think they're going to do, or they're not what they're cracked up to be. They just don't do it that way. You can see some of the bombs that hit installations today, no matter where. They have to really be on them. If they get a glancing blow, they don't do the job. You've got to put it on target to be sure everything works.

Q: Doesn't some of this show up in the testing of bombs?

Adm. M.: Yes, and today we're getting bombs that are much more accurate, much more powerful, and that really seek out their target, like Walleye that has a television camera in it. It seeks the target, hits it, and does a good job. That's what you call pinpoint accuracy. And a bomb that's coming along now, much bigger than the Walleye, the same in principle, is the Condor. It will also be a pinpoint job that seeks out, hits it on television, goes right down to the target.

Q: What kind of briefing did you receive before an operation like that? Who was in on it?

Adm. M.: Prior to ever coming close to the target, as soon as leaving port, our intelligence people would start briefing us on coming operations, the topography, the water conditions around the shoreline, any mountainous areas, the culture of the people, the natives of that particular area, what we could not eat if we were shot down and living off the land. We covered just about everything that we'd be concerned with in order to, say, hit that target and for surviving if we got shot down, including weather, time of year, all this. It was a very comprehensive briefing on all the information that we had at that time, and we had some pretty good information.

Q: The naval commander was in charge until the actual landing, wasn't he?

Adm. M.: Yes, then when the Marines got ashore they took charge there, and the Navy gave them support. They would ask for air support or ship bombardment, and they got it. We gave them as much as we possibly could. You know, it's a funny thing, but we used to work like the devil to really provide the support for those Marines who were on the beach. We knew that they had to have all the support in the world, so we worked a little harder to give them that support, and we lost more airplanes in close support of troops than we did on the big strikes, because we took more chances to help those Marines. I always remember that. They have a tough job. They had to go in there and seek out, go after the Japs and either kill them or get them to surrender. We supported them one hundred percent.

Q: In a place like Tarawa, what was the extent of the Japanese AA defense?

Adm. M.: Their AA defense wasn't worrisome. Their defense was against invasion from the beach area, and they had set up their defenses in grand fashion. The Marines had to pay a pretty stiff price for taking Tarawa. And you might say, later on, on the whole Central Pacific operation. They finished up Tarawa in December. We went back to Pearl. The Princeton dumped us off at Pearl Harbor and they went back to the States for Christmas, to Bremerton, Washington, to get a vibration fixed up in one of the shafts.

Q: Your stay in Pearl was something in the nature of a leave, was it?

Adm. M.: No. See, we were - I had the whole air group and they sent us over to Maui. They had regular training areas

H. L. Miller #1 - 69

over there, fields and everything. But we were a little bit peeved because they go back to the States and leave us out at Pearl.

Q: To eat your Christmas dinner out there!

Adm. M.: Yes. First of all, I went over to the Navy, Naval Air Force, Pacific Fleet, at Ford Island, and I asked the flight surgeon if he had any ranches where we could send some of the pilots to get a rest. He allowed as how there wasn't any. In the meantime, I had Chris Holmes Rest Home, which was down on Waikiki Beach, for a week for the pilots. I couldn't get anything from the Navy, so I went over to see the Army at Hickham Field, even landed down wind at Hickham. The special services officer there said, I was a lieutenant commander then, "You know, Commander, I have a ranch over on the big island, but Mrs. Mona Holmes, who owns it, can't use any of her help for your people because her mother is sick and they have to care for her. So, it you could, say, get some stewards . . ." I said, "I'll get them off the ship right away." With that, I had two ranches because I had the Theodore H. Davies Company ranch. I knew the Russells of the Davies ranch, and they invited us. Well, you can't send the whole air group on two ranches, and I had to keep some flying, so I ferried them over in torpedo planes to the big island of Hawaii, and I split up the leave period to give the whole air group, say, three, four, or five days at one of the ranches over Christmas and New Year.

H. L. Miller #1 - 70

So, really, we had a wonderful time. Everybody was relaxed, we got our flying in. When the <u>Princeton</u> came back, they were all mad at each other because at Bremerton it snowed and rained, and, here, we came aboard looking like a million dollars. So, really, Hawaii did us an awful lot of good over that Christmas.

Q: You really were doing your job, weren't you?

Adm. M.: That's right.

Q: What about some of the men? Were they suffering from strain as a result of the . . .

Adm. M.: After a certain length of time in combat, you've got to take some time off just to relax. You know, the flying game was pretty hard, too. You've got to relax and get away from it for a while, and then, when you pick up again, you're hot, you're ready to go. My kids were tired. We'd been going at it for quite some time. So, in January, when the <u>Princeton</u> came back, we were really ready to go.

We left Pearl Harbor and had an exercise with the <u>Saratoga</u>. Then we were going to go to the next big operation, the Marshall Islands, take Kwajalein, then go on up and take Eniwetok. Well, we landed aboard the <u>Princeton</u> before going back to Pearl to load up and head for the Marshalls, and here was a set of orders for me to go as the air officer to one of these little CVE carriers, midget carriers.

H. L. Miller #1 - 71

Q: This was the <u>Hancock</u>?

Adm. M.: No. I had a set of orders to a little jeep carrier. They didn't have an air group commander to take over my job right then, so I asked the skipper if he would ask Admiral Radford - Admiral Radford had shifted up to Air Force, Pacific Fleet, staff - if I could go on this operation to the Marshalls, because I knew if I got out of Pearl, way out there in the open sea, they'd never get me back to take over as air officer of a CVE being built up in Bremerton, Washington, or in Takoma, or some place.

Q: What was the wisdom of a set of orders like this, to a little jeep carrier, at this point?

Adm. M.: Don't ask me. It was idiotic for me with all my combat experience to be yanked out of the Pacific with important operations coming up, and you could have gotten 500 officers from some of these shore establishments around the country to take over as air officer of that little CVE.

Q: Was it, by chance, the fact that the jeep carrier was just making her way into the Pacific then, was she not?

Adm. M.: No, they had quite a few jeep carriers. Anyway, I got permission to go. We finished up the Marshall Islands deal . . .

Q: Would you focus on that for a minute?

Adm. M.: Well, we went in and we made strikes on Wotje, some

H. L. Miller #1 - 72

darned good strikes there, and Eniwetok, and the Marines had a comparatively easy time, walking right in and taking over Kwajalein.

Q: What kind of aerial opposition did you meet in these operations?

Adm. M.: After the first brush, we shot down all the Japs and shot their planes on the ground. So you might say aerial opposition was easy. We wiped them out and they couldn't come from any place.

Q: They had aerodromes on all of these places?

Adm. M.: Oh, yes, Sir. So, with that, we used Kwajalein and that area as a base of operations to pound Eniwetok to death and support the Marines and Army going in to Eniwetok, and that was a tough operation because at that time of year we had these swells in the Pacific and they're always sort of at cross purposes with the wind, so that you'd be landing into the wind but the ship would be rocking back and forth. It was difficult to get aboard, and it worried the devil out of some of the kids. So, I used to take the experienced pilots and we'd take most of the hops because we knew hot to take care of these little incidentals of coming aboard.

Q: What is the scientific explanation for these swells -- seasonal swells?

Adm. M.: I don't know. You don't have swells in the Atlantic like you do in the Pacific. We were talking about this yesterday. It's an entirely different picture. But we supported the operations there and we took over Eniwetok. And then we had permission and we went in and landed at the field just to see what we had done. It was very interesting. As a matter of fact, I took five pints of whisky from the ship's sick bay to give to the Army and the Marines there on Eniwetok for souvenirs. We also took, believe it or not, gallons of ice cream from the ship, plus sandwiches, candy bars, and what not.

When we landed we told the Marines to come and get some ice cream, and they didn't wait for a spoon, they'd just go in with their dirty hands and scoop it out. There was nothing but dirt and dead Japs on the island. I went over and I said to a Marine, "Here's a pint of whisky from the good ship Princeton." One pint had broken as we were shot off the catapult. I went over to the Navy and Captain Bat Cruse, who was the big Navy man there. His aide was a classmate of mine, and I gave both of them each a pint, and I said, "Now, I have a pint for the Army brigadier general." They said, "Don't give him a pint. Don't flash it in front of him because he'll take it and break it right in front of your face. He hates whisky and he hates smoking." So I said, "O.K. give this to the next guy in the Marines."

Well, we took a look, and they were just stacking all the dead Japs in a big hole. The stench was terrible. We asked about souvenirs and they said we could have the whole island if we wanted, guns and everything. So we piled a lot of this stuff back into two airplanes, my fighter and a torpedo plane that came with me. We took it on back to the ship, clambered aboard, got all washed and disinfected and then gave it to anybody who wanted it. But Eniwetok, in our opinion, was a comparatively easy operation.

All during this time I had permission from the Admiral to delay my going back. But after that operation was over, I had to go higher for permission. It was Easter Sunday, the whole fleet had congregated at Majuro, and the next operation was going to be Palau, Hollandia, in support of General MacArthur's landing operation, and then hitting the island of Truk on the way back. I knew that was going to be our last operation, so I wanted to stay out there. So I went over on Easter Sunday morning to the USS *Lexington* to ask the commander of Task Force 58, Admiral Pete Mitscher, who had been the skipper of the *Hornet* when I had the Doolittle boys on board, for permission to stay out for this operation. This got to be quite a game because I would get these dispatches, as I'd come back from a strike, saying, "When is Miller going to be detached to carry out his set of orders?" Well, Admiral Mitscher gave me permission to delay until this last operation, then I had to go and execute those orders.

We got down to Espiritu Santo before going up to Palau,

and I ran into then-Commander Tommy Blackburn, who had a fighter squadron down there. He was leaving and going back to Washington, and he said, "Is there anything you want me to tell them in Washington?" And I said, "Yes, tell them I am more experienced as an air group commander than any other group commander in the Pacific, so I want a big air group when I get back and I don't want that CVE. This is a waste of talent. Would you tell them? Then call my wife and say, hi for me." So Tommy went back and he told them and they said, O.K., and they assigned me to Air Group 6, but I didn't know anything about this for quite awhile.

Q: Because this operation was still coming up?

Adm. M.: Sure. So we went from Espiritu Santo up to Palau. We hit them, and we hit them hard. We hit the jackpot there, too. Then the task force went up in support of MacArthur's landing and that was an easy operation. From there, we came on back and on the way back we hit Truk for two days and we hit it hard.

Q: Truk was really a bastion, wasn't it?

Adm. M.: Yes, they were pretty well entrenched there.

Q: But we had no intention of taking Truk?

Adm. M.: No, we had absolutely no intention of taking it.

H. L. Miller #1 - 76

We just wanted to wipe out all the airplanes there and get any of their ships in the harbor, plus wipe out air installations, radars, any buildings, anything we could hit. We did a pretty good job of it. The Japs really didn't use Truk very much from there on in.

Q: It was more or less bypassed, wasn't it?

Adm. M.: Yes, Sir.

Q: Tell me, did you learn any lessons, new techniques, or what-have-you in these islands, these different operations, that then became a matter of policy?

Adm. M.: Well, before each different operation, of course, we'd learn, but there were certain fundamentals that you learned in fighting a war right from the very beginning that you carried through forever and ever, and when you started breaking those rules, you either got shot up, you got killed, or you were lucky that you got by with your life. These are some of the fundamentals that you learned in flying. The same thing in driving a car. The safety precautions, the speed that you're supposed to go, your turns, your G limits, all this, and you either stuck to the rules and did it right or you were going to be in trouble. Just like in one operation - we all gathered together on the flagship and said, OK, this is the way it's going to be, and here was this one air group commander who - you just couldn't talk to, and I said, you know, that fellow's going to be dead, and fast. He was killed the next day. You can do it wrong and get away with it if you're lucky, but you're not going to be able to get away with it forever. There are ways to do it and ways not to do it.

Q: Those were basic things. Over and above the basic, were there any special insights gained by any particular operation that one could put into effect in the future?

Adm. M.: We learned from each one. For an amphibious operation, you do certain things. For the big strikes, where we went in to hit, shake them up, and get out, you had other rules that you went by. For air support of Marines or Army ashore, there were certain fundamental rules which you went by, and certain safety precautions. So, you might say that for every type of operation, you used the basic rules and then the extra special rules for that particular situation. You learned and you kept them right up there in your head, and you continued to keep them ready to execute any time you got into a ticklish situation.

Q: Was there any cross-fertilization from any other squadron commanders?

Adm. M.: Yes. We used to send our combat reports after every operation, to everybody, and we would read these reports from all the air groups, from all the units that were participants. There was a very good exchange of information. Additionally, whenever we left the Pacific, coming back to the States maybe to new duty or to another outfit, we would talk to the air groups, say, at the Hawaiian Islands that were getting ready to go out or those in training on the West Coast. We'd keep passing this information all the time.

Q: Was that a voluntary sort of thing, or was it demanded of you by the over-all command?

Adm. M.: A lot of it was demanded, but there were a great many aviators who took it upon themselves to be sure that a lot of the ones that had never been in combat got this word.

Q: Were there any flyers who came into the Pacific at that time from the Atlantic theatre and, if so, did they have to re-learn certain techniques or were the basics the same for them, too?

Adm. M.: They had to learn all the tricks of the trade that we had learned in the Pacific, because if was a different war out there than in the Atlantic. The Atlantic was primarily an antisubmarine war. Sure enough, in the landings in North Africa and Normandy, they had strikes and air support, but it wasn't comparable to the operations that we found in the Pacific. It was a different ball game.

Q: Does this mean, then, that they had to unlearn some of

the things they had been doing?

Adm. M.: You might say they had to re-learn the new techniques, or learn the new techniques, that they were going to find in successful operations in the Pacific. We used to send all these memos and reports over to the Atlantic, too. But you really don't get into it or absorb it all until you know you're going there and have to do it. So in the Pacific, from combat operations out there, we sent our reports in to Hawaii, all the air groups there, to all the units there, we sent them to the West Coast, and we sent representatives to talk to these people. Furthermore, for the Atlantic sailors that came out there to participate in the operations, we used to go over and talk to them, just force feed them all this stuff right along, because it takes an awful lot of teaching to cover a big war and all the techniques that you use in it.

Q: Was it in a sense, then, perhaps, at least with some of them, a handicap to have served in the Atlantic first and then to have come to the Pacific?

Adm. M.: I'd say yes, when you're fighting a Pacific-type war. I remember some of the squadron commanders and air group commanders that came from the Atlantic, had to learn how to fight the war in the Pacific the way we did it and the way we had been doing it successfully for three years. It was altogether different.

Q: Since we are talking about the contrast between the two, did you in the early stages suffer because of the Atlantic conflict, did you suffer from a lack of equipment and so forth coming on to you?

Adm. M.: I think at the start of the war and for quite a while afterwards certainly we suffered from lack of equipment, but that was all over the Navy and the other services, too. We just didn't have the war machine, it wasn't putting out enough equipment and spare parts . . .

Q: In your sphere, were there any specific instances that you can cite where you lacked, at the moment, something that you should have had?

Adm. M.: Well, with my first air group on the Princeton, I had one extra pilot for my airplanes. Later on, of course, we had 150 percent pilots. We were short of pilots at the start, we were short of airplanes. They shifted more airplanes around to keep the units that were going out filled up. Those that weren't going to move for a while were always short of airplanes. But when the backlog was taken care of, the second time I went out, I had 162 percent pilots. I had pilots coming out of my ears. I had all the airplanes I wanted. I had everything I wanted, but that was when the war machine was really grinding 100 percent and turning out everything that we wanted. It was a different story as the war went on.

Q: Did you have any close contact with any of the well-known amphibious commanders in the Pacific, such as Kelly Turner?

Adm. M.: No, Sir. We supported lots of amphibious operations from the Marshalls, Tarawa, Eniwetok, Okinawa. We were there. We knew what they wanted, we knew the procedures. Whenever I was in charge of the air support from the air end of it, the air support coordinator calling in planes to hit these targets, or assigning them targets, the guy on the ground gave me those targets, I was in communication with him, and we had a very fine workable system. But I was way down the line from, say, the Admirals like Kelly Turner and Admiral Blandy.

Q: But didn't they, for a given operation, say, like Saipan or Okinawa, wasn't there a grand pow-wow on one occasion of all those who had a responsible role to play?

Adm. M.: Only of the top echelon. You really couldn't find a ship around there in the Pacific that had space enough for all the various echelons down to, say, people like me.

Q: And the command ships were usually small ones, weren't they?

Adm. M.: That's right. They were all small. They were chock-a-block all the time. They just had too many people. But because of working in these operations and the knowledge that we gained, we became very proficient in air support of troops and in all those other operations. So we supported them 100 percent and we knew what was going on.

Now, as far as our own task group is concerned, whenever we had a big strike going in and/or support for amphibious operations, the air group commanders from these carriers would go over to the carrier flagship and the staff would go over the next operation to ensure that everybody understood, and we'd take copies of that operation order back to our particular carrier with us. So it was a closely coordinated operation to cut in all echelons of command down to the last pilot in the cockpit.

Q: It was rather remarkable how quickly that technique developed, wasn't it?

Adm. M.: That's correct. Furthermore, the air group commanders would come over to my carrier, get all the pilots and brief them, tell them what their air group was going to do, and I'd get in a plane and fly with them over to their carrier and I'd tell that carrier, all those pilots. We'd cover the carriers that way. They knew, say, for instance, that that carrier was under my charge in that particular operation. They knew who was the boss. It was me, and they saw me face to face. It's a lot easier that way because they know that you can do the job and they're going to be right behind you obeying your orders.

Q: Even in this area, a public relations job is necessary!

Adm. M.: That's right. For instance, they were knocking off air group commanders pretty fast, so we went over to the flagship . . .

Q: You mean the Japs were knocking them off?

Adm. M.: Yes. So we went over to the flagship - Admiral Mitscher's flagship - and his air officer, who was then Captain Jimmy Flatley, said, "We're losing too many air group commanders. I don't want you guys going in and dropping any bombs. You stand off and you run the show."

Q: Did the Japs consider you primary targets?

Adm. M.: No, they didn't know, but we just happened to be losing them. They were taking too many chances. So he said, "You can't carry any more bombs. I want you to stay out." Well, you really can't do that because if you're a squadron commander or an air group commander and you say, "O.K., now, kids, you go in there and give it the old college try, and I'll stay out here and watch," you can't do it, you can't fight a war that way. Captain Flately said, "Don't forget that." So I went back to the carrier and, of course, I told them about this, and I said, "He just threatened the whole bunch of us," and we had a big operation the next day or the day after. I was up before the whole bunch and I said, "Now, here's the plan of attack and everything else." Somebody said, "We took that bomb off your airplane." You could have heard a pin drop, so I said, "You put that bomb right back on."

Q: You lose status right there!

Adm. M.: You're right. This was one thing that you had to

H. L. Miller #1 - 84

be very careful about.

Q: Interesting! In some of those later operations, I believe the Japanese had begun their kamikaze attacks, had they not?

Adm. M.: Yes.

Q: Did you have any experience with that?

Adm. M.: After I got through with Air Group 23 on the <u>Princeton</u>, that was after Truk and we went back to Majuro and I got a letter from my wife and found out that I was going to get Air Group 6. So I got back to Pearl Harbor and I knew that ComAirPac was still mad at me because I didn't carry out that set of orders, so I sent the torpedo skipper up to the staff to find out the lay of the land. I'd flown my plane in, see, but I stayed down with the CASU unit, and he called me up and he said, "What will you give me if I tell you?" And I said, "Give me the word over the phone."

Q: Who was ComAirPac? Towers?

Adm. M.: I think he was. He said, "Well, you have Air Group 6 and some other guy has the air job on the CVE." I said, "That's great."

So I went back to the States and took over Air Group 6. It was based at Santa Rosa, California. They'd been out and they were back getting re-formed, and when I left with them I was assigned to the USS <u>Hancock</u>. We went out to Pearl and

H. L. Miller #1 - 85

we had some more training on the big island of Hilo, Hawaii. I also formed another fighter-bomber squadron there of F-4U airplanes.

Q: Was this a supererogation on your part? I mean, was this something optional on your part?

Adm. M.: No. They ordered it from AirPac to form another squadron in the air group. Well, we had to do it in record time, so we all pitched in and I shifted to the F-4U so I could help out with the training of the new squadron.

We went aboard the USS <u>Hancock</u> in Ulithi. We went out in two Jeep carriers for transportation and I had the biggest air group in the Navy. It may have been the biggest air group in the Navy. I had 186 officers, 162 pilots, and 103 airplanes. We went aboard the <u>Hancock</u> in February of 1945, and in March of 1945 we proceeded right on up the chain making strikes because they were going to make the big landing on Okinawa. Well, we went in, we supported the landing on Okinawa and I remember Easter Sunday morning 1945, I think the first time we used napalm in combat. It was a beautiful morning when we took off. I looked back and I watched pilots who didn't make it with those belly tanks of napalm, they hit the water, and blew up, and there was fire all over. The guys just burned up.

We went in with the air group. I was one of the air support coordinators, and I watched the landing on West Beach.

I looked out at all the boats coming in. We had shot up planes on the field and everything else, and I said, "This is the hell of a way to spend Easter, to watch everybody shooting everybody else." It looked like it was just easy. The landing was easy, but then it was getting the rest of the island after that, the pillboxes, the fortifications that the Japanese had set up. Okinawa was a tough one to take.

Q: George Dyer made a similar remark. He was involved in the operation. He thought it was some way to celebrate Easter, too. On that occasion, the kamikaze did begin to operate, didn't it?

Adm. M.: Actually, the kamikazes started coming before that. When we were in Ulithi, we got aboard the Hancock and we went to the movies that night, and all of a sudden general quarters went, we rushed up, we looked over at the Ticonderoga and a Jap kamikaze had come in low - mind you, everybody was at the movies on the hangar deck of the Ticonderoga, you could see through the hangar deck, you know, the door was open. And that kamikaze, if he'd flown into the hangar deck, he'd have wiped out a thousand people. That ship would have been decommissioned, as far as people were concerned. But instead, he hit right by the stern. I never could figure that out. He could have gone right into the hangar, killed all those people, started fires that would have been too tough to get out because they didn't have the people to do it. They were all at the movies. They were very lucky, and it wasn't long before they had some jury rig and the Ticonderoga was operative.

Q: I suppose one could speculate that even a kamikaze pilot was not immune to emotion, which might obscure his reasoning about an attack?

Adm. M.: I just think he must have made a mistake, because I know if I'd been a kamikaze pilot I'd have said, OK, I'm going to kill myself, but if I saw that whole group on the hangar deck, I'd have gone for them. I think he just made a pretty bad mistake. The kamikazes started there and they continued. Okinawa was one kamikaze after another in all of those task groups around there. Following that, as we proceeded up the chain, it was the same story.

Q: They were a psychological factor, as far as our men were concerned, were they not?

Adm. M.: No, not the way I saw it. We knocked down an awful lot of kamikazes, and you might say day after day in some of those operations the ship's fire would get them, and then our combat air patrols would be after them. It was certainly a rough go for them. Of course, they got some pretty good hits on our ships.

Q: The Princeton came to grief, didn't she?

Adm. M.: Yes, but that was after I left. On the Hancock they launched the whole air group to go up and hit the Japanese battleship, the Yamamoto, I think it was. The big one. I remember we went up and that poor old ship was really sunk. Then when we got back, I'd been in the air for four hours and a half, as I circled the carrier coming in for a landing, I thought, "The air officer promised me he'd clean the flight deck, get all that grease off of it. Boy, it looks funny." Then, as I looked further, here was a great big bomb hole in the deck. The carrier had been hit by a kamikaze. They said, come aboard, so we landed aboard, taxied right around the bomb hole, surveyed the damage, asked how many people had been killed, and all that. It was pretty tough going. Other ships had been hit from the opening day in March up near Kagashima, the southernmost island. The day after, we went up in a fighter sweep to clear the Japs out of the air at Osaka and Kobe and to hit the airfield at Osaka, Itami Airfield. There were just a few Japs in the air, and they stayed way up above us - they were afraid to come down - so we hit the field at Itami. I had taken a fighter sweep from my own ship, the Hancock, my own air group, and one Marine squadron from the other carrier. The other carrier was the Franklin, and when I started on the way home, the air group commander in the Franklin called his troops and said, "Save your gas," don't do this and don't do that, and I thought well, what's he telling those troops with me, I'm in charge of this outfit, not him. But I didn't say anything. When I got back to where our task group was supposed to be, I could only count two carriers, and I said, "Gee, whizz, there was the Princeton, and the Franklin, and this other one. I wonder, have I missed the boat?" Then I looked over on the horizon, and there was a carrier burning like the dickens. That was the Franklin.

Q: Wasn't that Mitscher's flagship?

Adm. M.: No, that was Admiral Jerry Bogan's flagship. I looked at that thing burning. We landed aboard the Hancock and I had to cancel myself out of the flight schedule because we had to take over for the whole task group operations. You see, the Admiral and his whole staff were getting off the Franklin. They almost suffocated to death from the smoke. They told Hancock to take charge of all the task group schedule. We had to take airplanes, and we said, OK, this has more holes than the other one, throw it over the side, and make room for the good ones coming aboard. We also sent some over to the Bunker Hill. These were things that you had to make up your mind to do and do in a hurry to keep the flight schedule going.

A kamikaze had come in on the Franklin that morning as they were launching. They were lucky they got in there and when they hit a plane or two on that flight deck the bombs went off and it was a mess all over - fires and explosions, everything.

Well, as we went along, we still saw the kamikazes, but then as we shot, you might say, hundreds of them down, the Japs started hiding their airplanes, and as we moved on up to the Japanese mainland, when we would go in to hit we would search out, hunt for, some of these camouflaged planes around those fields. When you found one or two, it led you to a whole bunch of them, so you'd form a circle and start firing at all these airplanes and burn them up.

Q: Was the camouflage defective, I mean, inadequate, or what?

Adm. M.: Some were good and others bad.

Q: Similar to our methods?

Adm. M.: Yes, but there was the plight. For instance, if you took a look down there now, and you said, there's nothing there, then you went over on the other side and the sun hit something over here, and it was an airplane, so you went down there, you found not one but twenty-five. So when we started searching for them, we got hundreds of planes on the ground which is just as good as getting them in the air. The Japs were saving them - they still hadn't given up. I remember at that time there were three targets we couldn't hit. It's a funny thing, but when I was in Hawaii at Christmas, Mrs. Russell said, "Don't hit Kyoto." I said, "Why?" and she said, "It's a city of culture. It's a beautiful place." And it just so happened that Kyoto was one of the three targets we couldn't hit. The other two were Hiroshima and Nagasaki. We didn't know why, but I suspected Kyoto because it was a city of culture, but I didn't know the other two. Of course, when the first A-bomb went off, we knew why. Also the second.

During this time we still knew that the Japs would let go, they were out to give it the old college try again. So we kept on hitting Japanese installations all the way up through Hokkaido. Then that big day came. I had the task group of planes from our three carriers to go in and hit the electronics plant southeast of Tokyo. We had hit it before and were hitting it again. And all this time everybody was sweating it out, drinking coffee, and saying, "Is the war over?" I got about 40 miles from the electronics plant and the task group CIC officer called me and said, "99 Jamboree, this is Christopher. Over." And the guy who was calling from Christopher was none other than John Connally, now Secretary of the Treasury. He was a lieutenant then and fighter director officer. I said, "Christopher, this is 99 Jamboree. Go ahead with your message." He said, "99 Jamboree, have all your planes drop their bombs in the water and return to base. Do not attack, repeat, do not attack any targets in the Tokyo area. Call and get acknowledgements from the three fighter sweep leaders (who were in there right then) and tell them not to strafe or bomb anything, but to come back, return to base. Watch out for rats in the air (those were Jap pilots). They've taken off to give it the go for just one last try. Watch out for rats in the air." I asked Connally if the war was over. He said he didn't know but them were your orders.

I repeated back and about that time the pilots started singing "When the war is over, we will all go USN." I said, "Get the hell off the air. I've got to get this message across," which they did. I got acknowledgements from my three fighter sweep leaders. I told everybody else to return to base. People were dropping their bombs, they were doing loops, and everything. And about that time, my fighter sweep leader, Lcdr. Neff Bigelow, called me - we had code names but he wanted to be sure. Well, Neff Bigelow said to me, "Hank, this is Neff. There are seven Japs over me and it looks like they're going to attack. What do?" I thought, gee shizz, I don't want to start World War III, but I don't want to lose any of my kids, so I said, "Neff, this is Hank. If it looks like they're going to attack, shoot them down gently." He got four out of the seven. That quote six or seven years later was in Reader's Digest, and my wife said, "Hey, look what they have here," and they had attributed it to Admiral Halsey. Neff Bigelow was sitting here about two months ago, and I said, "Hey, Neff, I want to check with you." He said, "Yes, it wasn't Halsey. It was between you and me." But with that, I got everybody going back to the carrier.

Q: This was the interim period while they were waiting for the effect of Hiroshima to sink in and the armistice to come?

Adm. M.: Actually, the war was over, but I didn't know that. So on the way back to the carrier - one has to check with the picket destroyer there. They sanitize you. They de-louse you, to be sure no Japs are following you.

Q: Is that a kind of a picket ship?

Adm. M.: Yes. You circle, then they give you clearance to go to your particular carrier along the corridor. So everybody did that and when it came to my turn, I came down and I said, "Tomcat one, this is 99 Jamboree. Circling your base. I have lots of gas left, so you clear anybody that's in trouble and I'll circle here until you make up your mind." He said, "OK, 99 Jamboree." About that time, this kid said, "Tomcat one, this is 311 zebra. Over." "311 zebra, this is Tomcat one. Go ahead with your message." "Tomcat one, this is 311 zebra. Is the war over?" "311 zebra, this is Tomcat one. We don't know if the war is over. We got the same message as you. Return to base." "Tomcat one, this is 311 zebra. If the war is over, some Jap bastard didn't get the news because he just shot my ass off." But the poor kid got on back to base. He was OK, but some Jap had really corraled him. He was lucky.

When we got back to the ship, we found out that the war was over and from there on in we ran prisoner of war missions and we dropped supplies on the POW camps all over Japan.

Q: May I ask you a question, lapping back? You said that there were three targets that were tabu to you and Hiroshima and Nagasaki were two of them. How far in advance of the dropping of the atomic bombs were they designated as the targets?

Adm. M.: My only recollection is after we were hit on the Hancock we went back to Pearl and we got fixed in Pearl. We came back

H. L. Miller #1 - 94

again hitting all the way up the Japanese chain of islands, and when we came back in June - because we hit Tokyo on the 10th of July, that was my wife's birthday, and we hit on the 18th of July, my birthday, that's why I remember - and at that time we knew those three targets weren't to be hit.

Q: By that time it was fixed. I read recently - and I'd never known this before - that the second city was bombed in order to say to the Japanese, yes, we have more than one bomb. Was this the interpretation at the time?

Adm. M.: I don't know. I just had no information on that. We didn't know anything about an A-bomb.

Q: Did you have any knowledge of the B-17 raids, the Army Air Force raids, on various islands, under Admiral Hoover's command, I believe?

Adm. M.: The only information I had on the B-17s, was when we joined the Hancock in March of 1945 in Ulithi, we went over to Admiral Mitscher's flagship and, as I told you, Captain Flatley said, "We're losing too many air group commanders." Well, he also said this, "General LeMay's (General LeMay was in charge of the bombings) staff is over here wanting to get information on low-level attacks." (Remember, at that time they were bombing the Tokyo area with B-17s. They were doing high-level bombing and they weren't hitting), so the Navy told LeMay's staff how they did it in the lower-altitude bombing. I heard that right after that LeMay went to low altitude bombing and wiped out huge areas in the Tokyo area. He went from the high to the Navy way of doing it much lower, and he put his bombs in there. That's the only part of it that I know.

Q: Tell me about the specific attack on the Hancock while you were with her.

Adm. M.: On that specific day, as I said, when I came back from the big strike on the Japanese battleship, I saw this big hole on the deck of the USS Hancock. We landed aboard, taxied around the hole, parked our airplanes, and we asked how many were killed. There were some 80 people who were killed when that bomb hit. A Japanese kamikaze came down and dropped two bombs, one went right past the athletic officer as he was standing by his gun. It brushed his shoulder, went through an opening, and exploded down on the hangar deck. The second one hit the flight deck, went through it, and exploded on the hangar deck.

Q: Did he attempt to crash, too?

Adm. M.: He crashed in the water, astern of the ship. The fires that resulted really looked like we were going to lose the Hancock. It shook up the Number one elevator to such an extent that they couldn't use it, but the damage-control officer of the Hancock had his crews so well indoctrinated that the fires were under control in twenty minutes, and that ship was saved. Lieutenant Commander Slacks was - he's dead now - the damage-control officer. He had trained his crews, he was very hard-nosed about damage control,

H. L. Miller #1 - 96

closing doors, closing hatches, dumping debris over the side, not allowing any oily rags to accumulate so that fires could start. I had the officers who weren't flying in the wardroom, we used that as a ready room, we had two ready rooms aft of the wardroom. Lieutenant Commander Slacks was the first officer in the Navy that, without Bureau of Ships approval, moved the ready rooms from topside, where pilots were killed all the time, down below the armored deck. So, on that attack, all my pilots were below that armored deck in the wardroom, and my air crewman, too. They were in the ready rooms. They were scared because they were breathing some of that smoke through wet handkerchiefs, but we didn't lose a single person in that explosion and fire, simply because we had them under the armored deck.

Q: That calls for some further remarks on this special breed of men, damage-control officers. Some of them were pretty remarkable in the techniques they developed. Do you have any other observations or experience with such men?

Adm. M.: Lieutenant Commander Slacks, of course, asked me when I came aboard, do you have any objection to my putting the ready rooms under the armored deck? I said, "That's the smartest move that you could make. I'll back you 100 percent." So he did it, but it was months before all that information of all those procedures and ways of doing business were approved by the Bureau of Ships, and the go-ahead was given to others. But we had seen this all the way through. The pilots that were killed aboard the Franklin and the other ships that were hit by bombs right there by the ready rooms. They were cremated. They didn't have a chance.

After, in the peacetime years, I ran into another remarkable damage-control officer who was a captain, retired, out in Honolulu. He is now a vice president for Dillingham out there. He's in charge of tugs and all that. He was a remarkable damage-control officer. He trained his crews. He made everybody damage-control conscious, and when they had the catapult explosion on the Leyte there would have been much greater damage all the way through if he hadn't - and more loss of life - if he hadn't such a remarkably well-trained bunch of crews. No one had to take charge. They knew exactly what to do. That was Lieutenant Commander Meredith C. Riddle. He's a tremendous guy.

Q: Does this say that, certainly in time of war, there should be greater flexibility and less control from the Department in Washington?

Adm. M.: Absolutely, because they don't see what you see in the war zone. It's the man on the scene who has to make the decisions and must make them, because Washington certainly can't dream of what's going on out there on the water in a particular battle area, and the conditions under which you're operating. So it's really essential that you have good idea men around who will make decisions, and dreamers who can dream the right thing and execute it.

H. L. Miller #1 - 98

Q: And with freedom!

Adm. M.: That's right!

Q: I suppose this is one reason for the wisdom in bringing back Admiral Lee in terms of ordnance for setting up ComDevFour, was it?

Adm. M.: It was a development group.

Q: Yes, but a man who had the battle experience could come back and pass judgment on what was being proposed to sent out to the fleet.

Adm. M.: That's right. He knew what they wanted out there and what they needed, so he was certainly the Number one man to put in charge of that group and give them the authority to make tests and make recommendations to the bureaus to get those things done.

Q: Another question came to mind as you were talking about the kamikaze. Was there any deterioration in the quality of the kamikaze pilot, the daring, the ability, and so forth, as the war came to an end?

Adm. M.: No, I wouldn't say there was a deterioration, because they knew what they had to do and what they wanted to do for their country. As a matter of fact, as I told you, the big day that the war was over, we still had combat air patrols in the air to guard against maybe one or four or five kamikaze pilots that got away from the field and wanted to give it the last try.

Q: Carry out their mission, regardless.

Adm. M.: That's right, and the British carrier task force was operating next to ours. There were really four carrier task groups operating, three U. S. and one U. K. I had a combat air patrol in the air and the Kamikaze came, diving on the British carrier. It was late afternoon of August 15, 1945, the day the war was over.

Q: Precisely what you were afraid of!

Adm. M.: And one of my pilots started after him. He pushed down and he shot that kamikaze out of the sky. The British admiral sent him over a case of Scotch.

Q: He had it in his power to do that! Which carrier was being attacked?

Adm. M.: It must have been the <u>Victorious</u> because that was one of the ones out there. But there was the Jap, and this was the day after the war was over, and my boy followed him right on down and shot him out of the sky.

Q: How did the British task group of carriers meld into the general command?

Adm. M.: Pretty well. They didn't have the smooth operations that we had. They didn't have the experience. Furthermore, they didn't have the discipline that we had.

Q: In what sense did they lack that?

Adm. M.: They didn't stick together like we did. They had too many lone rangers who would do it their own way, so they had a little trouble finding their own ship. From time to time, we'd have them land aboard ours. Ours would be the first one that they'd find. But that was all right. They still did a good job.

Q: Had they, by that time, as units of the fleet, mastered refueling and all those things at sea because they hadn't been accustomed to that?

Adm. M.: No, but they caught on and were very good in replenishment of fuel, ammunition, food, at sea, just like we did. And I think they got the American wrenches and couplings and all that, to be sure that they could take on fuel and ammo and food from all of our ships. They did a good job and they feel right into it.

H. L. Miller #2 - 101

Interview No. 2 with Rear Admiral Henry L. Miller, U. S. Navy
Commanding Officer of the Naval Air Test Station

Place: Patuxent River, Maryland

Date: Thursday morning, 25 March 1971

Subject: Biography

By: John T. Mason, Jr.

Q: Admiral, this second chapter should begin, I believe, with your return to Washington in December of 1945. You'd been recalled from Japan, and came back to the Department where your first duty was to write Air Operations Instructions. I'm rather intrigued about that.

Adm. M.: Well, there's one part of Air Group 6 - on the Hancock that I forgot to mention.

Q: Fine. Please include that now.

Adm. M.: It was in regard to your old friend, Admiral Dan Gallery. It just so happened that he came out and took over command of the Hancock just after the surrender was signed. Incidentally, he rode in the back seat of an SB-2C aircraft piloted by the skipper of the dive bomber squadron in this 1,500-plane review over the battleship Missouri while MacArthur and Nimitz were signing the surrender documents. It was really worth your life to be in that formation because there were so many planes and so few places to go in a cloudy sky that we had some pretty hairy scrapes that afternoon. Captain Hicky who Dan Gallery was relieving was accused by Dan Gallery of trying to put him up there to eliminate him so he wouldn't get command of the Hancock. It was quite a show. And, incidentally, too, on that USS Hancock we had as executive officer, at that time, Commander Red Raborn, who later on became a vice admiral . . .

Q: And a great R and D man.

Adm. M.: Yes, Sir, and, of Polaris fame. He was an outstanding officer and certainly did a wonderful job on that ship.

Well, after that, back to Washington, for the job of writing up air operations in World War II.

Q: I don't imagine you were too happy to return to Washington at that point, were you?

Adm. M.: As a matter of fact, I was tired. I had had a real bellyfull of war, and what I wanted to do was go back to some nice air station on some staff and just relax for a couple of years. But it so happened that an officer senior to me was supposed to have this writing job, but he wanted to go to a nice air station on the staff, too. So he won out and I got the job.

We did, over a year's time, produce a tactical publication called USF 4, which listed the procedures, the formations of ships and aircraft that we used in World War II.

Q: This was a kind of a summation, was it?

Adm. M.: Yes. It was the best procedures, the best formations, and the best advice that came out of World War II, and we put it into tactical publication.

Q: How did you go about distilling all of this information, all of this knowledge?

Adm. M.: We had some 20 officers writing various aspects of USF 4. Mine was writing from the air group standpoint, what we did in squadrons and air groups in fighting the war - our procedures for rendezvous, proceeding to the target, identification of the target, attack, re-rendezvous, navigation back, what to do in bad weather, formations around a single carrier or a multi-carrier task force. All these things.

Q: Much of this was a matter of knowledge with you and some of it, I imagine, was something you consulted with others about?

Adm. M.: That's correct. I had a very good working knowledge of all the formations that we used, but I was a horrible artist and I used a black-shoe captain to do the sketches I used, because he was a very, very good artist. Of course, you can write just so much every day, then you have to go and talk to someone, go visiting, and get it off your mind. In a way it was sort of a blessing in disguise for Air Group 23 people of the USS Princeton. At the start of the war, when it was tough, awards were scarce. People said, well, that's part of the job, fighting the war. But later on they were much more lenient and they allowed Air Medals and Distinguished Flying Crosses for the numbers of strikes in which you participated. Also, if it was an important strike, you could get a medal for that particular one.

A memorandum fell on my desk one day in the Navy Department while I was writing, and it said that all former commanding officers can resubmit recommendations for their pilots in accordance with

H. L. Miller #2 - 104

the strike flight system. Whereupon I broke out my Air Group 23 diary which showed the individual pilots of each flight. I also sent all the pilots who were still living a memo requesting verification of the data that I already had and, with that, I used the yeoman there to type up all these recommendations and as a result the pilots from Air Group 23 and crewmen all received a bucketful of awards that they never would have received if I hadn't been in that position.

Q: You say it took you a whole year to compile this set of instructions?

Adm. M.: That's correct and, as a matter of fact, some of the other officers stayed there longer than a year sending these instructions out to the fleet for comment before it was finally published.

Q: Did you do that with your sector?

Adm. M.: No, Sir, and I'll tell you the reason why. We had some of the most experienced talent in the Navy writing up these operations, and when I say the fleet - at that time, six months or a year later, after the war was over - it was the third and fourth and fifth team that was out there operating the fleet. They didn't have the experience.

Q: There were many johnny-come-latelys, I suppose.

Adm. M.: There were. So we didn't ask them for advice or comment because they didn't know enough to comment, and this was very significant because our boss was then Rear Admiral Jerry Wright, and when he said the fleet is coming in tomorrow, they're going to review your publication, and the fleet is going to be right, nobody said anything except me. I raised my hand and I said, "Admiral, that fleet that's coming in tomorrow is the fifth team. The first team is right here. They're going to change my writing over my dead body." And it held up, too.

Q: He would appreciate and understand that point of view, I'm sure.

Adm. M.: Jerry Wright and I are very good friends.

Q: To what use was this publication put?

Adm. M.: USF 4 was the bible as far as carrier task groups were concerned for the Navy.

Q: It came in handy for Korea, did it?

Adm. M.: Yes, Sir, all subsequent operations. It's been changed as we've gone along and improved our methods.

Q: Was this a part of a concerted effort of the Department to distill the experiences of World War II in every area?

Adm. M.: That's correct. The Navy Department pulled everybody in, submarines, air, surface ships and started them writing to collect all that information, put it down for posterity and to further refine it as they learned more. For instance, as we got into the jet age, USF 4 was refined to include changes that had to be made because of jet aircraft aboard carriers and in the air around carriers. This was really necessary, but it was very easy to change. As a matter of fact, our procedures that were put into USF 4 took care of jets. We'd looked ahead to that.

H. L. Miller #2 - 106

Q: For one year you were engaged in writing these instructions, but then you remained in the Department for a more interesting assignment even still. Tell me about that.

Adm. M.: Do you mean going to Alaska?

Q: Going to Alaska?

Adm. M.: Yes. Just at the end of the year that I was in the job of writing, the Navy asked me to go to Alaska for a period of about thirty days to the Fairbanks, Nome, and Point Barrow complex, and get some specific information that they wanted. Whereupon, I was briefed by a so-called arctic expert in the office of naval research who gave me a solid hour's advice on what to wear going up to the great northland. I kept telling him that I was born and raised in Fairbanks, that I had gone to school in 65 below zero weather, but he still kept on giving me all this wonderful advice.

Q: Was it accurate?

Adm. M.: Accurate by the books that he had read. He was no arctic expert. He had spent a total of about two weeks in the Alaska area but he did a magnificent job of studying his lesson and reading all the literature that had been written on the great northland, the arctic and the antarctic.

I did go up to Fairbanks, from there I went to Nome and in Nome I interviewed Mr. Lohman of the famous Lohman Brothers there, the colonel in charge of the Air Force base, and others. While there, the Lohmans invited me to dinner. After dinner we looked over old

H. L. Miller #2 - 107

photographs and, lo and behold, I asked who this dirty little urchin in overalls was and they allowed as how it was Jimmy Doolittle when he was a boy. He sold papers in Nome. His father was mining there.

Q: He was an Alaskan, too?

Adm. M.: Yes, Sir. I asked them if I could have this picture and they said, yes, they had the negative. I sent it to his secretary in New York who put it on his desk for a Monday morning review when he came in. He was very surprised to see it but had a hunch where it came from.

From Nome I went to Point Barrow. The Seebees had a detachment at Point Barrow. The Navy had the staff at the arctic research lab at Point Barrow. After we landed - it was November of 1946, pretty cold, but not too bad - we went over to one of the quonsets and I interviewed the civilian in charge of the Seebees. He had come from Port Hueneme, California, and after about three hours I said, "Well, thank you very much for all this good information." He said, "Commander, I have a bunk over there for you for the next two or three days. You can relax and see everything around here." I said, Mr. So and So, "After I get something to eat, see that little airplane out there, I'm taking off and going back to Fairbanks." He said, "So, you're another one of these Washington experts who come here and in three hours you know all about Alaska, you go back to Washington and make all the decisions." I said,

"How long have you been up here?" and he said, "Since May." And I said, "Well, I'll tell you. I was born up here and spent the first seventeen years of my life and when you get that kind of experience come and see me." He had a wonderful sense of humor. He just roared.

Q: What was the type of data you were seeking?

Adm. M.: Information on important people, important knowledgeable people, to contact in these three areas if anything started up in the arctic where the Navy had to participate and we could tap these individuals for knowledge and their expertise in mining, agriculture, transportation, defense, fishing, hunting, any information that you would need in Alaska if you had to live there and send troops up there.

Q: Human resources, then?

Adm. M.: That's right. At that time the Navy had an oil well drilling at Umiat, which was to the east of Point Barrow, and when we left Point Barrow we stopped at Umiat. It was night and we wanted to get a good meal. It just so happened that an Eskimo man and his wife were in the plane and they were going to Fairbanks, I guess for recreation, so they were in their Sunday-go-to-meeting clothes. They didn't have all the layers of clothing that they would normally have. When we got to Umiat a jeep came and took me and a couple of the others to the camp where I assumed they were taking everybody. We had a very good meal, came on back, the door of the plane was open, and here was the Eskimo and his

H. L. Miller #2 - 109

wife, sitting in the plane almost frozen to death. They didn't want to move because they knew they probably wouldn't get a ride down to Fairbanks. So we got the plane started up, the heaters going, gave them blankets, had them get up and stomp around to get the circulation going, and they were OK. But it was funny. They just didn't want to rock the boat and say could we come along.

But you know probably the most good that I did on that trip for the Navy, I ran into Navy personnel in the Fairbanks area who were supporting oil operations around Umiat, and these Navy people were getting about nine-dollars-a-day per diem. I lived at home, I had one of the family cars, I used to crack a twenty-dollar bill every day and spend it. That's how fast the money went, so when I came back to Washington the longest part of my report consisted of a detailed description of the cost of things and services in Fairbanks, Alaska, and pointed out to the chief of naval operations that he had a bunch of officers and enlisted troops up there who were practically starving to death because they just weren't making enough money to live. Immediately afterwards, the per diem allowance for all the Navy in Alaska was raised.

Q: That seems to be a most appropriate part of your report since you were dealing in human problems and human resources. Tell me, did the Navy at that time have all the acreage which they now have as oil lands?

Adm. M.: Yes. The Navy and the petroleum 4 area. The petroleum 4 area goes from the area around Point Barrow all the way over to the North Slope, so in reality they have as much or more oil-bearing land as the Great North Slope Oil Discovery has.

Q: When did the Navy acquire this?

Adm. M.: The Coast and Geodetic Survey sent a Mr. Foran up into that area in 1923. Bill Foran explored the whole area. He was a geologist and he, at that time, said there's plenty of oil here. The Navy put a uniform on Bill Foran in World War II and put him in charge of oil exploration in that area. It was known as the petroleum 4 area - short name Pet 4. Bill had a drilling team up there plus others. They brought the equipment, started drilling, they explored, and he told the Navy that they had one of the biggest oil finds in the world, but he didn't convince the Navy. Now, I think, the Navy is pretty much agreed that they have quite an oil find up there in the petroleum 4 area.

Q: So the interest of the Navy in the area was long before any of the private oil companies got involved?

Adm. M.: That's right. The Navy has been there for years. At the present time, the Navy supplies natural gas to Barrow Village and to the Navy Arctic Research Lab at Point Barrow, which is now a very modern little lab, looking at permafrost, ice floes, water, the ionosphere, communications, and all that. It's a very interesting operation.

Q: It's under R and D?

Adm. M.: Yes, Sir, that's under the Office of Naval Research. They run that contract through the University of Alaska, which is at Fairbanks, and the Navy has reaped great profit from that operation up there and it hasn't cost them much.

Q: Is the Navy operating the oil wells on its property now or only the gas?

Adm. M.: I don't know. I know the gas line is going, and they sank another gas line last year, but I do not know the extent of their future operations. The Navy has been in Alaska for many, many years, not only in Kodiak where the headquarters are and Adak where they have communications and an airfield, but also all along the Aleutians, from many years ago when they were looking for operating areas. They did this because they knew they were going to operate from Alaska.

Q: In terms of national defense?

That's right. They operated seaplanes out of those areas in the Aleutians, and, of course, land planes from the airfields there.

Q: Actually, it's the only place where we confront the Russians from our own soil, isn't it?

Adm. M.: That's right. They knew it wouldn't be the Russians they'd be confronting, it would probably be the Japanese, and they were correct.

Q: Does the Navy conduct such surveys in other parts of the world? It seemed rather unique to seek out human resources for future use. Is this an accepted policy?

Adm. M.: Of course, the services - and the Navy, being one of the services - obtain as much information as they possibly can on areas of the world and people, but they didn't have too much information on known arctic experts, people who had lived there, and this is what they wanted.

Q: So, you came back then and took on something else.

Adm. M.: I came back and made my report. Then I received a set of orders to the Office of Naval Research in Washington, D. C. The Office of Naval Research is commonly known as ONR and it had been established by public law in 1946 to get basic research started again in this country, and the scientists did this. They had the law put together and they had complete faith in the Navy to do this job, because the Navy was one of the leading research and development institutions in the United States.

Q: What was the thinking back of this, on the part of the scientists? Why did they urge this at that time?

Adm. M.: Well, with World War II we put all the basic knowledge into applied research to make the new weapons systems that we needed to get the job done, but we ran out of basic research, basic knowledge that had been going on for years. We took all those researchers and put them into applied research and engineering, so we stopped doing research.

H. L. Miller #2 - 113

Q: During the war?

Adm. M.: Yes, and we had to get it started again. The scientists knew this and they knew somebody had to take charge and get basic research going.

Q: Would you discourse on that just a little bit?

Adm. M.: Yes. How do you do it? Well, universities, of course, and industry did the preliminary basic research in this country before World War II. We took all those scientists and engineers and we put them in war-making machines. So, we had to get started and we had to go to the universities and say, "Will you get some of the basic research started again?" At that time, the universities, the scientists and the engineers had had their fill of the military in World War II. They wanted to go back to the laboratory and they didn't want to have anything else to do with the military. They'd had their fling and that was it. They wanted to go back to the lab or to the cellar to get immersed in their research work, and they didn't want to take their place in the community or anything like that. They wanted to be left alone. So the Navy's job was to go to the universities and get them interested, and this was a tough proposition because the first one was MIT, and MIT had been very active in World War II and have been ever since. Millions of dollars of defense money have gone to MIT.

At that time, Rear Admiral Luis de Florez took the first contract to MIT, to Dr. Compton. He parked on Dr. Compton's doorstep for three or four days and told him he could take the contract and

H. L. Miller #2 - 114

he could alter it any way he wanted, but, please, let's just get basic research going, and get affiliated with the Office of Naval Research. That was the start. Dr. Compton helped out, and the Naval Research Advisory Board, of which Dr. Compton was a member, helped the Office of Naval Research get these contracts going. They talked to universities, they talked to scientists, so in a very short space of time in a budget of about 20 million dollars, the Office of Naval Research got hundreds of basic research projects going around this country. And today, as a result of the integrity and dedication of the Office of Naval Research, they're known world-wide. It's a great institution.

Q: How did they succeed in being so persuasive with reluctant scientists and reluctant educational institutions at that time?

Adm. M.: They were successful because they didn't demand that the scientists come up with a report every quarter or what they did with their money. They let the scientist make his report, say, once a year or twice a year on how he was doing, how much money he'd spent, because we did have to go to the Congress and ask for money to keep all this going. In 1948 we asked for a 22-million-dollar budget. The Bureau of the Budget gave us 20 million dollars. We went back and recovered the 2 million dollars. What we did was to get our scientists from the Naval Research Lab who were working on projects - research projects that they could describe - to bring their experiments over and convince the Secretary of the Navy Forrestal right in his office; then we took those exhibits over to the Bureau of the Budget. The next day we had our scientists and exhibits right there showing the Bureau of the Budget what basic and applied research was all about. We got our 2 million dollars back and they asked us if we needed any more money because this was the first time they really ever knew what research and development was all about.

Q: Practical use of visual aids, wasn't it?

Adm. M.: Yes, and some very smart and intelligent scientists who knew how to sell.

Q: Tell me, did the Office of Research lay out certain areas that they were interested in for these various educational institutions? Did they assign MIT, for instance, a particular area to deal with?

Adm. M.: No, Sir. They asked the particular university what fields they would like to work in. The whole business was so wide open that you could practically tap any field and the Navy was interested in getting started in that particular area.

Q: Completely laissez faire, then?

Adm. M.: That's right, and this was one of the reasons that the Office of Naval Research was so successful, because it allowed that freedom of choice. It was a hands-off policy of letting the scientist do his work without somebody looking over his shoulder or telling him to hurry up. It was a very successful operation. It is to this day.

Q: Was the Army also engaged in this kind of operation?

Adm. M.: Not anywhere near as extensively as the Navy. For instance, I indicated how hard it was getting started. Well, in two years' time, we were really refusing very good research contracts, research proposals, because we had so many of them we didn't have the money to cover the costs. We threw great projects right in the wastepaper baskets because we couldn't support them all. The response was absolutely terrific from all the universities around this country.

Q: And you assign Luis de Florez as something of a godfather to this whole effort?

Adm. M.: Luis was an absolute jewel. He knew how to talk to engineers and scientists. He knew how to deal with them. Just as a matter of interest, at that time dental research was practically nonexistent. The most money that we could allocate or could spend on the dental research proposals was something on the order of 60 thousands dollars. The dentists were all filling teeth, they weren't interested in research.

Q: Was this effort in the late 1940s the beginning of the great outflow of subsidies to the universities of the country, this whole system which has come to grief since 1968?

Adm. M.: I wouldn't say a give-away program because we received, I think, much more in the way of basic or applied research from these universities than we really paid for.

H. L. Miller #2 - 117

Q: You got your money's worth and more?

Adm. M.: Oh, we got much more. It was a terrific program. Of course, we're not today getting the same for those prices. The price has gone up.

Q: And it's had to cease in so many of these institutions because of the student uprisings, and this has resulted in disaster for some universities.

Adm. M.: This is a good subject to bring up - the distinction between certain projects that go from the defense establishment. Whenever you talk basic research, you're not talking defense, you're not talking weapon systems. You're talking about knowledge that will be used for the whole world. So, no matter how militant you are, you just cannot throw basic research out of the window, even if the Defense Department is paying for it or Agriculture or who, what. That information will be used probably by the whole world, if it has application.

Q: But isn't it unfortunate that basic research has been lumped with military weapons and all the rest in the thinking of some of the militants of our time, because is it not true that even the basic research subsidies to universities have been withdrawn in certain areas?

Adm. M.: Right now I do not have any current knowledge on that. I don't know if basic research contracts have been withdrawn.

Q: What was your role in this? You were there at the beginning, weren't you?

H. L. Miller #2 - 118

Adm. M.: Shortly after the beginning. I was the executive officer in the air branch of the Office of Naval Research, and our job primarily was to talk with the scientists and the engineers to point out operational problems that we had in the Navy that needed solution and where, perhaps, applied research could be directed to help solve those problems. I think we all profited, because the Office of Naval Research consisted of scientists, engineers, technical naval officers and operational naval officers. Now, when you got the operational naval officer, that was quite a team. It was an unbeatable team, particularly if they kept talking and seeking out these areas that needed some solution.

We had a wonderful relationship with, you might say, all branches in the Office of Naval Research from mathematics to nuclear physics, the geophysical, the missile branch. We did have missiles way back then in 1946, 1947, and 1948.

Q: They were the outcome of the Goddard rocket idea, weren't they?

Adm. M.: Yes, Sir. We had several projects there in missiles. We also had proposed an all carrier flying system that they still don't have to this day in the Navy. We have a partially completed system. We had a big project with General Electric on controlling the weather, nucleation of clouds, seeding the clouds.

Q: What motivated you in that direction?

Adm. M.: We knew - or the scientists knew - that if you used silver iodide or dry ice or just plain water, dumping it on super-saturated clouds, you could get the reaction going for either snow or rain to clear that area and have unlimited visibility where just a short time before it was completely socked in. I remember these experiments were conducted in Schenectady, New York, by Drs. Langmuir and Shafer. Some experiments were also done at Arcata, California, and they do have some of that activity going on there to this day. The nucleation of clouds, that whole project, has had its peaks and valleys over the years and today there's more effort going into the problem of controlling the weather. I think an awful lot can be done in this field.

Q: Is there general cooperation with scientists from other countries in an area like this, even with scientists in Russia?

Adm. M.: As far as I know, there is very little exchange of information between other scientists and ours in the business of nucleation of clouds for controlling the weather. Why? Because there's so much involved if you find the answer in controlling the weather.

Q: You mean, then it gets into the realm of national defense?

Adm. M.: Politics and national defense.

Q: Tell me about some of the ideas which you were able to formulate resulting from your wartime experience and some of the areas where research was necessary in your own mind.

Adm. M.: The biggest project was carrier all-weather flying. We let a contract to a research agency in New York to look at the whole problem of carrier all-weather flying. By this I mean, from take-off from the carrier, the rendezvous, navigation to the target,

H. L. Miller #2 - 120

identification of the target, attack of the target, re-rendezvous of the planes that attacked, navigation back to the carrier, the approach, the break-up, and the landing, all to be done automatically. That was the problem that we gave to industry.

Now, we sent a team of scientists and engineers to every industry in this country at that time to find out what they had in the way of instruments and/or techniques to apply to the components of that tremendous problem. For instance, what do you have to solve the navigation part of it? What do you have to come aboard the carrier automatically? What directional gyros do you have in your company that will contribute to the solution of a piece of it? So we covered industry. We found out what they had and we gave them credit in this over-all problem for various pieces that they had that would do the job. There was nothing that we found in, say, taking off automatically. We put a red ball at that particular part of the problem. If some of the solution was there, we put a yellow ball. If we had the solution, we put a green ball. We made this presentation December 11th, 1947 in the Interior Department auditorium, showing the Army, the Navy, and the Air Force, the Marines, and any interested people around Washington how much of that problem we had solved, how many pieces contributed to that, and how much of every component we had to have solutions for.

Q: That was a tremendous research project to initiate, wasn't it? To find out that present status?

Adm. M.: That's correct. For instance, from the study. The study was so technical that the average naval officer didn't even know what some of the terms meant. They were all new in the electronics game. So when we got this highly technical study, we sent copies to the officers that we felt could read it and contribute, but we weren't getting any replies simply because it was too technical and it was Greek to a lot of people.

Q: You'd have to attach a glossary to go along with it!

Adm. M.: Absolutely. So I went to one of the big bosses and I told him that we had to put this into a presentation that the newsboy on the street corner could understand. He gave me $3,100 which I needed to get this presented on great big boards. Presentations Incorporated of Washington, D. C. did it. They had some good artists, they also had a mathematician, a physicist, and some good engineers in that company. They knew how to do it. They knew how to present it so you might say the dumbest guy in the world could understand.

That was one of our projects that we really worked at and we did a lot of good in getting the carrier all-weather system started.

Q: What about another project?

Adm. M.: We actually dabbled in a great many of them. An amusing one was computers. One of the institutions that belonged to us was the Special Devices Center at Sands Point, Long Island, New York. They put on trainers - simulators - to do all these things on the ground so you didn't have to waste money charging around in the air.

H. L. Miller #2 - 122

They had a very smart capable engineer by the name of Perry Crawford, and Perry was absolutely sold on computers. Well, at that time, computers were just starting. Perry used to tell us about computers, sell us on computers, that computers were going to do millions of things for this country, but he had a hard time selling it to everyone. As a matter of fact, many people said Perry Crawford was a nut, but he was a very smart, capable guy. He was years ahead of his time. Today, of course, we have computers for everything.

Q: What commercial outfit was in the field? Was Sperry Rand?

Adm. M.: I forget. I think they were. I can't remember the name of the mammoth computer that they built at that time. They said, OK, here's the papa of them all. Since then we have table sets the size of a small table that does more than that great big job that they built at that time.

Q: One of the Sperry Rand outfits was the Univac which was tremendous in size.

Adm. M.: They're still putting out lots of Univacs. Univac is still one of the best computers available. Sperry Rand has done a wonderful job in it.

Q: Did you explore the possibilities of any of the so-called think tanks that were in existence like the Rand Corporation?

Adm. M.: Rand Corporation at that time was just getting started. They were subsidized by the Air Force and Rand wanted to, you might say, exchange information with us. We said, great, what are you doing? Well, they were just getting started. So they, at that time, didn't have much to offer. They had some very smart talented people that they hired to get started in the think tank business. But you might say in the Office of Naval Research we had quite a few think tanks right there. We used to get together and talk out these problems. We used to have sessions in mathematics, each week there was a meeting by everybody in the Office of Naval Research and one of the scientists or engineers would come up and brief us on his latest project, and some of them were most interesting. This was the way we kept our finger in the pie of what everybody was doing at ONR. It was very interesting.

Q: It must have been not only interesting but stimulating to one's intellect!

Adm. M.: Oh, yes. Then if we got tired of listening to the scientists at ONR we could go across the river. The Naval Research Lab belonged to us and that's one of the oldest labs in the country. They had some tremendous people there. Really you could get lost in NRL for a week or two and still not scratch the surface, they have so many interesting research projects going.

Q: Also the Taylor Model Basin.

Adm. M.: The David Taylor Model Basin is an old institution and there was lots going on there. And the Naval Ordnance Laboratory at White Oaks, Maryland, that's a very famous institution. But the granddaddy of them all was the Naval Research Laboratory. To this day, they're one of the best, if not the best, in this country. They still belong to the Office of Naval Research.

Q: You, as an individual, were very fortunate to get involved in that area, were you not?

Adm. M.: I certainly was. I had known nothing about the research business until I got in the Office of Naval Research. That was a very rewarding and stimulating, you might say, two-and-a-half year tour.

Q: Was it an assignment that you had sought or that you knew anything about?

Adm. M.: No. I didn't know anything about it. I was assigned there. There were a couple of officers that I know were hoping that I would come to the Office of Naval Research because I did have a good operational background that they could use in talking to the scientists and engineers in pointing out these things that we had needed in the aviation Navy.

Q: I take it you'd established a reputation as something of an astute observer of things in the operational field.

Adm. M.: Well, I had a pretty good background in the operational field because I'd been out in bloody World War II, you might say, from start to finish so I was bound to learn something.

Q: You were telling me how you first met Luis de Florez?

H. L. Miller #2 - 125

Adm. M.: I met Luis de Florez when he was a commander in the Navy. He was in charge of the Special Devices Center which, at that time, was in Washington, D. C. He took over a building, he put these simulators or trainers in this building . . .

Q: This was under the Bureau of Aeronautics?

Adm. M.: This was at that time under the Bureau of Aeronautics, and Luis, you might say, was a pioneer in the simulation, the trainer, business. He really had a great imagination. He hired smart, capable, creative people who had ideas and he let them run as far and as fast as they wanted in getting these ideas and machines to make it easier for the pilots, the gunners, everybody else that had a job to do in the war, to do it better than then could find in any other method. So I had just commissioned my squadron at Willow Grove, Pennsylvania. I went down to Washington and talked to people about certain things I needed, and one of the officers, who was going to be the executive officer of the USS Princeton, the ship we were going to be on, told me to go over and see Luis de Florez if I wanted some trainers for my air group. There were gunnery trainers, identification trainers, how to shoot, how to fix a flat tire, or anything like that.

So I went over to see Luis and he said, well, what do you need? "First of all I said I'd sure like to see what he had in the way of trainers." With that, he showed them to me, and he had a man come along to jot down all these things, and he said, "Well, which ones do you want?" I pointed them out and he said, "When do you want

H. L. Miller #2 - 126

them?" Well, by that time, I was getting a little bit suspicious because it was so hard to get anything in that war, and here was a guy offering me the moon. So I told him I wanted all these trainers at Parris Island, South Carolina, because that was the air station - Marine Corps air station - that we were moving to right after the first of the year. He told me where he had these trainers and that he would get them airmailed or have somebody fly them and install them at Parris Island, South Carolina, and they'd be there when I arrived with my air group. And that, mind you, was in about twelve days.

Q: Did you accept that as the gospel truth?

Adm. M.: Well, I was hoping, but I wasn't counting on those trainers being there. But I tell you, on the 4th of January when we arrived at Parris Island all those trainers were in place and the next day we were using them. Luis was a can-do man. He waded through the red tape. He got everything done. He was a master at all that. He was a very persuasive man and a very smart - brilliant - man. Luis more than anybody else got the simulation, the trainers, going as a big business in this country. He was a great individual.

Q: Many things were begun at that point in naval research.

Adm. M.: Yes, Sir. Many things started in the Office of Naval Research and also the Naval Research Lab at that time that paid off for the Navy. One of them that was of tremendous interest was non-flammable hydraulic fluid. We did have hydraulic fires in aircraft. Hydraulic fluid would catch fire and we'd either lose the plane or lose people. It also had tremendous application for hydraulic catapults aboard ship and before we could get non-flammable hydraulic fluid into our catapults aboard ship, there was a tremendous explosion aboard, I think, the USS Bennington, Captain Red Raborn's ship, because the hydraulic fluid went bang. This was before we could get non-flammable hydraulic fluid into big time production.

But there were many other things, many other fallouts. For instance, in missiles, basic systems, components for future missile systems were, you might say, born in the Office of Naval Research through the contracts that we had at that time. And when we talked about firing missiles, when we talked about computers, when we talked about some of the advanced all-weather flying systems, there were a lot of non-creative officers over in the Main Navy Department who thought that we were really a bunch of nuts, that we'd gone off our rockers. This was never going to be for probably another fifty years, and here we were talking about it as though it were here tomorrow. It was quite a change.

Q: Was China Lake fully developed at that point? What was your relationship with them out there?

Adm. M.: China Lake was coming along. It was primarily, at that time, this was the Naval Weapons Laboratory at China Lake, it was the Naval Ordnance Test Station, Inyokern, California. Their big forte was testing, not research. Now they do have the Michaelson Laboratory out there and they do some basic research in weapons, weapon systems, bombs, guns, explosives, along those lines. But in 1946, 1947, 1948, they were primarily a test ordnance station, and a good one.

Q: You worked very closely, I take it, with BuOrd?

Adm. M.: Oh, yes. The Bureau of Ordnance owned the Naval Ordnance Test Station at China Lake, at that time. All the laboratories, the Naval Electronics Laboratory at San Diego, the Naval Ordnance Laboratory at White Oaks, the Naval Research Laboratory, the Office of Naval Research, the David Taylor Model Basin, Naval Weapons Lab at Dahlgren, Virginia, all of these laboratories exchanged information, they worked closely together. They were very fine institutions, and they still are to this day.

Q: Since it has come to the fore as one of the paramount areas for research, what was being done at that time in the realm of oceanography?

Adm. M.: Oceanography at that time was split and, you might say, divided into many, many fields. We had one of the finest oceanographers in the business in the Office of Naval Research at that time.

Q: Who was he?

Adm. M.: Dr. Roger Revell. Roger is a great big likeable gent. He reminds you of a St. Bernard dog. He's an expert in his field. He's well known all over the world. At that time he was a commander in the Navy in the Office of Naval Research and he represented ONR at many international conferences. He did a masterful job of getting oceanography organized in ONR. From there, he branched out to Scripps, San Diego and La Jolla. He's affiliated with many agencies around the country. He's been on presidential committees, Department of Defense committees, civilian committees, National Science Foundation committees, all this.

Incidentally, a fallout of the Office of Naval Research was the National Science Foundation. Our chief scientist at the Office of Research was Dr. Allan Waterman. The Navy and other scientists in the government realized that we had to have a National Science Foundation, so they worked toward that end and finally got a public law passed to establish the National Science Foundation in Washington, D. C., and our chief scientist, Dr. Allan Waterman, was nominated and appointed the first head of the National Science Foundation in this country. Dr. Allan Waterman is now dead. He did an outstanding job of getting the science foundation organized, staffed, operating, and its influence felt not only in this country but also around the world.

Q: As the executive to this whole research outfit, did you get involved in selling the idea of something like that to the congress?

Adm. M.: My boss, Captain Eddie Wagner, and I helped in our budget presentations, presentations to other departments and other agencies in the Navy - other offices in the Navy in Washington, D. C. and to other offices in the Department of Defense, on what ONR was all about, what we were doing, what our principal projects were, where we were going, and how much money we needed to keep going. So we did get heavily involved in the presentations and selling ONR.

Q: Can you recall anything of real interest in that area that you might like to include?

Adm. M.: Well, the example that I mentioned prior to this was getting a 2 million dollar reclamma back from a 22-million-dollar budget. Now that budget would probably be on the order of 150 million dollars today. But we had many, many projects that were on tap at that time that paid off. We could see all this. We knew it was going to come and we just wanted the Navy to get on board and help out.

Q: Did you work with Hyman Rickover?

Adm. M.: No, Sir, I didn't work with Admiral Rickover until I got in the nuclear power business with the USS Enterprise and that came many years later.

Q: Tell me this. You and all of those who were involved in the Office of Naval Research and many beyond that in the Navy came now to appreciate the great value of basic research and specialized research that followed upon that, why, then, was it allowed to lapse in the later years? I mean, once under way and appreciated and understood, why, then, was it allowed to lapse?

Adm. M.: As far as the Office of Naval Research and our other laboratories in the Navy were concerned, research wasn't allowed to lapse after ONR did such a magnificent job of getting it started.

It progressed. We had more and more and more research projects that were started every year, and today the fields of interest, the disciplines that we look at, the areas, both the basic and applied research projects have expanded greatly in many, many areas, more areas than we ever dreamed of in the 1946-48 days.

Q: I suppose one of the problems with research and with actual developments in the terms of newer and better ships and so forth, is to keep the two in a kind of tandem relationship, and this is pretty difficult, isn't it?

Adm. M.: It certainly is difficult because there's a big valley between the basic research man and the applied research man who wants something fast. Basic research may take years and years and years, and you really don't know what you're going to use that basic research for until you find it and then you can see applications for it. But many times, of course, the operational sailor, the technical officer, the industry man who's looking for a quick solution, wants to try to direct his research to the solution of these problems. In the industrial world, that's the bread and butter, the pay-off. But a scientist who wants to be left alone to work at basic research is really the individual who has to be left alone, who is going to eventually contribute immeasurably to the welfare of the world.

Q: These, indeed, are two different types of mentality.

Adm. M.: They are. They're two different breeds of cats.

Q: Isn't it interesting that you, as an individual, have an understanding of both areas? This is not usual, is it?

Adm. M.: Well, if you're working in an organization like that, you must understand that these differences exist. Otherwise, you just won't be able to do your job, you won't be able to get your points of view across to those individuals, unless you understand their thinking. And, believe it or not, after you do realize that in your conversations, your work with these individuals, you have absolutely no problem of communicating.

Q: Was this knowledge hard to come by on your part?

Adm. M.: No. I think probably because both my boss, Captain Wagner, and I talked to the scientists and the engineers every chance we got, and Captain Wagner was a boy from Brooklyn. He had a little of the Brooklynese in his speech. He went over big with every scientist that walked into that office. He was a natural communicator. The first thing he offered you was a cup of coffee, and from there on it was one idea after another that they discussed. They discussed basic and applied research, development, gadgets, ideas, and there were times when scientists who had to catch a train to New York at two o'clock in the afternoon never got out of there until six o'clock that night, because they were exchanging ideas with a very smart and capable Navy captain who knew how to communicate with them.

Q: He was able to meet them on the level of the intellect which they appreciate most?

Adm. M.: That's right. And he was an operational naval officer, but he got down to various levels, and he got up to various levels. He had that intellect.

Q: That's a rare ability because so often the scientific mind can be a very arrogant mind and if it is dealing with somebody whom it doesn't think its equal . . .

Adm. M.: That's right. That was a very good tour in the Office of Naval Research. I've always kept up with a lot of those individuals that I worked with at that time. A great many of them are still in very important positions around the government and around the country. Others are retired.

Q: Do you want to mention any of them?

Adm. M.: Of course, Dr. Allan Waterman was one of the outstanding ones. Dr. Waterman, as I mentioned, was the first president of the National Science Foundation. He's now dead. We had Dr. Lanny Pierrie, who was on one of the president's scientific committees. We had Dr. Roger Revell, who had made a great name for himself in oceanography and many other fields. He's been on various national committees, at Scripps and other institutions. Dr. Erner Liddell, who was our nuclear physicist. Dr. Liddell was in the Defense Department, in their engineering. He contributed immeasurably to the nuclear physics program in the Office of Naval Research. And, of course, Admiral Luis de Florez who did so much for the Navy and so much for ONR. Well, the list goes on like that. Dr. Mina Rees, a mathematician. She was very brilliant. She went back as the dean of graduate studies, City University of New York. Mina Rees was well known in the mathematical world. We had a great number of people like that, really outstanding.

Q: Looking at your biography, you went on to a quite different assignment but equally fascinating. You begin to develop into a kind of a renaissance character with different facets!

Adm. M.: From the Office of Naval Research I had the shock of my life. I received a set of orders to report to the staff of commander-in-chief of the Atlantic Fleet. The boss there was Admiral Blandy. I was to be his public information officer.

Q: Had you known Admiral Blandy before?

Adm. M.: I hadn't known Admiral Blandy, I hadn't been a public information officer. I got the job and I didn't want it.

Q: Was there any connection between the Office of Research and the fact that Blandy had been head of BuOrd? Was there any connection there at all?

Adm. M.: No, Sir. Admiral Blandy had been chief of the Bureau of Ordnance in World War II, he was also an amphibious commander in World War II, he was in charge of the Bikini A-bomb tests after World War II was over. He was a very capable man and I think he did get the word that I didn't want that job and I tried my darndest to convince everybody that I was not the man for the job.

Q: Why didn't you want the job?

Adm. M.: Well, I was much more interested in aviation and, research and development, but as long as I was going to sea I wanted to go to an operational job in the Navy or to a staff job where my aviation background would be useful.

Q: You wanted to go on a carrier?

Adm. M.: Certainly not as a public information officer! But I reported aboard and, at that time, the Navy was in a fight for its life with the Air Force on the subject of aircraft carriers. So, in order to get our story across to the press and to certain members of the congress, both representatives and senators, we set up weekly cruises aboard one of our carriers down at Norfolk. We would fly the congressmen and the press to Norfolk on Saturday morning. We would board the carrier, shove off, do air operations Saturday afternoon, and just a wee bit of night flying, showing them what carrier operations were all about. That was followed by a movie Saturday night. They were briefed too during the day. Everybody went to bed thoroughly tired but with a pretty good idea of what aircraft carrier operations were all about, how the Navy did things. They met pilots aboard, enlisted men, they got to ask anybody any questions they wanted. Nobody held back any information from them, and on Sunday morning, after church, we'd come in to port. Everybody would disembark and they'd fly them back to Washington.

Admiral Blandy and I would get in the limousine and go home. We did that for twelve consecutive weekends. We did take one weekend off, and that was Easter Weekend. It got to the point where, later on, the congressmen and the press wanted to bring their young boys along, and the Navy set an age limit of, I think, about 12 years of age. So we had a lot of kids of 12 and above who got their carrier indoctrination in the Navy from those cruises.

Q: It would be interesting to follow through and see how many of them became - eventually wore uniforms! You had to organize all of these tours?

Adm. M.: I helped organize them with Commander, Naval Air Force, Atlantic Fleet, who was then Vice Admiral Felix Stump, and his air operations officer was Captain Jimmy Flatley. So we were all very close friends and we worked all this stuff out together. But along with that I realized that we had to sell an awful lot of Navy. I wasn't interested in selling Admiral Blandy because I knew that if you sell the Atlantic Fleet and the Navy that sells Admiral Blandy, too. He knew that. I organized seminars at the type commands in the Atlantic Fleet, a Mine Force seminar down at Charleston, South Carolina, the amphibious and the air at Norfolk, the destroyers at Newport, and the submarines at New London, Connecticut. I brought in specialists from the Office of Information in Washington. I brought myself - I had a presentation to make on the Atlantic Fleet public affairs program. Then I also got some well-known media representatives from Washington and/or

New York to come to those presentations, and they would give a pitch from the media point of view - what they were looking for in the way of Navy news and what they wanted when they called up.

Q: Was that helpful and was it the sort of information the Navy could impart?

Adm. M.: Oh, yes. These seminars were very helpful. They got the word across to the Atlantic Fleet on what we wanted. They also helped us disseminate the word to the officers and men of the Atlantic Fleet on what the media were looking for, that they were out to help us, not to cut our heads off.

Naturally, a naval officer is always afraid of the press. You might say the Defense establishment is afraid of the press, but they're not all bad. They have a job to do, they want the information. If you give it to them straight, they'll print it straight. So this is the word that we tried to get across.

We also had an annual big-fleet exercise. It would always take place in the latter part of January, February, March. We would leave Norfolk, go south. We would have antisubmarine warfare exercises, air strikes, submarine warfare, amphibious landings working with the Marines, the Army, and the Air Force. We'd go down to Vieques, San Juan, Guantanamo; and, in certain phases of the exercises, we took up to 250 media representatives, not only hitting the national news, but the biggest number came from weekly newspapers through the United States.

M. L. Miller #2 - 138

Q: May I ask, as a kind of a footnote, how you went about selecting these men, or did they nominate themselves?

Adm. M.: We asked the Office of Information in Washington, D. C. - the Navy Office of Information - to help us select the media representatives that went. In other words, all the national media could come if they wanted, but they all didn't come, so we filled in those that we had open with weekly newspapers or radio stations. At that time, TV was just starting.

Q: How were your delegations of VIPs selected or invited? What was the criterion for them?

Adm. M.: They came from nationally used lists - congressmen, both representatives and senators, congressional committees, people in the Department of Defense. We also invited Army, Air Force, Marines to come and watch our exercises. We invited well-known industrialists in the country, bankers, top people who were interested in the defense of this country.

Q: When you organized the groups out of Norfolk on the carriers, this was obviously a sell idea, was it? I mean you were confronted with the public relations job of the Air Force and so you had to offset that, and this was a conscious effort?

Adm. M.: That's correct. We knew that we were, you might say, in a battle for our lives as far as the carrier Navy was concerned, and we wanted to be sure that we did our job in showing the great American public what aircraft carriers could do for the defense of this country, and we had to have them if we were going to project our power overseas.

Q: This was one facet of the program. The main thrust came before the congressional committees, did it not? Were you involved in that also?

Adm. M.: At that time there was a captain in the Navy by the name of Arleigh Burke who was doing a pretty fair job of getting the word across to a great many people in Washington on the value of aircraft carriers in this man's Navy. I worked for Admiral Burke later on. He had had a hard time when he was the head of Op-23 selling sea power. He made a lot of friends, he made a lot of enemies, but he did an outstanding job of fighting for the Navy.

Q: As I remember, it was at this time that Don Griffin was one of his subalterns and had to go before congressional committees and organize that aspect of the presentation.

Adm. M.: That's right, and I came to one of Captain Burke's meetings in Washington when I was at Norfolk. I also got him down to Norfolk to one of our type commanders meetings to talk to all the Atlantic Fleet type commanders and their principal officers on selling the Navy and selling aircraft carriers. There were many people who didn't want to be associated with Arleigh Burke at that time because they figured just the sight of him or to be seen talking with him and their chances of promotion were over. Arleigh Burke will never forget this, either.

Q: He had been so heavily involved, had he not, in the unification fight?

Adm. M.: That was it.

Q: Admiral, a question comes to mind since you've talked about the VIP delegations to the carrier. A young chap in our office a few months ago was invited to go out on a carrier and came back, and he was somewhat shaken by the experience and he had a large question in his mind which he proposed to me. He said one gets such a feeling on a carrier when it's in operation of overwhelming power, of invincibility. Is this automatically, then, imparted to the men who operate the carrier, who are a part of this war machine? Do they become imbued over a period of time with this sense of invincibility?

Adm. M.: I don't think so. I spent thousands of hours aboard aircraft carriers during my naval career. It's a powerful weapon system. It's a dynamic weapon system. Its growth potential is terrific. It has a lot of power. It looks like power. But nobody in his right mind will ever say that any system is invincible, that we have the ultimate weapon here. It is a powerful weapon system. It's done a great job in World War II, the Korean War, and the Vietnamese war. It does a remarkable job in showing the flag wherever it goes anywhere in the world. But I don't think the inhabitants of that aircraft carrier feel that it's so big and so powerful that it is an invincible weapon that the Navy has. We learn to respect every weapon of war, its destructive power, what it can do, but we're always cautious in advertising the fact that we think it's the ultimate, because no weapon system is the ultimate. There'll always be weapons that beat other weapons as long as we live.

Q: As long as man has imagination and ingenuity.

Adm. M.: That's right.

Q: In a slightly different vein, but it seems an appropriate time perhaps to ask you about it, since you were involved with public relations in the fleet, what about the Navy's policy on imparting information?

Adm. M.: At that time, most of the Navy was scared to death of media representatives.

Q: Why?

Adm. M.: They just weren't exposed to a great many reporters or radio men...

Q: Because they operated at sea and didn't see that many of them?

Adm. M.: That's right, and, remember, prior to World War II, there was very little interest in the media on national defense. It was mostly domestic. So the Navy didn't have much of an education and a training program for getting the officers and men interested or cognizant of the implications of media reps coming aboard or writing up the Navy. The Navy didn't care. The Navy figured that congress and the people were going to take care of them automatically, and they had been taken care of all these years. Before World War II, their champion, Franklin D. Roosevelt, came into power. He built up the Navy. The Navy didn't have to sell the American public. They had Franklin D. Roosevelt, they had him almost the whole war. So, they didn't have to sell. Then they realized that they were in a fight for their life in the aircraft carriers and they had to get out and pitch. Arleigh Burke recognized this.

Q: Because the Air Force had long since recognized the value of publicity.

Adm. M.: That' right, and the Secretary of the Air Force then was Stuart Symington from Missouri, and he hired a professional public affairs officer to head up the office of information in the Air Force.

Q: Why was the Navy so slow to come out of its cocoon in terms of the press and so forth, because there were a number of flagrant examples during World War II where the Navy would have gained by being more vocal? Midway is one.

Adm. M.: Well, they had never been trained, never been informed that this was what you had to do. The Navy didn't have to sell before World War II. So whenever you find an outfit like that, it's going to take a lot of shaking up of the system to get those people to change their whole attitude and to adopt a new course of action of seeking the press and selling their story to the press. It's an entirely different ball game.

Q: And it really involved another generation of naval officers, didn't it?

Adm. M.: That's right. They didn't want to do it. To them, to the Navy at that time, selling yourself to the press was a dirty game of pool.

Q: It was cheap and vulgar, I suppose!

Adm. M.: That's right. They didn't want to have anything to do with it. So, when I say that we ran seminars in the Atlantic Fleet it was to get this word across. It was tough. It was really difficult.

Q: You met resistance and you met it from naval officers?

Adm. M.: Oh, yes, Sir. We met resistance right along. Even though I was working for the boss, Admiral Blandy, and this was his policy. As a matter of fact - and this is a very pertinent item - I made out the first public affairs manual, you might say, bible, in the Atlantic Fleet. Now, there's a professor at Old Dominion College in Norfolk right now, Dr. Grant Meade. Grant was the public information officer for Commander, Amphibious Force, Atlantic Fleet. Grant and I locked ourselves up and we put that public information manual, the instructions, together for the Atlantic Fleet.

To show you how backward the Navy was, the office of information -

the Navy office of information in Washington, D. C. - used that bible, our bible, to prepare the Navy manual of information for the whole Navy. That's how lousey we were in public affairs.

Q: Your manual was developed after all these groups had been organized and brought on? Did you base some of your experience on that? Some of your thinking?

Adm. M.: Yes, Sir, and lots of talking between Grant Heads and myself on what we observed and what we felt had to be done.

Q: What were some of the essentials that you included in your manual?

Adm. M.: We had, at that time, an internal program of talking to our own people and selling them on the Navy. It was a morale program, too. Doing things for our own people, because you're not going to sell the Navy yourself unless you like it, and unless you're happy in it. So, one of the things that you had to do was get other programs started, morale-wise, to include the morale, housing, athletics, more liberty, more boats, get all these things going, because if a happy man likes his organization he's going to do a lot of selling by himself. That's the internal program. The external program - selling the Navy to the media and to the great American public. How are you going to do it? Speeches, press releases, inviting those people aboard ships for demonstrations, cruises, other means of getting the word out externally to the great American public - open houses on Armed Forces Day

H. L. Miller #2 - 145

or Navy Day, speeches, dinners, Navy League ball, got the Navy League organization going again, it was pretty poor in those days. Getting other Navy organizations going.

Then, the third part of it was the international program. We had Navy ships visiting ports all over the world. Some ships did a marvelous job, others were absolutely terrible. They left some horrible tales around the world.

Q: The wrong impression?

Adm. M.: That's right, and others just did a magnificent job. They sold the Navy. They sold the good ole USA. So, we said, OK, when you go to the Mediterranean, you reinforce the Sixth Fleet over there you you're visiting these ports, these are some of the things that you should do. And this is the bible for those people to follow. We, I think, built a very sound basic manual of information for the Atlantic Fleet and for the Navy.

Q: And it was based on your experience and Dr. Meade's?

Adm. M.: That's right.

Q: Combined, you developed a manual for that?

Adm. M.: We put it together.

Q: How did you feel the need for the existence of such a manual?

Adm. M.: Because nobody had any instructions. Nobody knew what the policy was. There wasn't any uniform policy out. You did it your way. I did it my way. Another guy didn't do it at all.

This way, they had a bible to follow wherever they went. They had some help and some guidance. Prior to that they didn't. It was every man or every ship for himself.

Q: A very interesting development which led ultimately to Chinfo, didn't it?

Adm. M.: I guess so.

Q: Admiral, the fact that you did so much in this billet as public relations officer says something about you as a person, at least it does to me. You told me off tape that you got there and there wasn't anything, it was a great void, and there was much opposition, and this caused you to dig in and really accomplish something at a job that you didn't want. Do you want to say anything more about that?

Adm. M.: Well, as I mentioned previously, the Navy never had to sell anything. The congress gave them what they wanted. It was easy. Now there was a fight, and still there were thousands of naval officers who hated public relations. They thought it was a nasty business, trying to sell the Navy. The great American public should know that they needed a Navy, so, why sell? Well, they had their heads in the sand and they just wouldn't look up. And it was quite a battle right along with quite a few officers on the staff who hated public relations, public affairs. Admiral Blandy recognized the fact that you just had to have a good public information program. If it hadn't been for him and his deputy, Admiral

Goodwin, I wouldn't have got to first base. They supported me 100 percent and backed me to the limit. I also got some splendid support from Commander, Naval Air Force, Atlantic Fleet, Vice Admiral Felix Stump. He believed in public affairs, public relations, public information, and he supported us 100 percent.

It was interesting because you had to fight your own people. There were a great many naval officers who just refused to give a speech on anything Navy or to open their mouth in defense of the Navy. They figured that that was somebody else's job, not theirs.

Q: It's interesting to observe the fact that that was only twenty years ago, and it's hard to conceive of naval officers or anybody else lacking in understanding of the force and power and necessity to have the media with you today.

Adm. M.: Well, at that time, as I mentioned, Admiral Blandy realized that you just had to keep selling if you were going to exist, you wanted support from the public and, as I said, for the fleet exercises we invited VIPs, we invited many media representatives, we went on these cruises to San Juan, Guantanamo, Vieques. We held seminars along the coast. We went on a fleet exercise to Canada. We gave speeches in New York City; Detroit; Michigan; Washington, D. C.; even Springfield, Illinois, a Republican stronghold, sponsored by Adlai Stevenson at that time.

Admiral Blandy did a wonderful job of public affairs for the Navy. He gave many speeches, he sold, sold, sold. But there were a great many people on his staff who didn't take the hint. They still felt it was somebody else's job to do it.

Q: I suppose, Sir, it would be less demanding on a naval officer or any other career man if the situation which existed some years ago in the Navy prevailed still.

Adm. M.: It still prevails in a great many circles, because there are many officers, including flag officers, who will not give a speech. As a matter of fact, a three-star admiral told me three years ago that he hadn't given a speech in three years and he wasn't at all anxious to get up there on a platform and tell anybody about the Navy. We still have thousands in the Navy today who won't spend five minutes of their time giving a speech.

Q: I know, Sir, that you're convinced that a naval officer should be able to speak out and he should be able to write. He should be able to present his point of view. Would you say something about this area and the need for training new officers to be fluent...?

Adm. M.: When I was going to the Naval Academy, our public speaking course consisted of, I believe, two occasions when we were allowed to speak a total of about five minutes each time at a dinner, and that was the extent of our public speaking course. The Navy didn't speak at that time. It wasn't part of the Navy life. We went to social activities, but I just never did hear admirals or captains sounding out or telling anybody about the Navy. In the present world we know that one of the jobs of the Navy and the Department of

Defense is to keep the public informed of what we're doing. We asked them for money to do all these things. We should tell them why we need that money and what they're getting for that money. If we expect 100 percent support, we have got to tell the people what we're doing around the world today and how we're using their money.

At the present time at the Naval Academy, look at all the elective courses. Look at the opportunities that they have to speak. We also find that today in the Navy in Washington, D. C. at the headquarters hundreds of naval officers have to make presentations every day, around the Navy Department, in the Department of Defense, and up on the Hill. The congress demands a very detailed explanation of why we need monies for all these various programs, and no more can a naval officer go up on the Hill and just tell them, well, we need that money because . . . They'll never get it. It has to be a detailed explanation, and they have to answer to the appropriations people, the armed forces committees in the congress.

Q: And it should be done persuasively.

Adm. M.: They've got to be convincing. If they're not, they don't get the money.

We also have a continuing job of telling the great American public all these things and answer their questions. So there's a real need, a continuing need, for naval officers to tell the story of the Navy.

H. L. Miller #2 - 150

Q: May I be permitted a footnote? In my dealings with retired officers, I find an equal need for an ability to speak. They're called upon to do all sorts of things in the communities where they live and usually to assert leadership, and this necessarily requires an ability to get on one's feet.

Adm. M.: Yes, Sir.

Q: Your tour of duty as public information officer must have involved some getting around the Atlantic area. You weren't stationed in Norfolk constantly.

Adm. M.: I went to various commands in the Atlantic Fleet. I visited all the cities where the Atlantic Fleet commands were stationed, Charleston, Norfolk, all around Norfolk - Little Creek, Newport, New London, all of these areas, plus various aviation activities that were along the Atlantic coast. As I mentioned, too, I accompanied Admiral Blandy every time he gave a speech in any of our big cities.

Q: And made your own share of speeches, I take it?

Adm. M.: Yes, Sir, I had to make presentations and speeches right along, to our own commands and to various organizations in Norfolk, and Washington, D. C. We kept moving pretty fast, pretty consistently.

Q: Did you during all this time manage to get in some flying time as well?

Adm. M.: Oh, yes, Sir, we still had to keep up with our flying but that wasn't very difficult there because the big field at

H. L. Miller #2 - 151

Norfolk was a stone's throw away. So we kept up with the flying business.

Q: This was, of course, simultaneous with the Korean conflict, was it not?

Adm. M.: No. Just after I left the Atlantic Fleet the Korean War started.

Q: Oh, yes, I'm sorry. Well, at this period, as you mingled with the public as well as the naval personnel at the base, what did you learn from the public? What was their high degree of interest in the Navy, or had there been a let-down as a result of World War II and the aftermath?

Adm. M.: After World War II certainly there was a let-down as far as the American public and the armed services were concerned. It's that way after every war. However, in 1948, 1949, and 1950, while I was at CinCLantFlt, there was a renewed interest in the Navy and what we were doing, how we were doing it, and I found people very observant, very interested, very inquisitive. They asked many questions. They wanted to know what was going on. And I found this particularly from the weekly newspapers around the country. Of course, the general American public, the ones we talked to, the organizations, we found that they wanted to know more about what the Navy was doing.

Q: How did you manage to get yourself in contact with weekly editors?

H. L. Miller #2 - 152

Adm. M.: Through our office of information in Washington. They have a listing of the editors of weekly newspapers. There were certain numbers of editors of weekly newspapers who wanted to come and see the Navy. They wanted to see what happened on an annual fleet exercise. They wanted to see amphibious operations, submarine operations, air operations. Really, when you go aboard a carrier and see the airplanes operating day and night, jets and prop planes, helicopters - it's really the most interesting and the greatest show on earth. The air crews are on that flight deck, some of them a month before coming aboard ship as brand-new sailors. You pray the good Lord that nothing happens to them, you lead them by the hand, show them everything, tell them to go slow, learn, don't rush around or there'll be an accident. It isn't too long, a month, a month and a half, and those kids that you led around by the hand are now operating that flight deck with million of dollars' worth of airplanes, and you wonder how the miracle happened, but it happens every week out there on the briney deep.

Q: And those boys came originally from the grass roots of America, so I suppose that answers the question how you get back to the leaders of the grass roots, these local county editors?

Adm. M.: We always send write-ups on the sailors that we have aboard ship back to their home town newspapers, tell them what that boy is doing on that particular ship, what he makes if he makes a higher rate, if he gets an award for something, a letter of commendation, or has done something unusual, we let the home town know about it.

H. L. Miller #2 - 153

Q: In this immediate post World War II period, was there any recruitment problem, and did this tie in in any way with your public relations job?

Adm. M.: At that time we did not have a recruiting problem. We had many volunteers to fill up all our quotas, and we didn't have numbers of people resigning from the Navy. It was a different atmosphere than we have now, different times. We weren't at war.

Q: You didn't have the problem the Navy has today with the young officers who choose not to stay in the Navy very long, who have family ties pulling them away from service aboard ship? You didn't have that problem then, in the early 1950s?

Adm. M.: We had more people signing up in the Navy at that time, more percentagewise, than we have today.

Q: How do you ascribe . . .?

Adm. M.: I wish I knew all the answers to that. The Bureau of Naval Personnel would probably hire me as a consultant! But I think one of the big factors is we're in a very unpopular war at the present time in Vietnam - that's a big factor, and people are changing, times are changing. It isn't the same world we used to live in. The younger generation are asking for more answers. I don't know what the solution to all this is. All I know is that we do have more of a recruiting problem today and there are fewer people shipping over in the Navy, percentagewise, than there were at that particular time, 1948.

Q: Even though you had no problem in terms of recruitment then, did your program tie in with recruitment?

Adm. M.: Absolutely. This is one point that we made in our public affairs program in the Atlantic Fleet. We had to tie in with recruiting or, I should say, retention and morale. We didn't recruit. We helped, you might say, by the favorable publicity that we obtained. That always helps. Retention and morale were two big factors that we pointed to. That was our internal relations program. We pointed to it because we knew that we had good people who were happy with the Navy and were staying in the Navy. They were going to be some of our best sailors when they went back home on leave, or in any city on liberty in pursuit of happiness. They're your great salesmen.

Q: You were, in effect, applying modern psychology, were you not, to the job?

Adm. M.: Yes. We knew that that was a fact of life. Those sailors were going to bring a lot of people into the Navy if they were happy with the Navy. As a matter of fact, we still point to that, and I made it a big program later on when I was chief of information.

Q: I should imagine that, even though you were reluctant to take this job, it was of very great value to you in future commands, was it not? The experience gained there?

H. L. Miller #2 - 155

Adm. M.: Absolutely, because wherever you go in this world, no matter what the job, there's a big chunk of public relations that has to go with every job. If you don't have it, if you don't recognize it, you're going to lose out in many areas. But in the Navy, like any business, you have to keep on selling if you're going to survive, and within the Navy you've got to maintain good public relations on every job that you go into.

Q: Admiral, after you left your public information office with all sorts of new talents acquired, you went on to something else which was very interesting. Do you want to tell me about that - Composite Squadron No. 7?

Adm. M.: Composite Squadron 7, was an A-bomb squadron. As a matter of fact, one of the officers that you are now interviewing in New York City, Admiral Chick Hayward, was at that time a commander and he got the Navy's A-bomb squadrons organized. He set up training programs and did a truly remarkable job in organization and getting an awful lot of people into the program. This was in 1950, and first I went to A-bomb school for two months at Albuquerque, New Mexico.

Q: Will you tell me how you got involved in this area?

Adm. M.: In 1950 I was due for rotation from Admiral Blandy's staff going to a tour of active sea duty.

H. L. Miller #2 - 156

Q: Did you come away from his staff with a commendation for the kind of job you did?

Adm. M.: He gave me good high fitness reports. That was enough. They were looking for pilots for these A-bomb squadrons, and Chick Hayward asked me if I'd come into it. I said I'd be delighted, I wanted to go to an operating squadron. So I received a set of orders to Composite Squadron 7, but first we had to go to A-bomb school and get checked out as qualified bombardiers. Why, I don't know, because really we weren't concerned with all the details of how that bomb was built, the wiring, etc., but we had to go through this course.

Q: You weren't about to be called upon to bomb another Nagasaki, were you?

Adm. M.: No. We had a group there of about 15 officers who were going to be in VC-7, going to school. Two months of concentrated study and workshop routine . . .

Q: What did this actually involve? I mean, this study?

Adm. M.: The two months' course was in all the theory of the nuclear bomb, the neutrons, the protons, the atoms, the structure, how it was set up, how to fix things that went wrong with the bomb - very comprehensive. As a matter of fact, when we got through with the two months' course we could take an A-bomb to pieces and put it together again.

Q: Who conducted the classes?

H. L. Miller #2 - 157

Adm. M.: The Atomic Energy Commission set all this stuff up at the base there at Albuquerque, and it was a school that was jointly run by the Army, Navy, and Air Force. There were instructors - officers - from the Army, Navy, Marine Corps, and Air Force there. There were also Army, Navy, and Air Force detachments out there. We stayed in the BOQ, we attended classes five days a week, we tried to play golf the other two days, and keep up with our studies. That was two months, and afterwards I proceeded to Corpus Christi, Texas, and got an additional three weeks there in all-weather flying. My wife and youngster met me at Corpus Christi. They had been down in Alabama on leave while I was going to A-bomb school.

After Corpus Christi we proceeded to Moffett Field California, where VC-7 was formed.

Q: This all-weather flying course, did this teach you anything new? I mean, you had such vast experience in wartime?

Adm. M.: Well, it was sort of a refresher on airline techniques, flying various beams, the new systems that were coming in at that time. So, it was a refresher, I enjoyed it. I learned a lot more and we used all that in the P-2V type airplanes that we were flying.

We had a separate compound at Moffett Field. We were set aside from everybody else. They couldn't come in to our particular tight area because we had a lot of secret A-bomb literature that we had to hold very closely.

Q: Security became a factor, I suppose, the moment you went to Albuquerque?

Adm. M.: Absolutely. As soon as we became associated with the A-bomb, there were many, many more security precautions that we had to be cognizant of. Moffett Field was a very enjoyable tour. We were there from about September 1950 to May of 1951.

Q: And this is where Hayward was?

Adm. M.: Hayward, at that time, moved from Moffett Field to Norfolk, Virginia, with his squadron, VC-5. It was planned to have two squadrons on the East Coast and two squadrons on the West Coast, but as it turned out, three squadrons were sent to the East Coast, and I don't think the fourth squadron was ever formed. There were VC-5, VC-6, and VC-7, three A-bomb squadrons.

Q: Were these tied in in any way with SAC?

Adm. M.: No, sir. We were three Navy A-bomb squadrons that would be operating from aircraft carriers. They had nothing to do with SAC. We got our initial training in the P-2V airplane, and we were shifted to the A-J, a North American plane that Chick Hayward was instrumental in getting, in pushing.

It was very interesting. We had a great bunch of people. All the youngsters that were coming up at that time were just like the ones today. They were a lot smarter than we were. Their college education was a lot different. There were more mathematics and more science.

Q: Did you find that kind of duty a greater strain than previous squadron duties?

Adm. M.: No. It was the same. It was very enjoyable. We got lots of flying in. We had a great deal to do and a great amount of work had to be spent in administration in organizing the squadron because starting from scratch, there's an awful lot of paper work to do.

Q: Why more paper work in that?

Adm. M.: Because you have to establish your instructions, your routine, your organization, your names, get your inspections started. You have to start from scratch. When you walk into an organization that's already been formed, it's comparatively easy.

Q: The traditions are going.

Adm. M.: Yes. It just takes thousands of hours to do all that paper work and get organized.

Q: At the same time, the standards for the personnel in such a squadron were somewhat higher, were they not? More selective?

Adm. M.: Yes. Chick Hayward had screened quite a number of people for those three squadrons. But it was really nothing startling. It was something new - the A-bomb, but in a way they made too much of the deal. They put so many restrictions on the operations and the people - they had to be this and they had to be that, I think it cost the government and the Navy a little bit more that it should have. Looking back, we didn't require all those restrictions and precautions, wire fences, and all that sort of thing.

Q: But that was in the early period of the A-bomb and, I suppose, understandable.

Adm. M.: Yes, I guess so.

Q: There was a great awe and fear of the A-bomb, was there not? Did you feel this as a person getting involved in this area?

Adm. M.: No, I didn't. I felt that they were going a little bit overboard on the whole business. I still feel it. I felt it at that time and I told them I thought they had too many unnecessary precautions and procedures. They set up their own supply system. And when you do all that and you set up another Navy, it costs an awful lot more, and this is practically what they did.

Q: Was this largely due to the attitude of the AEC, or was it the Navy itself?

Adm. M.: It was the Navy. The AEC would go along with our recommendations. I think the Navy put too many precautions on paper for us to follow.

Q: In retrospect, after the program inaugurated by General Eisenhower in December of 1953, "Atoms for Peace" - in retrospect, did this change the situation any? Did it make the atom bomb and atomic energy less formidable as a weapon?

Adm. M.: In my opinion, I didn't see it change a bit. It was still the same.

Q: Is there any aspect of that squadron's experience that should be a part of your story?

Adm. M.: Not especially, because it was such a short tour of actually flying in the squadron that we really didn't have much opportunity to get the old fire and fight in the squadron's spirit that you would in a two-year tour.

Q: This was true of all the men?

Adm. M.: No. Most everybody stayed there longer than I did. During the time I was there the two biggest operations that we had, I loaded about eleven pilots into one of those airplanes and flew non-stop from Moffett Field around a hurricane in the Gulf of Mexico to Guantanamo Bay. This was to go aboard the aircraft carrier Franklin D. Roosevelt and watch Chick Hayward and his outfit make the first carrier take-offs and landings of the A-J airplane, and on that first operation they were lousy. They lost one plane and lost one pilot, too.

Q: Was it a particularly difficult version to operate?

Adm. M.: No, it was really an easy plane to fly, but they hadn't practiced enough and the pilot that went in sure must have been scared to death when he was taking off. He was one of those pilots who didn't have much carrier experience. He went down the deck, mind you, with his elevator tab, which was electrically operated, out, so it was physically impossible for you to take that stick and hoist that airplane in the air. You had to have power to help you. His was locked, you might say, and he just kept on going and ran off that deck. I watched him, and I said, "Boy, if that had been mine, I'd have stopped just like that," which I've done on carriers, you know. When I'd see anything went wrong, I'd stop right away and say, "hey, this has to be fixed." But evidently, you know, he was just scared to death.

Q: He was as frozen as the elevator!

Adm. M.: That's right, and in the carrier business you've got to be pretty alert, because you have to make up your mind in a hurry sometimes.

Well, we watched that operation and we learned how not to do it. Then, shortly after that, we had to move the whole outfit from Moffett Field to Norfolk, Virginia, and a new base of operations. That was a very rushed period of time, because we had to pack up and move, get the families out of school, and all that sort of thing. But I was fortunate there because the house that I owned in Norfolk was being vacated at just the right time by the tenants, so I could move in. Of course, they only caused $1,000 worth of damage, but at least I was able to move back into the house.

It wasn't long after that that I received a phone call that said, you go down to Guantanamo Bay, Cuba, and take over as executive officer of the aircraft carrier, USS Leyte. With a cheery "Aye, aye, Sir", I wrapped up the executive officer's job on that squadron in a hurry and got going.

Q: This you found more desirable?

Adm. M.: No, I enjoyed the flying in VC-7. I always enjoyed the flying and I wanted to stay in the squadron, but Washington told me that if I wanted to be promoted to captain I'd better get head of department or executive officer aboard ship. So I said, "Aye, aye, Sir", and went.

Q: Who was the skipper of the Leyte?

Adm. M.: The skipper of the Leyte was Captain Paul L. Dudley, who had been my commanding officer in Ellyson Field, Flordia, when I went on the Doolittle raid. He was a great skipper, and we had a marvelous time on that ship. They were going through their training at Guantanamo Bay. Following their inspection, their operational readiness inspection there, they returned to Norfolk, had one week to get ready and sail for the Mediterranean to relieve the carrier USS Oriskany and take their spot in the Sixth Fleet.

That was a wonderful cruise, and we had a lot of fun on that ship. It was a hard-working ship. We did everything. We had a good air department, good engineering department. Everybody turned to and were very proud of the job that they did. We visited all the ports there in the Mediterranean, we sent tours to Paris and the Swiss Alps, Rome, everywhere.

Q: Who was the commanding officer of the Sixth Fleet then? Was it Ballentine?

Adm. M.: No, Admiral Ballentine was then in command of the Naval Air Force, Atlantic Fleet. It was Admiral Max Gardner who was in command of the Sixth Fleet at that time.

We certainly enjoyed it. We visited Nice, Genoa, Naples and went from there to Rome, Algiers, Suda Bay, Crete, Izmir, Turkey. We really had a wonderful Mediterranean deployment.

Q: Showing the flag and ...

Adm. M.: Exercises.

Q: At that time, the Sixth Fleet was undisputed lord of the Mediterranean, wasn't it?

Adm. M.: It certainly was, and we took advantage of all the fine tours that were set up. Can you imagine, at that time, 1951, we could go from Naples to Rome on the train, stay in a very nice hotel in Rome, all meals, two nights, two days of touring, return to Naples and it cost us $23? It was fantastic! So we just had great numbers that signed up for every one of the tours, and we told our sailors if they got in trouble, no tours, because we had to put our best foot forward and they were our best feet. And I tell you, we were proud of our sailors because they didn't get in trouble. They were darned good ambassadors. One sailor missed the train in Paris, the tour train, caught an express train and beat the tour train back to Naples. He was going to be sure and be there on time.

Q: Here you had, I suppose, an opportunity for some practical application of your manual, as developed in Norfolk.

Adm. M.: Yes, Sir. At that time, we did everything we possibly could to enhance the relations of the Sixth Fleet and the Navy with all those countries that we visited. We went all-out to do this. On United Nations Day - I think that's October the 24th - we made speeches in France, Nice. I gave a luncheon speech over the radio in French. That evening, we put on a big show for many VIPs from Nice aboard ship and for all the ships that were in at Nice with us, cruisers, destroyers, a couple of amphibious ships, and we had a great time. We put on that same show in one of the other ports. We went on tours, we gave speeches, we invited hundreds of people aboard ship. We felt as though we had done our part and sold a little bit of the USA wherever we went.

Q: There was no indication at that time of present-day Russian naval policy in the Mediterranean, was there?

Adm. M.: Absolutely not. We didn't see one Russian ship that I can remember, and Americans were well received. As a matter of fact, Americans had done such a good job of doing so much for those who were homeless in Italy after World War II, helping kids and families, business get started - because the Sixth Fleet had a lot of money to spend in comparison to the money that was available in those countries at that time. People were still poor. They were trying to get industries going. Money just wasn't available. For instance, two of the very fine artists in Naples had a contract with the Sixth Fleet. They would paint pictures for us at these set prices, including beautiful framing. Later on, they got to be, you might say, as far as art is concerned, the Sears Roebuck of Italy, right there. They got their start right from the Sixth Fleet. So the Sixth Fleet really helped out in a great many areas in the Mediterranean, but no Russians were in sight. Stalin and Company were still holed up in Russia and shouting at the world.

Q: The Sixth Fleet was under NATO, was it not?

Adm. M.: Since NATO was formed, the Sixth Fleet is still attached to NATO. When NATO plans are executed, the Sixth Fleet is in that chain.

Q: At that time, when you were there, General Eisenhower was in Paris, was he not?

Adm. M.: Yes, Sir. General Eisenhower was in Paris and Admiral Carney was what they called CinCSouth, a NATO organization. He was at Naples.

Q: Did you have much contact with Carney?

Adm. M.: No, we didn't have any contact at all. I've seen him many, many times since then, and still see him. He's a great man.

Q: Tell me about some of the diplomatic calls that you got involved in.

Adm. M.: Well, we made it a point that wherever we went with a tour - you see, we had an Italian agency handle the tours for us - we sent a tour officer with the group of officers and men. He was a combined tour and shore patrol officer. I'll give you an indication of how it worked. We went to Florence, and I happened to go on that tour. The damage-control officer that I mentioned before, Lieutenant

Commander Riddell, was assigned as the tour officer and the shore patrol officer. He had a certain number of men assigned to him who were paid for by the tour and who went with that tour to Florence. As soon as we got there, I put my baggage away at the hotel and I went over to see the American Counsul in Florence. I told them that I was Commander Miller from the aircraft carrier the USS Leyte, we were anchored off La Spezia, I had brought about 30 or 40 officers and men from the Leyte for a two-and-a-half-day tour of Florence and I was checking in with him. He said, why, and I said, "You are the senior U. S. representative in this city. I and your armed forces are over here and it's incumbent upon me If I bring any tour of sailors over here that I check in with you. One, you'll know of our presence here in the city. Two, you might have certain places that you would like to put out of bounds, where our sailors shouldn't go to keep out of trouble. Number three, do you have any pamphlets on good places to eat, reasonable places, entertainment, or where to buy things?" He said, "By gosh, now I'm glad you came, because on the other side of the river tell the sailors to keep away. At sunset don't cross that bridge because they'll find themselves over there in the morning either dead or robbed of everything that they possess." I said, "Thank you. We will put that information out because no sailor is moving away from the hotel headquarters, no officer or man, until I get back from this visit with you, so I'll pass that word. I just want you to know that these are the phone numbers at the hotel for my shore patrol officer and there'll be somebody on duty there twenty-four hours a day, so you have immediate contact with our people and with me." He said, "Thank you."

This is what we attempted to do, and we did, in every port that we visited because we wanted to be responsive to the highest American official representing the USA in that particular port. This was what you might call standard operating procedure that we initiated - to check in with our State Department wherever we went.

Q: Did this also pertain to the ambassador in Rome?

Adm. M.: In Rome, we had our tour going there, and we called up the ambassador's office in Rome and the naval attaché there. The naval attaché met us, or one of his subordinates, so that's the way we checked in with them. They knew we were there, and they knew where we were staying. They had a big American delegation there in Rome.

Q: Did you do the same sort of thing when you visited Greece?

Adm. M.: In all these places, we would always check in. We'd always send somebody ahead to set up tours and to make the contacts, and by the time we got there we either called on the ambassador or the ambassador came on out to the ship or there was an automatic invitation and the skipper and the ambassador would talk at the reception that afternoon. One of those options. We always checked in some way with the State Department in every port we visited.

Q: How were you received in North African ports, in former French territory?

Adm. M.: Just great. In Algiers, we were invited to dinner by the American Consul there, and he had some of the French there. Captain Dudley, you see, had been the former commanding officer at the Naval Air Station at Port Lyautey, so he knew some of these French and he could speak French and understand it. He spoke very fluently. So that made it easy.

Q: Did you visit outlying places, like the Balearics?

Adm. M.: No, Sir, we didn't have that opportunity. We went, as I said, to some of the inland places - Rome, beautiful, lovely tours, shopping, but I think that Florence was the nicest shopping city. In Greece, we visited some of the ruins, took tours out in the country. It was tremendously interesting. We were a wonderful bunch of tourists. There were more shoppers on that ship, more sightseers, I think, than I've ever seen. They wanted to see things.

Q: Where was the fleet based, actually?

Adm. M.: The fleet kept moving, but you might say that the base was at Naples. They didn't stay long, they kept moving from port to port to port, and exercises between ports. They would meet, have exercises, split up - one group would go to one port and another group would go to another.

Q: Did you use any Malta facilities?

Adm. M.: We didn't use them. I don't know if the Sixth Fleet did.

Q: Perhaps, Admiral, because of your experience in the Mediterranean at that time, you might say something about the withdrawal of the

Royal Navy, in large measure, from the Mediterranean and what that did to the whole picture.

Adm. M.: Well, the withdrawal of the Royal Navy from the Mediterranean is just a continuation of their withdrawal from all other water areas of the world. Britain has pulled in her horns from Asia, Singapore, the Persian Gulf. They found it difficult to maintain a defense establishment on a world-wide basis. There's no longer a showing of the flag of Great Britain around the world. This void that they left in the Mediterranean is just like the voids that they are leaving now in the Persian Gulf and the Indian Ocean, the South China Sea, or Singapore. They have to be filled by somebody if we don't want to see the Russians moving in. So, what's happened? The Russians are now a big power in the Mediterranean. They have the bases to operate from Egypt, North Africa. They're in the Indian Ocean. They are really out to get that foothold throughout the Middle East, and the only nation that is showing any opposite strength is the United States with the Sixth Fleet in the Mediterranean, our poor little old seaplane tender in the Persian Gulf with an occasional destroyer or destroyer escort down there. Nothing in the Indian Ocean. We hope that one of these days we will have something operating in the Indian Ocean, more than the seaplane tender that we have in the Persian Gulf. These are all very real problems that the world should be facing up to vis-a-vis the Russians. The only one that is shaping up to it is the United States.

Q: Does it say that the Royal Navy's withdrawal was so precipitate that we were not really ready to fill the vacuum? That we didn't have the ships and men to do it, or that we were not prepared mentally for taking over this burden?

Adm. M.: Sure, we, over the years, relied on the British to hold up their end of the deal, but when they pulled out, we filled the gap there pretty fast. We weren't the most professional Navy in the Mediterranean at this time, but we learned in a hurry. We've maintained very good posture in the Mediterranean since then. However, witness the demonstrations against us now in Italy, in Turkey, in other ports there are demonstrations we never did see before. So the climate is changing and some of this Communist movement is still dynamic, it's against us, and the Commies are still getting those demonstrations going.

Q: It's changing with some assistance, then?

Adm. M.: That's right. Remember, we've given all of these countries in Europe billions of dollars' worth of military aid and economic aid - billions. We still are giving more aid than we should.

Q: That's really not the basis for friendships, is it, giving?

Adm. M.: Absolutely not. We helped get Japan back on its feet. We almost did it for them, and the same for Germany. Germany still wants us to maintain troops, more troops, there, and it's getting much more difficult for the great American public to reason why they don't supply people for their own defense and for the defense of Europe. They just aren't doing enough, and the same goes for Italy.

Q: In retrospect, would it have been to our advantage, to the advantage of the Western World, if perhaps through judicious financial help we had assisted the British in continuing to remain in some of these areas. It was a financial crisis for them which, in large measure, caused them to withdraw. Could we have bolstered them in any way and saved us some grief?

Adm. M.: I don't know what the bill would have come to, but it's just an aspect of keeping forces anywhere, and I don't think it's a very helpful situation if we're paying Britain's bills to keep some of their forces in a particular area. They've got to want to do it, I think. If they don't, then we have to look at some other source of providing the troops or the arms or the ships, even if they supply just a few, but I just don't believe in paying the bill for everybody. And we're still doing it. We're still supplying Korea with lots of aid. Chiang kai-shek, and he's got a viable economy going in Taiwan. They can all do more.

Q: Admiral, do you want to talk about your period at the Industrial College for the Armed Forces, which happened in July of 1953? Would you preface what you did there by telling me about the Industrial College? How does it rank in comparison with the National War College, the Naval War College? What is its particular objective?

Adm. M.: I went to the Industrial College for the Armed Forces in 1952 to 1953. One of our most illustrious alumni at the Industrial College was General, then President, Dwight D. Eisenhower. He was there in the early days of the formation of that college. It is one of the finest institutions of the armed forces. It provides an outstanding course of a year in management, research and development, production, natural resources, test and evaluation, everything that goes into industry and defense. They have an outstanding staff of instructors, they have correspondence courses, they hold seminars all over the country, they have outstanding speakers on various subjects, and in addition, the students at the Industrial College have the opportunity of listening to the lectures at the National War College next door. So you might say that we get, at the Industrial College, a big chunk of what the National War College gives plus the outstanding course that the Industrial College offers. It's, I think, the best of all the armed forces' colleges. The National War College is, I think, in comparison, number two, the Naval War College farther on down the line. They don't hit as comprehensive a curriculum as the Industrial College.

Q: Where does the staff come from? I mean how are they selected? The Teaching staff?

Adm. M.: The teaching staff consists of civilian professors and a certain number, a small percentage, of military officers who have a broad educational background, degrees - some of them have masters and doctorates.

Q: Anybody from industry?

Adm. M.: The Industrial College has outstanding lecturers from industry, but no teachers or professors that have been associated with industry. The professors that they have are professionals who have been teaching various aspects of Industrial College curriculum for a long time.

Q: What about the complexion of the student body? How many are there, and what do they represent?

Adm. M.: The student body is about 150 a year, representing Army, Navy, Air Force, Marine Corps, Coast Guard, State Department, Labor Department, Commerce Department, and now probably, Transportation. Quite a cross section of students and quite an exchange of information between those students on various committees. It was one of the most interesting and profitable years that I spent in the Navy.

Q: What sort of qualifications do you have to have to be eligible for this assignment?

Adm. M.: I don't think the Navy has much of a criterion set up for a position description, so to speak of who they pick. I think when your time comes that you should go to school, the Navy fills the holes up of the National War College, the Industrial College, the Naval War College, the Air Force College, and the Army. I think they just fill up the holes.

I had never heard of the Industrial College for the Armed Forces when I got this set of orders as the executive officer of the Leyte. I immediately inquired as to what they did, and I was delighted that I was going to have this year's sabbatical to go study. I enjoyed every bit of it and learned an awful lot. I think the Industrial College has contributed greatly to the management and the professionalism of the military officers in the Department of Defense.

Q: Did you have to prepare a special paper and, if so, what did you focus on?

Adm. M.: We had to prepare several papers during the year. As we finished one broad area, we would prepare a paper on our thoughts, our opinions, on that particular area. So, you might say, we covered quite a bit of territory in our deliberations. We were assigned to various committees during the year, we were shifted from one committee to another. We had seminars with outstanding leaders in industry. We had some of the finest lecturers in the land, including some foreign talent. We had field trips, very outstanding field trips, to industry, to research and development establishments for the Department of Defense. I remember we visited Birmingham in my group. United States Steel down there and various other industries, the pulp industry, paper. It was a truly outstanding year spent at that school.

Q: It's wonderful that they have that system where officers can go back at a much higher level and get educational information. Did you find it difficult to go back as a student at that point?

Adm. M.: Not a bit. As a matter of fact, the first group that I was assigned to, we had a Marine colonel, an Army colonel, an Air Force colonel, I was a Navy commander, was just selected for captain that I wouldn't make for another year. We had a fine spirit

H. L. Miller #2 - 176

of cooperation in that group. We helped each other. We got along well. I found it very easy to go back to the books and thoroughly enjoyed it. I enjoyed the trips, the briefings, the lectures, the discussions with the various professors at the college, and the committee meetings. We had many meetings and case histories.

Q: How long has that College been in existence?

Adm. M.: I think it started before World War II, when it was the Army Industrial College. That's where Ike graduated. Then, after World War II, when the Department of Defense was organized and unification of the services, they established it as the Industrial College of the Armed Forces, instead of the Army War College.

Q: And was that almost simultaneous with the setting up of the National War College?

Adm. M.: I think so, and the two schools are right next door to each other. Their only competition during the year is in athletics.

Q: Which is friendly!

Adm. M.: We always beat the National War College in soft ball! You assume that when the year's over, with that wonderful background in research and development, management, production, quality control, logistics, certainly you will end up being in the logistics office of the Navy Department or the Joint Chiefs of Staff, or some tremendous R and D organization, or a procurement office. Of course, the Navy doesn't do things like that. They sent me to the strategic plans division of the Navy Department, and that's where I got back to dear old Admiral Burke.

Q: But you were an exception, in that your experience before the Industrial College had been so broad that, maybe, you were qualified for this special assignment!

Interview No. 3 with Rear Admiral Henry L. Miller, U. S. Navy

Place: Naval Air Test Center, Patuxent, Maryland

Date: Wednesday, 19 May 1971

Subject: Biography

By: John T. Mason, Jr.

Q: Admiral, the chapter today will begin, I believe, with your tour of duty in the Strategic Plans Division in the CNO's office. You went there in 1953 after having had a very stimulating course at the Industrial College of the Armed Forces. Would you tell me something about your job sheet there in the Strategic Plans Office? What were your particular duties, what were the issues that you were called upon to deal with?

Adm. M.: After graduating from the Industrial College of the Armed Forces, commonly known as ICAF, I expected that because ICAF gave us a predominantly logistics-production management-RDT & E course that I would end up in logistics planning in the CNO's office somewhere, but I was assigned to Strategic Plans which was then Op-30, changed subsequently to Op-60, under at that time Rear Admiral Arleigh Burke.

Q: I should think that would have been a very pleasing to you, perhaps more so than logistics.

Adm. M.: Well, at the time, I didn't know what to - how to take it because a classmate of mine told me to break away or do anything to keep out of Op-60. I didn't break away. I took the assignment and reported in to "31-Knot" Arleigh Burke's shop. I was assigned to the policy branch of that division under, at that time, Captain Sandy MacGregor, then Captain Benny Bass, and, finally Captain Corky Ward, who later turned out to be a four-star admiral.

My first assignment, I was part of a three-man team to come up with a new look for strategy for the Eisenhower Administration, and Admiral Burke gave us a week to do this. Subsequently, he had a turn of heart and gave us three extra days.

Q: That was good of him. Did he give you any guidelines?

Adm. M.: No, he didn't give us any guidelines. We were supposed to get together and come up with a new look. It was quite a shocker because of the time element involved. It was actually ten days and nights of hard work.

Q: This he actually expected of his "think" people, didn't he? I mean you could work day and night as far as he was concerned.

Adm. M.: Oh, yes. As a matter of fact, after that initial pressure push, Op-60 wasn't too bad, but Admiral Burke was a real driver just like his nickname "31-Knot" Burke. A terrific guy. He was always thinking ahead. He was always driving himself just as hard as anybody else.

After that my job over the next two years in the division was in NATO planning, in over-all policy, and liaisoning with the Department of State and the Secretary of Defense's office on world-wide problems. In other words, the State Department would come up with U. S. policy with respect to a particular country, and that policy would highlight the political, economic, military, and psychological aspects. We, of course, would contribute to the military part of that policy. However, we were asked to put our ideas into any of the other areas, political, economic, and psychological, because in the end State culled all the comments that came in and finally arrived at the new policy that was approved by the President.

Q: In this particular section in the Navy, you were more or less what we now term a "think tank," weren't you? I mean, an idea man who generated...

Adm. M.: Well, I think just about everybody in the Strategic Plans Division is an idea guy. He has to come up with new solutions in double quick time to take care of particular situations that arise all over the world.

Q: Tell me about your first assignment, this assignment that was limited to a week, for a new naval attitude for the Eisenhower Administration to adopt and pursue. Tell me something about that.

Adm. M.: We stressed the importance of sea power in the over-all picture and, naturally, as a part of sea power the aviation Navy, including aircraft carriers, patrol squadrons, and all that. The new look administration did emphasize the nuclear deterrent, more bang for the buck, a big strategic bombing force. We weren't against strategic bombing and the A bomb because it was doing a pretty good job for us, but we stressed the importance of and highlighted sea power in over-all defense.

Q: And stressing sea power, did this mean control of the seas? Was this considered to be imperative?

Adm. M.: That's correct. We emphasized the policy that we're doing right today, control of the seas, projecting our power overseas, controlling the submarine threat, showing the flag, all of this.

Q: Actually, in the early 1950s, was there any considerable naval force in existence that could challenge us?

Adm. M.: Yes, as far as naval forces Russia had more submarines than probably the whole world had at that time. They had close to 450. We had about 125, most of which were diesel boats, not nuclear, and had a very limited capability.

Q: At that point, had the Eisenhower doctrine of massive retaliation been developed?

Adm. M.: Not at that particular time, but we had to come up with a concept. The Eisenhower doctrine of massive retaliation originated a short time later. It was proposed by the Joint Chiefs of Staff and the chairman at that time, as you recall, was Admiral Radford. And this plan of massive retaliation was advocated by Secretary of State Dulles and Admiral Radford.

Q: How much did your outfit contribute to the development of this plan?

Adm. M.: Our contribution to the development of the plan for massive retaliation was to show what our aircraft carriers could do with the planes that we had aboard in carrying A bombs wherever we went on the oceans of the world. The aircraft carriers made a very significant contribution because they could be near the potential enemy, and launch planes in a matter of minutes. They didn't have long distances to go. So the Navy could contribute immeasurably and this is what we pointed out. That was before polaris submarines.

Q: As a matter of a bit of digression, I suppose, this whole idea of massive retaliation was something that the citizens of the United States bought with much eagerness, did they not?

Adm. M.: Oh, yes, because they felt that we'd have less of a defense bill and we'd get more for our money, and at that time the A bomb was a very wonderful deterrent. So it was probably a darned good policy to have at that particular time in our history.

Q: But, Admiral, did we in our thinking go so far as to conceive of the A bomb actually being used? Did we think that we might be called upon to go the limit with this policy, or was it merely held over the heads of the potential enemy as a threat?

Adm. M.: Well, you can't have a weapon and a policy without the determination to use it, if you have to use it. So I don't think President Eisenhower was kidding when he said we have the A bomb, we have our plans, and if we have to use it, we will.

Q: A further digression, our friend George Miller feels that when the moment came and the threat was real with the Suez crisis, we backed down and did not employ this policy, and as a result our current problems began to grow.

Adm. M.: I don't think the Suez situation was the right one to use an A bomb. We took care of that without the use of it. Lebanon followed right after Suez - is that the one you're talking about?

Q: Yes.

Adm. M.: And we put the Marines ashore, we airlifted some troops and airplanes over there, we reinforced the Sixth Fleet in the Mediterranean, and we took care of that particular situation at Suez. Certainly, to my mind, it wasn't the place to use the A bomb.

Q: Was there any thought given to the results of use of the A bomb? The whole world was somewhat shocked and horrified by what happened in Nagasaki and so forth. Did we not think in those terms, too? The results of the employment of the ultimate weapon?

Adm. M.: Oh, yes, Sir. Every one of our plans looked at the effects of the various megaton bombs that we had in our arsenal and every aspect of strategic A-bombing was taken into consideration - radiation effects, the heat, the pressure, all of those results of bombing were given great consideration. We were thinking about how industry would be levelled and how many of the population would be killed, maimed for life, or affected for life. That had to come into our plans.

H. L. Miller #3 - 184

Q: Was it also a part of the understanding of the populace? Did they know this, too?

Adm. M.: Well, the great American public normally will not take too great an interest unless it's almost hitting them between the eyes. Certainly, an awful lot of information went out on the effects of the A bombs. Some read it and forgot about it. Others didn't even take time to see what the effects would be. And, I believe that you can back that statement up by the apathy in the civil defense program. There weren't very many people who were rightly concerned for helping out in civil defense. It was a hard chore for any of our civil defense leaders to get people interested.

Q: As I recall, at the end of his first year, President Eisenhower addressed the United Nations in December and his thought was "atoms for peace," atomic power used for peace. Maybe this was responsible for redirecting the thinking of the people?

Adm. M.: I really don't know, but President Eisenhower wanted to do something with the A bomb that would help the world instead of devastating the world, and his proposal was to use the atom in medical research, underground explosions to clear areas, for other things as a weapon-not to kill people. He also approved the building of the SS Savannah, the first nuclear powered merchant ship to again show the world another example of "atoms for peace."

Q: In your planning, which was worldwide in scope, what role did you assign to the British Navy, the British Air Force, our own Air Force? What sort of cooperation did the Navy expect in the thinking and planning for certain operations, what share was given to them?

Adm. M.: The NATO planning was done by groups of allied officers and naturally the armed services of those particular countries were all fitted in to the over-all NATO plan for that area of the world. So every branch of the armed services of a particular country was planned to be used.

Q: Tell me more about your own personal operations in Op-60.

Adm. M.: We put heavy emphasis on the Far East, Southeast Asia, and South Asia. It was all a tremendous education because sooner or later we were concerned with United States policy with respect to almost every country in the world. And Admiral Burke kept everybody on step. I had met him previously out in the Pacific when he was a commodore, and chief of staff to Vice Admiral Marc Mitscher, who was Commander, Task Force 58, and who had been the commanding officer of the USS Hornet when I took the Doolittle raiders aboard.

I saw Admiral Burke several times around the Pacific during the war. As a matter of fact, I have been in touch with him off and on ever since. I think Admiral Burke operated on the theory that the busiest people would always produce, so he gave them the work. At times, it was pretty frustrating. He never let up. He was a driver. He had tons of energy. He was absolutely dedicated to the Navy. He knew no hours, he set no pattern of work. If he thought you could do the job for North Africa planning even though you were assigned to the Far East planning, you got the North African job.

Q: In addition to Far East?

Adm. M.: Absolutely. One never knew what assignment he was going to get next, day or night, and it was, I thought, a pretty disorganized operation, but we got the job done. Admiral Burke used to hold weekly meetings, almost every Friday, to keep the whole shop up to date on what was going on, and he told us many of his most intimate secrets and some of the real top secret stuff that was going on, just to keep us cut in.

Q: That came from the Joint Chiefs?

Adm. M.: That's correct. He even told us about some of his own personal life, particularly when he was Op-23 leading the Navy campaign to keep aircraft carriers in the United States Navy, and he was out-and-out fighting with the United States Air Force. During that time when he was Op-23, I attended a few of his private meetings on what we should do in selling the aircraft carriers. He got quite a name for himself, both good and bad, and a great many of his friends didn't want to be associated with him because they figured that there was a good chance to get passed over. This really hurt Admiral Burke because he was fighting for the Navy and there were a lot of naval officers that weren't supporting that fight.

Well, after one year with Admiral Burke there, his relief, Admiral Dennison, came in. He is a brilliant man, more relaxed

H. L. Miller #3 - 187

than Admiral Burke, and a great leader. He knows strategy and tactics and he went from that particular job to four stars.

Q: I understand that Admiral Burke is quite a gardener and used to think as he worked in his yard. You must have had an affinity with him there?

Adm. M.: No. In fact I didn't see his garden, if he had one. I know that he couldn't have had much time to spend on the garden because he was always working on strategic plans.

After a year with Admiral Dennison, springtime came along and there were many rumors on who would be the new chief of naval operations to relieve Admiral Carney, and when somebody said Arleigh Burke was being considered I made the statement that if he was selected as chief of naval operations, this was going to be a very disorganized Navy. Of course, I lived to eat those words later on because he did a tremendous job as Chief of Naval Operations.

Q: Why wasn't Admiral Carney himself re-appointed? He wanted to be, I'm sure.

Adm. M.: I don't know all the details, but primarily I guess because the administration didn't like him. There were probably other reasons but I don't know.

Q: Or was it SecNav?

Adm. M.: Well, SecNav is part of the administration.

Q: During that time I think there was a certain amount of attention devoted to re-designing aircraft carriers, was there not? For different uses, antisubmarine warfare?

Adm. M.: We had at that time what I consider a major effort going into antisubmarine warfare. Subsequently, we did have aircraft carriers for heavy attack, that's the A-bomb business and for supporting our troops ashore. In addition, we had aircraft carriers, assigned exclusively to antisubmarine warfare. This was the change, but I forget what year it did come in.

Q: Was it a reaction to the build-up of the Russian submarine fleet?

Adm. M.: It resulted from the increased emphasis that we put into antisubmarine warfare and what was needed in antisubmarine warfare. We had a very poor over-all effort going into antisubmarine warfare at that particular time. We needed to do something about it.

Q: What about the realm of naval aircraft? Were there any significant developments in the period that you were there? It was a time when we were cutting down on expenditures. Did this affect naval aircraft?

Adm. M.: Certainly. Whenever they cut the Navy aircraft, numbers and types of aircraft were cut. Additionally, during that period of time starting in 1952, we put an angled deck - and this was a British invention - on one of our aircraft carriers to try out the angled-deck concept. It was so good that everybody bought it, bought the idea, and plans were then made to re-configure most of our aircraft carriers with the angled deck, since it did provide increased safety of operation. It would save us an awful lot of money and lives.

Q: So this led into the planning part and it had some effect on the Navy budget, too?

Adm. M.: Definitely. Any changes that are made in aircraft or aircraft carriers are very expensive. Any of those cut right smack into the budget.

Q: Were there any developments in the realm of submarine missiles? I know it was before Polaris, but were there any beginnings in this time?

Adm. M.: Yes, we did have the Regulus I missile that had been tested out at the Navy missile range at Point Mugu, California, and we had a certain number of submarines specially built and configured to carry the Regulus I missile. This was a good idea for that particular time. Later on, they planned for the Regulus II missile, which would go farther and faster and carry a bigger payload, but that program, after it was initiated, was canceled simply because it wouldn't be a big enough pay-off for the money put into it. We had Regulus I and we had already decided that we were going whole hog for Polaris.

Q: Then Regulus I must have entered into your strategic planning? And in the development of naval doctrine for the Eisenhower administration?

Adm. M.: Oh, yes. In all strategic planning we take into consideration the entire arsenal we have in the way of weapons, whether it be our planes carrying A bombs, strafing and supporting troops ashore, any missiles that the planes carry, any missiles that the ships carry, guns, people, and all that.

Q: This period in time was the start of the developments involving Formosa, the Formosa Resolution in the Senate. Did this have its repercussions in your planning group?

Adm. M.: Yes, in Far East planning.

Q: Tell me about that.

Adm. M.: All of that was cranked in to our Far East planning. We had to maintain the line of bases that we had, you might say, to this day, starting with bases in Japan. This is the line of bases in Japan, Okinawa, Taiwan, and the Philippines. Following that we started the SEATO organization, the Southeast Asia Treaty Organization. This was an organization that was brought together for planning purposes and to talk over the problems of defense that were involved in the whole Far East and Southeast Asia area, including Pakistan and South Asia. But the line of defense was Japan, Okinawa, Taiwan, and the Philippines. Guam was too far back of that line to really be seriously considered as a stronghold.

In Japan we had a certain number of bases that we held onto. We had certain forces in Korea as a result of the Korean War. We had bases in Taiwan and a heavy military aid program to them, also to Korea, and a pretty hefty military aid program to Japan. Then, coming down to Okinawa, we put many, many millions of dollars building Okinawa into a formidable base. This was for strategic bombing and for a training area, primarily for Army and Marines . . .

Q: And we surely intended it as a permanent base, didn't we?

Adm. M.: Oh, yes. We intended it as a permanent base and we built it with permanent construction. The Navy had very little construction there at Okinawa. The Navy had Okinawa at one time but gave it up and were sorry that they gave up all that area to the Army, the Air Force, and the Marines.

Coming down to the Philippines, the three principal bases there were Clark Air Force Base, north of Manila, Sangley Point, just across the bay from Manila, and the naval air station that was being built at Cubi Point in the Philippines. Cubi Point is right next to Subic Bay, which is about fifty miles away from Manila. As far as the Philippines were concerned, and their own armed forces, they had very few. We, over a period of time, built up their Army, Navy and Air Force, but it wasn't a really effective force. We supplied them with lots of military aid, as we did Taiwan, Japan, and Korea, but not as much as any of the other countries, and one of the reasons was because they couldn't afford to keep a large army, navy, and air force. They couldn't afford paying the troops. So our military aid was in much smaller proportion than to the countries up north of them.

Q: Was there any carry-over in know-how in the Philippines from before World War II? General MacArthur spent a great deal of time there training military forces. Was there any carry-over of this in the postwar years?

Adm. M.: The Philippines armed forces had some of those people left. They were used as a nucleus in building up the armed forces in the Philippines, but, as I said, they didn't have large numbers because the Philippine economy could not support them. Now, going farther south, at that time, we did start a military aid and advisory program in Saigon for the South Vietnamese.

Q: Well, Admiral, at this period when you were with the strategic planning division in the Navy Department, a lot of very important things were happening in the Far East. Do you want to mention some of them, like setting up SEATO and the beginnings of our involvement in Vietnam?

Adm. M.: Just keeping the dates straight when you asked me about weapons and weapon systems, it's significant that in January of 1954, the *Nautilus*, the first atomic-powered submarine, was launched at Groton, Connecticut, and, following that - remember the war in Indochina had been going on for about seven and a half years - in May of 1954 the French outpost Dien Bien Phu fell to the Vietnamese Army of Ho-Chi-Minh. This was followed shortly by the Geneva Conference on Far Eastern affairs, where 19 countries were represented, including Communist China.

Q: And that set the stage for the picture in Vietnam down to the present day?

Adm. M.: Not exactly because in August of 1954 the armistice was signed which ended that war in Indochina that had been going on for that seven years, and it was also the time of the French withdrawal.

Ho Chi Minh won 62,000 square miles and 13 million population in North Vietnam. And, remember, Cambodia and Laos became independent countries. Less than one month later, in September, the Southeast Asia Treaty Organization, SEATO, formed by these countries, the U. S., Britain, France, Australia, New Zealand, the Philippines, Pakistan, and Thailand. That treaty was signed in Manila on September 8th. The Far East and Southeast Asia was very much concerned with what had been going on in Korea and all the way through Indochina. Other countries were thinking about it, too, and one of them was Indonesia. Sukarno, as you recall, was a very flamboyant guy. He whipped up an Afro-Asian conference of 29 nations. They met in Bandung, Indonesia, in April of 1955. And it was primarily for these countries to have a platform to voice their new nationalism of 29 young and developing nations. On the other side of the world, West Germany, in May of 1955, became a sovereign state and not be outdone, a short time later in May of 1955, the Warsaw Pact, a 20-year mutual defense treaty, was signed in Warsaw by the countries that Russia had taken over. So all of these sort of set the stage for a lot of things that came later, including, of course, the summit meeting between the U. S., Great Britain, and France. It was a proposal for those three countries and the USSR to meet and talk over world affairs. President Eisenhower was the top U. S. negotiator at Geneva.

Q: This must have been of some concern to the planning section in the Navy Department. It must have had some bearing on new problems. Did the plans that you developed there originate in your own office or were suggestions handed down to you from the Joint Chiefs? How did you begin to work on a problem in a

H. L. Miller #3 - 194

given area?

Adm. M.: Take, for instance, the Southeast Asia Treaty Organization. The initial planning for SEATO plans and all these various contingency situations came from a joint planning group that was established by these countries in Bangkok. And that planning group on SEATO plans has held forth every year since they were established in Bangkok. Twice a year, the top military people and the heads of state of those countries get together in either Bangkok, Pearl Harbor, or Washington, D. C., or any one of those countries to okay the plans that have been promulgated or produced by that planning group, and any changes that have been recommended since the previous meeting. Additionally, the heads of state now are talking along economic lines in addition to the military planning that this group does. But the detailed military planning must come from the planners assigned to that joint group in Bangkok, where the headquarters of SEATO is established. Nevertheless, because CinCPac more or less rules the Pacific, the SEATO group looks to him for leadership. He, of course, checks his planning guidelines with our JCS.

Q: That's interesting. Now, your tour of duty in the Department came to an end in 1955 and it was perfectly logical, I expect, that you went on to the next in the Philippines.

Adm. M.: Not necessarily. The Navy has different ways and different reasons for detailing an individual, but it happened that I was assigned as commanding officer of the Naval Station at Sangley Point in the Philippines, right across Manila Bay. I had never been stationed overseas, so we looked forward to a nice leisurely trip out there...

Q: Did this assignment come as a surprise to you, or had you sought it, really?

Adm. M.: You might say every assignment in the Navy to me is a surprise. I never know where I'm going until somebody calls up and says there's a set of orders that's waiting for me. But we had a nice trip out. On the same boat we met the new commanding officer and his wife of Clark Air Force Base. When we got to Guam, the Commander, Naval Forces, Philippines, at that time, Admiral Goodwin, had flown over and he yanked me off the ship. I was given briefings by the Commander, Fleet Air, Guam, staff, and I was informed that I would take over as Commander, Fleet Air, Philippines, and Naval Air Bases, Philippines, and Commanding Officer of Sangley Point.

Q: Why these additional jobs?

Adm. M.: Well, the Commander, Fleet Air, Philippines, job was primarily to take care of the Seventh Fleet squadrons that came in there from the carriers of the Seventh Fleet, to provide services to the aircraft carriers, to provide logistic support for the Navy squadron that was in the MATS organization, carrying the mail and logistics from Clark Air Force Base to Saigon, Bangkok, Calcutta, New Delhi, Karachi, and Dhahran, Saudi Arabia. I provided logistic support for that outfit and also the MATS detachments that were in those locations.

The primary job was Commander, Fleet Air, Philippines, and in that job I did not work for Admiral Goodwin. I worked for Commander, Fleet Air, Western Pacific, who was then Admiral Fitzhue Lee out in Japan. The Naval Air Bases, Philippines, job was responsible for two bases, the one being built at Cubi Point and I was immediately placed in charge of the completion of construction - of that base until it was commissioned the following year, 1956, and my own station of Sangley Point.

Q: They really needed you out there, didn't they?

Adm. M.: Looking back on it, there were about six or eight agencies that were building Cubi Point, and it seems that nobody was in charge, so I was the guy. I sent a message and said I'm here, I am bringing the Fleet Air, Guam, squad over here as the staff, that will be the Fleet Air, Philippines, staff, and that's the way I got in the business. I didn't know anything about the construction business and neither did the staff, but they were the best little staff that got into the swing of it all, learned their lessons, and were absolutely terrific.

The job as commanding officer of Sangley, I guess I was supposed to do it on Sunday afternoon, but if you want to know the truth of it, that was the toughest of the three because the base had deteriorated in almost every department. The Filipinos were stealing the place blind and we had very poor relations with the mayor of Manila. He was one of the key guys there. It seems as though the Admiral of Naval Forces, Philippines, and the mayor of Manila, Mayor Lacson, didn't like each other. Lacson was a brilliant, tough, cussing mayor. He liked women and he really did love our former ambassador there in the Philippines, Admiral Spruance. They got along beautifully. He was a pretty straightforward guy. I met him at a special celebration in Manila and, after shaking his hand and sizing him up, I asked him if he was ever a boxer, and he said, yes, that was right, he was a boxer. I told him I was on the boxing team at the Naval Academy and from then on we were big buddies and we agreed on everything. As a matter of interest, when we left the Philippines two years later he personally cooked the luncheon that he gave for me at the Manila Hotel, and he was a darned good cook.

Q: So, having established that relationship with him, matters at the base began to progress?

Adm. M.: Oh, yes. We had projects that had been hanging fire for a couple of years that we had to get his okay on over in Manila, and it didn't take long after that to get his personal okay on all the things that we wanted done. Lacson was a good mayor. He did a lot for Manila and for the Filipinos, and he made no bones about cussing any Filipino who was doing a bad job. He'd cuss him out right on the spot.

Q: There must have been some interesting experiences during that two-year sojourn. Tell me about some of them.

Adm. M.: As far as Sangley Point was concerned, one of the biggest problems was to maintain good relations with the little town outside the gate, the chief of Police there, the mayor of the town of

Cavite, and the governor of the province. It didn't take long to get good community relations going with those three and, believe it or not, here it is almost twenty-five years later and those are still the same three people in power in that area.

Q: How did you go about establishing a good rapport with them?

Adm. M.: We had certain problems between the base and the community and we would immediately call the chief of police, the mayor and the governor, or just the governor and let him get the mayor and the chief of police together, have a meeting and see what we could do about those particular problems right now, and it might be any time, day or night. But that's the way that we kept good control over relations between Sangley Point, the Navy, and the Filipinos.

Q: How did you communicate, in Spanish or in English?

Adm. M.: They could all speak English very well.

Q: Did you know anything about the Filipino character which would give you an insight in dealing with these people beforehand?

Adm. M.: The only thing that I knew about the Filipinos were the ones that I had seen in the United States Navy. They're different from us, but certainly if you get together with them you can iron out your problems just like with anybody else, any other ethnic group. And after you get together with them it's pretty easy to maintain good relations.

H. L. Miller #3 - 199

Q: How closely were you tied in with the commander of the Seventh Fleet?

Adm. M.: The commander of the Seventh Fleet in the Far East gets top priority from any Navy installation in the Far East, or anywhere. He's got a big job to do and we're there to provide him with all the services that he needs. So for his requirements, we turned to and produced for him.

Q: Did he during your tour of duty make periodic visits at Manila?

Adm. M.: Oh, yes, he made visits up and down the chain with his flagship. He had to meet the principal military people in the Far East and the heads of state. The Seventh Fleet job in peacetime is a big diplomatic job, for one has to be able to communicate with the top leaders in all of those foreign countries.

Q: What was the attitude of the Filipino generally toward Americans?

Adm. M.: At that time the Filipinos had great respect and admiration for Americans. I think MacArthur left his influence there, so did Ambassador Spruance. Ambassador Spruance did a marvelous job, but we had some other top people there in the Embassy that left their mark with the Filipinos. We had many military leaders there who were respected and admired by the Filipinos. So I'd say, all in all, Americans and Filipinos got along great. Also at that time General Romulo was ambassador to the U. S. and also head of the U. N., and General Romulo was a great friend of Americans.

Q: Did you know him as a man?

Adm. M.: Yes, Sir. I met him through friends of mine from San Francisco and I've seen him many times since then.

Q: He's a very dynamic individual, isn't he?

Adm. M.: That's right, and his son, Carlos, Jr., and his wife were guests of ours on a couple of occasions at Sangley Point. After we left the Philippines in October of 1957, Carlos, Jr. was killed in a plane crash. His wife, Mariles, in accordance with Philippine custom never re-married. I've seen her many times out there and in the States. She always travels with the General now, since his wife, Virginia, died a couple of years ago. So every once in a while I see the Romulos.

Q: During this tour of duty you said you were called upon to set up a supply depot in Saigon, a commissary? Do you want to tell me about that?

Adm. M.: It wasn't a supply depot. In October of 1955 I was directed to set up a small commissary-px in Saigon and Bangkok. This was primarily for the military assistance advisory people that were there, U. S., Army, Navy, Air Force, and Marine Corps, and for the U. S. Embassy groups in those countries.

Q: How did this group come about?

Adm. M.: After the armistice that was signed on August 11, 1954, the United States was requested to set up a military assistance/advisory group to the South Vietnamese armed forces.

Q: Requested by whom?

Adm. M.: Requested by the government of South Vietnam. The Joint Chiefs of Staff and the President of our country sent this group to Vietnam. A military aid program was set up to provide them with guns, ammunition, tanks and all the things that you need to fight a war, including some airplanes. This was the start of the military assistance program that is now a major part of the Vietnamization process in South Vietnam today. I set up that commissary and PX principally for those military advisers and the Embassy group. You might say the American colony there consisted of the military assistance advisory group, the State Department people, the Aid people, and all those Americans who were concerned with the Vietnamese government.

Q: How large a contingent were they?

Adm. M.: I forget how many people were involved, but they were most appreciative of the American food and spirits that I sent over to that commissary. As a matter of interest, down in Bangkok they said they were short of meat and I couldn't get anything down there in a ship, so I flew 10,000 pounds of meat in an airplane packed in dry ice and it got there in good shape.

Q: You couldn't get hold of a refrigerator ship.

Adm. M.: No, not at that time.

Q: In Saigon, did you have a chance to call on President Diem?

Adm. M.: No, Sir. In the first part of 1956, I made an inspection trip all the way to Saudia Arabia with some Air Force people from the MATS organization. The first stop was Saigon. I was primarily concerned with inspecting my commissary over there to find out how they were doing. There was a young ensign and his wife in charge. They were most enthusiastic. I think they did an outstanding job. The rest of my inspection trip was going to the places we supplied, checking with the detachments of the MATS organization, to find out if anything was needed.

Q: You were, in a sense, showing the flag, too, were you not, in these places but in a very concrete fashion?

Adm. M.: Since we had Navy planes that went to all those cities, delivered cargo and mail for the Embassy people and for our military aid people in those countries, you might say we were in a small way showing the flag.

Q: Burma was not on your route at all?

Adm. M.: No, Burma was not.

Q: You've talked essentially about two of your hats, but you had a third hat in the Philippines.

Adm. M.: As commander, Naval Air Bases, Philippines, I was charged with the completion of the building of Cubi Point which was commissioned in July of 1956. Since Cubi Point was Admiral Radford's project, they used to call it "Radford's Folly," because we moved more dirt in carving out a landing strip on that hillside than they moved in building the Panama Canal. The Seabees did it, and they did a wonderful job. We had a commercial construction company from Hawaii doing most of the building of the structure there, but the Seabees moved the dirt and built the airstrip.

Q: If it was such a difficult location and difficult operation, why was it chosen over other possible sites?

Adm. M.: It was chosen because it's right next to Subic Bay, the Naval Station at Subic Bay, and that beautiful anchorage for ships, we had our planes, ships and aircraft carriers all together in one locality. So it was a natural spot for an air station that we really needed, and certainly it's paid off tremendously during this war in Southeast Asia as a logistics support center and a recreation center. From Subic Bay and Cubi we got many of our people up to Baugio, which is the beautiful resort center in the Philippines. It's a lovely place. And in July of 1956 I got Admiral Radford to come out to the commissioning plus quite a few other celebrities, including President Magsaysay of the Philippines. It was a beautiful day, a beautiful ceremony, and we commissioned Cubi Point.

Q: How much did the base cost in terms of American dollars?

Adm. M.: It was about a fifty-million-dollar base, paid off many times over through this Vienamese War.

Q: You spoke of importing a contractor from Hawaii in order to accomplish the job there. Did this create any feeling among the Filipinos? Did they not have contractors in Manila who could have done it?

Adm. M.: You open up a whole new question and answer period here! That's a good question for the Philippines at that time. The Filipinos had built quite a number of good solid structures in Manila. They were building all over the city - a new city - but we did not have on contract with the Filipinos in any minor or major construction either at Sangley Point, Cubi Point, or Subic Bay, and the American company from Hawaii was Pomeroy, Hawaiian, and they were operating mostly on cost-plus-fixed-fee basis, and their prices were high. I had some construction at Sangley Point so I investigated the Philippine construction firms in Manila. First, I had to get a contract form approved by the Pacific Division of Yards and Docks. I sent my Public Works Officer to Pearl Harbor to get this. He brought it back approved. We let out bids in Manila to about six companies for a small minor construction job at Sangley Point. The bids were sort of ridiculous in their estimates because it was a very small facility, but we did find that one company came through with a very reasonable bid. So we asked the others why they were so high, and they said they could come down lower if we would tell them how much they had to kick back to us. And we said we didn't do business that way. All but one company didn't believe it, so this one company took a chance on us and they did a beautiful job of construction. We were so pleased with what they did that we even threw in a few extra sacks of cement to help them out.

From that day on, you might say, we broke the bubble as far as construction by the Filipinos was concerned. Later, they built the 1.3 million dollar BOQ at Sangley Point for about 1.1 million dollars. The American company, Pomeroy Hawaiian, wouldn't touch it unless we paid them much more than that.

Q: But the Filipino experience with contracts, had this been based on earlier contacts with Americans?

Adm. M.: No, contracts with Filipinos. That's the common way of doing business in Manila. You have to kick back a certain amount of money.

Q: Tell me something about President Magsaysay who certainly was famous in Philippine history.

Adm. M.: Magsaysay was a great man. He had real control of the Philippine government and the people. They worshipped him. As a matter of interest, I think that President Magsaysay could have set himself up as a dictator for the rest of his life and the Filipino people would have loved to have him sitting right there. He took action, he was a great leader, he got along well with both his friends and his enemies. He was very patient, tolerant, he saw the big picture. He, you might say single-handedly, defeated the Huks who were out to kill him when they almost had control of the Philippines. He persisted and he won out. He was a brave man and an intelligent man in every respect. When he was killed there were, I think, as many Americans out there as Filipinos who burst out crying. He was a great loss to that country. At the time he was killed, I was on another inspection trip with the MATS organization. I landed at Karachi and was told that the Embassy wanted me to call them. I did, and they requested that I pick up the Vietnam detachment from Saigon to go to the funeral. I said, "What funeral?" And they replied, "Don't you know that Magsaysay was killed in a plane crash?" That was the first time I heard it. I stopped by Saigon, picked up the Vietnamese group there, which included the Vice President, but I really didn't know who all I was picking up, and I took them to Clark Air Force Base where they were taken care of by the Philippine government.

The Philippines have never had a president since then like Magsaysay.

Q: Was it Osmena who succeeded him?

Adm. M.: No. I forget the name of the Vice President who succeeded him. I knew him well, but his name just skips me now. But he really didn't do a good job for the Philippines.

Q: Tell me about the papal nuncio you got to know there.

Adm. M.: One of the Catholic missionaries who was in the Philippines used to come to Sangley Point on Saturday to hear confessions, stay over and hold Sunday masses for us at Sangley Point. He asked me one day if I would like to meet the papal nuncio, Monsignor Vagnozzi, who was the senior diplomatic representative in the Philippines. Whereupon, I said, sure I'd like to meet him, and the next thing I knew my wife and I had an invitation to a dinner party at his residence, and he had some wonderful Italian cooks, so it was always a big treat to be invited to the papal nuncio's house. He was a great friend of the Americans during World War II. He traveled on several trips with Mr. Taylor - Myron Taylor - who was Roosevelt's representative to the Vatican. He had great respect for Myron Taylor and told me about some of those trips where they were nearly shot down. When Cardinal Spellman came out to the Philippines, the papal nuncio had a big party for him and we were invited. That was quite an honor to a layman and we reciprocated. We took him out on a beautiful yacht that we had there. We invited quite a number of the people from Sangley Point, Protestants and the Baptists and everybody else, and when the women with their swimming suits and shorts on, saw those long robes coming down the dock, they all screamed. They thought I was really embarrassing them. But he quickly got into a sporty outfit and we had a great time with him. Later on, he was the papal delegate to the United States and his house on Massachusetts Avenue was right across from the Chief of

Naval Operations. In the latest round-up, then-Monsignor Vagnozzi is now Cardinal Vagnozzi and is in Rome.

Q: Would you tell me about the visit that Admiral Burke made to the Philippine area when you were there?

Adm. M.: Admiral Burke had recently taken over as the Chief of Naval Operations and he was on a trip throughout the Far East with Admiral Felt, who was going to be his Vice Chief of Naval Operations, Admiral Libby, who was his Deputy Chief for Plans, and several others were in the party. They asked me in the Philippines what he would like to have in the way of briefings. I told everybody that, one, he wanted a brief description of the place; two, what the problems were; and, three, what they were doing to solve the problems.

Admiral Burke arrived with his whole group. At Sangley Point, we gave him the ComNavPhl brief and the Sangley Point brief. He was so pleased that he said, "All right. Now, do you want me to tell you what is happening and what has happened in Washington?" We said we'd be delighted, and he told all of us, including the ensigns sitting there, some very top secret information. That's the way he operated. When we took him over to Subic Bay, the commander of the Naval Station apparently hadn't gotten the word because he gave him a very basic briefing of the base functions saying that he had a commissary to feed families, a school so the children could learn their lessons, and he had a million problems. These were the problems, and now, Admiral, will you help me? Admiral Burke turned to Admiral Switzer, who was then Commander, Naval Forces, Philippines, and said, "He's got to go," and that Navy captain was out of the Philippines in about two weeks' time. That's how Admiral Burke operated. He would help you, but he wanted to know what you were doing to help yourself.

Q: And his aid was supplementary to your initial efforts?

Adm. M.: That's right.

Q: Your tour of duty came to an end in two years, did it not? Were you reluctant to leave the Philippines?

Adm. M.: I really was because even though we had a lot of work to do, we met a lot of fine people, fine Filipinos. We worked and met with a lot of fine military people who were competent and dedicated, and we met a great many State Department and other civilians in the Philippines who were doing a great job in the Philippines and were a great credit to the United States.

We really did hate to leave. It had been a fine, wonderful, and busy two years.

Q: Did you know what you were getting back into?

Adm. M.: Yes, Sir. I had a set of orders that told me to report to the staff of the Joint Chiefs of Staff in Washington, D. C. I was not thrilled to come back to Washington, D. C., but those were the orders and I felt that from my previous duty in Strategic Plans and knowing something about the Far East, I would be able to do a pretty good job on the staff of the Joint Chiefs. However, it didn't turn out that way. I was on leave in Alabama and received a phone call from the Bureau of Naval Personnel telling me that they were canceling my orders and I was going as the new aide for Admiral Burke. Whereupon I said, "I really wouldn't like to have that job, but I will call his aide and find out more." I did call his aide who was a friend of mine. He wasn't in. He was at his son's graduation, but I left word for him to call me any time during the night that he got back. He did call and he told me that I had been superceded in that job because Admiral Burke had to leave for Europe the next day and needed an aide, so he was taking another captain and I would take that captain's place. I said, "Who is that captain working for? Who is he working for now?" and he said, "Admiral Burke, but you'll like the job that you're going to." And that turned out to be 100 percent correct.

Q: And that next job was with the Progress Analysis Group, a rather enigmatic title. What does that mean?

Adm. M.: The Progress Analysis Group was supposed to keep track of various programs, large programs, in the Op-Nav organization. They really didn't know what they were supposed to do because each director who came into that spot changed the job. I came in as the Number Two man to then Captain John S. McCain. Jack McCain took on as his primary job putting together sea power presentations and selling sea power to the great American public. This had Admiral

H. L. Miller #3 - 211

Burke's 100 percent approval and I think it was a wonderful move.

Q: It was a PR job then?

Adm. M.: Basically, the way Jack McCain started it, it was a PR job, but I'll tell you later that we got into the other part of the job which had never been touched. Maybe I should tell you about that first.

We had an operations and logistics section. We laid out the Navy for the next fifteen years in the four big programs of shipbuilding, plane procurement, missiles and guns, and manpower. We put specifics into those four big programs. We put operations, research and development, and shore establishment, in other blocks. Now, we time-phased and priced out for fifteen years the numbers and types of ships, aircraft, missiles, guns, and ratings of people that we needed in the Navy. And at that time, in terms of 1958 dollars, we showed that we needed 18 billion dollars a year to organize and bring the Navy up to date. We put that presentation on all over the Navy department, the various bureaus, and several places around the country. It was interesting. Take, for instance, the airplane field. We showed that there was going to be a tremendous increase in helicopters in the Navy, all types, in the next fifteen years. Mind you, this was 1958 when we finally put this tremendous study and presentation together. The aviators that didn't like helicopters laughed and said we certainly wouldn't have those numbers or those types. We have many more than that now because helicopters have come into their own.

As far as manpower is concerned, we had the only long-range manpower program in the Navy. It was very significant that BuPers did not.

Q: Did the director of BuPers ask you about it?

Adm. M.: It was the Assistant Chief of Naval Operations for personnel or manpower. He was Admiral Ira Hobbs. He asked me if I knew of any place in the Navy that had a long-range personnel plan. He said he couldn't find any in BuPers. I told him, yes, we had one and he could see it if he came down to the shop and went into my back room where the group was working. Whereupon he did and backed us 100 percent in pushing this plan from the long-range viewpoint.

Q: How did you go about making this study? How much time was consumed in it? What was the feed-in to the whole thing?

Adm. M.: Believe it or not, we had five people - only five people - working on this study. It took several months, and the director was a captain in the Supply Corps. The other four were civilians who were experts in shipbuilding or ship-construction planning, missiles and guns, airplanes, and manpower. Those four civilians, as a result of the outstanding work they did, were all jumped a grade and rewarded with other things. The captain in the Supply Corps received no reward until I came back to Washington years later when I was Chief of Information and wrote up a Legion of Merit award for him, which he received.

Admiral Russell was then Vice Chief of Naval Operations and said that it was the finest study that he had ever seen in all his years around Washington.

Q: You had a lot of built-in knowledge within this small group. You brought a lot of experience and knowledge and I suppose the director did and the rest of the personnel, but there must have been some more feed-in. I mean did you call in people, did you have hearings?

Adm. M.: No. Our people knew which offices to go to get this basic information. They also were in on the future planning that was projected and we did a little of our own future planning in the study, and it turned out that we were pretty accurate in our over-all estimates in every one of these areas.

Q: Then the PR job you spoke about previously came after this study had been completed?

Adm. M.: No. The PR job came first. This study group didn't get started and in business until, perhaps, four or five months after I reported to the office of Progress Analysis

Q: Did you generate the idea of the study yourself?

Adm. M.: That's right. Captain Twitchell, my Supply Corps Officer, and I talked about this and we had many discussions on how to proceed, then we said let's go and see how it works out. A lot of creative thinking and new ideas went into the long range study from all of us, civilians and military. However, the other part of the office that really sold the Navy was what we called the sea power shop. We built sea power presentations projecting the jobs that the Navy was supposed to do in the entire spectrum of war, from a peacetime status to little brush-fire wars, to wars like Vietnam, Korea, World War II, to the all-out war, or a nuclear war. We pointed out the job that the Navy had to do in this entire spectrum of wars and the missiles, ships, manpower, planes, and other things that we needed to do that job for this country.

We put this into a script of about 30 pages, sixty-five to eighty color slides, or vuegrafs. We had about 2,000 of these presentations made. They were sent to a distribution list that we made out, to reserve groups in the country, to commandants, to other commands in the Navy, and told all the recipients to get out and preach the gospel. We gave thousands of presentations all over this country and I even continued it when I went overseas. This was selling sea power as it had never been done before. As a matter of fact, Captain McCain, at that time, did an almost impossible job of getting that sea power presentation approved by the Navy and the Department of Defense. In other words, getting it out of the Pentagon and getting it on the road.

Q: Who was Secretary of Defense, McElroy? or was it Gates?

Adm. M.: Gates was Secretary of the Navy at that time, and McElroy was Secretary of Defense. Gates backed us 100 percent, but when the selection board met in July or August Captain McCain's name wasn't on that list, so he had to go to sea. He received a rush set of orders as commanding officer of the cruiser USS Albany and I relieved him in his job in the Progress Analysis group, commonly known as Op-09 Dog.

I continued with Jack McCain's philosophy of getting the word out, getting our people and everybody else in the Navy to learn that sea power presentation, and to sell it to the great American public. I also prepared a new sea power presentation. I finished it in January 1958. I presented it to Admiral Burke for approval, and to a whole group of naval officers that he invited in. He said to put in theirs and his suggestions, wrap it up and put it out on the street. We put it together, I took it home over the weekend and I learned every word of it. On the Monday morning following, I presented it to the House Military Affairs Committee. I must have given that presentation 300 times after that over the next year and a half. However, before the House Military Affairs Committee, it was the only time that I ever gave it without a hitch.

That sea power shop is still going on. They're doing an outstanding job in getting presentations on various aspects of sea power to the public--oceanography, antisubmarine warfare, the importance of logistics, the merchant marine. the merchant marine and the Navy, everything that's concerned with sea power. They're also getting out short movies on the same subject. It's something that we have to continue to do for ever, as long as we have a Navy, because once we stop selling we won't have a Navy.

H. L. Miller #3 - 216

Q: Is this Op-09 Dog something that Admiral Burke set up?

Adm. M.: When Op-09 Dog was set up, it was the Progress Analysis Group, but each director more or less assigned his own terms of reference to that job, and when Captain McCain took over and said he wanted to really sell seapower, Admiral Burke gave him a 100 percent okay, and I continued it because this should have been done years before, and now Jack McCain had started it. Let me tell you that there are a lot of naval officers that didn't like to see this.

Q: Why?

Adm. M.: They didn't think that we should demean ourselves by getting up and pounding the table and selling sea power. That was for some public relations firm to do in New York. They had no conception of what you should do to keep the American public informed about what the Navy is all about, how we're spending their money, et cetera.

Q: What was the reception you received before the House Military Affairs Committee? How did they react?

Adm. M.: It was good. You would normally expect them to be very critical and ask very searching questions. They asked a few general questions and thanked me.

Q: You spoke of the preparation of the whole thing as it had been prepared going out to various groups, I suppose the Navy League and

Reserve officers and so forth. They heard it and then were told to go out and preach the gospel. What kind of a feed-back did you get from these presentations?

Adm. M.: Everybody was enthusiastic. They liked it. It was a power-packed presentation. Civilian groups liked it, and Jack McCain with that gravel voice of his almost like a bosun's mate's, could really get the story across. I recall one time some naval reserve officers who were speech experts sat down and wrote a comment, a criticism, of the way he gave the sea power presentation. When he got through, they just murdered him. But the important part of Jack McCain's presentation, no matter how many mistakes he made was that he got it across better than anybody else, better than any one of those reserve officers.

Q: The impact of his personality!

Adm. M.: That's right, and incidentally we have reserve officers who took it upon themselves to put on the uniform at night and give that presentation in various places around their locale. Some of them did a tremendous job. They were great, and they spent many, many extra hours giving that presentation. It did help them, though. A great many of them got increased stature in their community, in their working areas. They were known as Mr. Navy.

Q: Did you begin to see any noticeable results from the total impact of the program throughout the country?

H. L. Miller #3 - 218

Adm. M.: Yes, Sir. We could sense it. We could feel it. We had more requests coming in. We had more naval officers speaking sea power. We had many, many more reserve officers who were talking sea power and making these presentations around the country. The requests went up, oh, I'd say, a hundredfold from when we started out. We used to have people report back by card the numbers of presentations they made, the audience, and the audience reaction.

Q: Well, now, Admiral, this happened toward the end of the decade of the fifties and it was certainly a terrific program to promote the interests of the Navy, and yet we find that at the end of the sixties we talk of a Navy a large percentage of whose ships are obsolete. What happened in between? Why didn't this go on?

Adm. M.: I think primarily three very important factors are involved. The first, Polaris submarine. This was a strategic force that we, the Navy, paid for. We didn't get any extra dollars. We took it out of our other hides in the Navy and paid for Polaris, but it was such a wonderful concept that nobody kicked. It did cut an awful lot of other ships out of the shipbuilding program.

The second factor was the rise in prices. Ship after ship went up in price, sometimes half as much again as what was estimated to start with. So we had to cancel ships that were approved because we didn't have the money to pay for them. And then, come 1964, we had a massive buildup in the Pacific following the Gulf Tonkin incident, and from there on in we spent all our money, or a big chunk of our money, on the Vietnam War. We just didn't have the money for all the ships that we needed.

Q: That's a very interesting analysis of the reason it got sidetracked because it seemed to have been well launched.

Adm. M.: And then from the initial Polaris I we had Polaris II, Polaris III missiles, and following that, right now, we are outfitting those submarines with a Poseidon missile, which is a terrific concept.

We are getting more new ships but certainly not as many as we need, and the prices are still going up in every field.

Q: That was the main thrust, I take it, of the Progress Analysis Group during your time there, the preparation of this study and the publicizing of the need for a more modern Navy, but there must have been other issues as well, other questions. What were some of them?

Adm. M.: Some of the other things that we did besides produce sea power presentations and other presentations on various aspects of naval warfare, plus this fifteen-year study of the Navy, was to help out in legislative liaison on the Hill. In late 1957, I think it was October the 4th, when the Russians launched Sputnik, Lyndon Johnson's subcommittee took on the job of investigating the readiness posture of the armed forces. Normally, the Office of Legislative Affairs - it was then Legislative Liaison - does all the work in getting the answers to all the questions that they want up on the Hill and briefs and debriefs the principal Navy representatives that are talking up on the Hill.

Q: Is this under . . .?

Adm. M.: That is under the Office of Legislative Affairs now, but at that time it so happened that most of the legislative liaison shop was either in Europe or on leave, and Admiral Burke got very peeved, so, with that, he appointed my Program Analysis Group and the JAG group which was headed at that time by Admiral Chester Ward to handle all the appearances of the Navy people on Capitol Hill for that Lyndon B. Johnson subcommittee investigation.

We had to murder board all the principal witnesses, including the Secretary of the Navy, Tom Gates.

Q: That's a sort of dry run of the testimony?

Adm. M.: This was a dry run on the testimony. We asked the questions, if they didn't know, we told them the answers, and when they went up on the Hill we got copies of the Congressional Record the next morning and distributed them to our previous witnesses to show them what they said, and also to those who were standing by to go up on the Hill and testify.

Q: Some of them must have had stage fright at this process!

Adm. M.: As a matter of fact, Tom Gates in our questions got all mixed up and became sort of peeved, but we told him that this was the murder board, he was going to have to go through this up on the Hill so we were just going to keep at it. He was a pretty good sport.

Q: In this kind of operation, did you have any contact with the White House liaison with Congress, Bryce Harlow?

Adm. M.: Bryce was a good friend of ours at that time and we kept in contact with him all the time that I was there. He was a very nice gent, too.

Q: And very understanding of military problems.

Adm. M.: That's right. And there were other naval reserve officers on the White House staff that we stayed in touch with.

Q: Did you work through Pete Aurand who was there then as the aide?

Adm. M.: Yes, we did lots of work with Pete. Pete Aurand was a very valuable Navy member up there on the White House staff.

Q: Admiral, would you tell me about the service you rendered the Secretary and the CNO through this office of yours, in terms of the relationships on the Hill, the summaries you supplied? This was an innovation, I would think.

Adm. M.: We had a very astute naval reserve officer who had previously worked with the Democratic National Committee. He was assigned to our office as a reserve officer. We would send him up on the Hill to all the hearings that pertained to the Navy or other big issues that the Navy was interested in. At the end of his day or half a day, whenever the Congress was in session, he would type up, double-spaced, in a page or two the significant decisions that were made or events that took place at that particular hearing that day. I would make up copies, give it to the Secretary of the Navy, the Chief of Naval Operations, and in most cases the Vice Chief of Naval Operations for their information, and I believe it's the best summary that anybody has ever got from the Hill. This man could really put it together.

Q: What else did you do in your imaginative shop?

Adm. M.: That was just about it. We had a small group of people and an innovative group. They had ideas, they had enormous energy, an awful lot of determination, they were persistent, and they were dedicated to the job of selling the Navy, and selling it all over the United States. They weren't afraid to travel, they weren't afraid to go anywhere anytime, day or night, and sell their product. It was a great outfit.

Q: I can imagine, Sir, that your path was not always strewn with roses because from what I've heard about the Navy Department at times, there are entrenched groups who pursue their own particular ends and have no willingness to see an over-all picture, which is what you were attempting to project throughout the nation. Did you have brickbats from some of these groups?

Adm. M.: Oh, absolutely. We had naval officers who thought it was disgraceful to put all this stuff together and go out and pound the beat and try to sell the American public on sea power. They thought it was demeaning, that Congress should automatically give us the money that we thought we needed to build a Navy and to keep that Navy going. And there are still a lot of those naval officers around today and some of them are admirals.

Q: Did they also think that their own particular pet project or area of operation would be neglected because there would be more emphasis put on some other?

Adm. M.: Yes. Admiral Red Raborn, was the chief project officer of Polaris and was probably the most optimistic guy in the world. He was determined that we were going to have Polaris and, he was successful. He did a masterful job, but there were submariners who looked on Polaris as stealing the money from the attack nuclear boats that they needed.

I had one submarine officer, who is a three star retired flag officer at the present time, sit by my desk and say, "You guys are selling the wrong horse, Polaris. We need the 'nuc' attack boats." And I said, "You know, you're talking to the wrong guy. We're selling Polaris and we're going to make Polaris work. That's what this country needs." Now that was a submariner. We had other officers who helped us tremendously. One was George Miller. When we'd put certain parts of our presentation together, we'd get murder boards together of dedicated officers who knew that this had to be done, to come in there, look at it, pick it to pieces, offer their suggestions, and then we'd go back to the drawing boards. We had others that would comment and were never satisfied with any product that we put out. They wanted perfection and you're never going to get perfection in any presentation, no matter what you do.

Another thing we did, we made movies of sea power. We got the money from the Bureau of Aeronautics and we made movies on amphibious operations, and we would make up our own scenarios of how we thought that particular war would get started. We made movies on carrier operations, on limited war operations, on mine warfare operations, all of these to show the various aspects of sea power.

Q: Where were these movies shot?

Adm. M.: We had private companies who bid on these pictures, much like they do at the present time, and we had an officer in charge who was the liaison between us and the movie company to ensure that they knew what we wanted, and we'd educate them in various aspects of sea power so that they'd put the proper stuff in that particular picture. And we got those movies out all over the country.

Q: And they used units of the fleet?

Adm. M.: Yes, Sir. They used animation, too. Real life plus animation.

Q: I remember in the early sixties having Admiral Charlie Lockwood tell me that he was in Hollywood as a consultant for various pictures. Was he involved in this effort, do you know?

Adm. M.: No, Sir. We had people from our own office who were the liaison experts and we had at one time Louis de Rochmont make a picture for us. Louis is the one who put "Fighting Lady" together after World War II. We sent Louis's crew over to the Mediterranean with this scenario. They put cameras in airplanes to get shots of coming aboard, being launched from the carrier, around the carrier, over land areas, and, believe it or not, when the Lebanon business went we had crews over there at the same time shooting a real live situation.

Q: And a successful one!

Adm. M.: Yes, that's right. We were really johnny-on-the-spot. The right cameras, the expert cameramen, and with full cooperation of Commander, Sixth Fleet, and everybody in the Sixth Fleet. You might say we scooped an awful lot of people at that particular time, and when we brought that picture back and put it together we had the whole story of the Suez crisis and Lebanon. So that picture sold on TV all over the country. By that time we'd learned that if you wanted to get a picture on TV, you made it about fourteen minutes for a fifteen-minute show, or twenty-eight or twenty-eight and a half minutes for a half-hour show.

We made quite a few movies on the money that Jack McCain bummed from the Bureau of Aeronautics, and he bummed it, too.

Q: That was a magnificent effort. So, Washington turned out to be not too bad after all! It was an exciting job.

Adm. M.: That's correct. We learned an awful lot. We know that we helped the Navy. We met hundreds and hundreds of people all over the United States, and two of the associations that we helped tremendously - to build up and help us sell was the Navy League of the United States, which at that time was not doing much, and the Naval Reserve Association, which was a very young outfit at the time. They were just getting started. So I think we did a pretty good job in jabbing the Navy League high command, in getting more umph behind their program, and pushing the Navy to the great American public and on the Hill.

Q: You gave them a project to work on!

Adm. M.: We helped them in a great many ways, in the magazine that they put out, and all that.

Q: This must have entailed a fair amount of travel on your part, being involved in a program like this?

Adm. M.: That's right. You might say we represented the real honest-to-God Navy more than Chinfo did. We attended all the big annual meetings of the Navy League, the Naval Reserve Association, Veterans of Foreign Wars, the American Legion, all of these.

Q: When you say "we"...

Adm. M.: I and one or two of my officers - three, because when you're giving a presentation somebody has to run the machine. We wanted to be sure. We set up everything, we took our own gear, and we gave presentations at all those organizations and also at their regional meetings. If the American Legion had a regional meeting in Indianapolis, we gave a sea power presentation to all their top people, so they knew what we were talking about. We did that with the Veterans of Foreign Wars, with the Catholic Veterans. Then we helped the Naval Reserve Association get their chapters started. They'd form a chapter, we'd go give them a sea power presentation, and say this is what it's all about, we'd like to have you help us. And we did this all over the country. Navy League groups, at that time, weren't as knowledgeable or gung-ho as these NRA chapters, guys that were comparatively young and had a deep interest in the Navy and were still in the naval reserve status. The Navy League top command were just too old to do anything, very slow, and it took the younger crowd in the Navy League who later took over as top officers in the Navy League and really get it started. And we worked hand in glove with those people. We helped them tremendously.

Q: Admiral Burke must have been very pleased with the direction this program took.

Adm. M.: He was.

Q: Did he maintain a close interest or a close watch on it?

Adm. M.: Absolutely. Admiral Burke always wanted to know how we were doing, so about once a week we would put everything into about a thirty-second report, go up to his office, and if he had thirty seconds to spare or if he was going to a meeting, we could walk alongside of him and tell him what was happening and what we had done to date. He also wanted to find out what we learned at some of the big meetings like Navy League, the American Legion, NRA, et cetera, whether or not we were getting the good old Navy support. Admiral Burke is a dedicated Navy man. He's still selling the Navy.

Q: As I say, you must have been somewhat reluctant to leave that job.

Adm. M.: Oh, yes.

Q: But you had a plum coming up, didn't you?

Adm. M.: That's correct. It's always good to leave a job and feel as though you've really accomplished something, and everyone of us in 09 Dog felt that we had contributed immeasurably to the future of the Navy.

Q: And if circumstances hadn't interfered, the results would have been much more evident by now.

Adm. M.: I think so. I think in the normal course of events if we had been assigned the money as the number one Service and if the Vietnam War hadn't come along, we'd be in much better shape as far as the Navy is concerned.

Q: One other question comes to mind. Since Navy was a part of a defense set-up, how did this aggressive program of selling the Navy tie in with the other services, and what was their attitude toward it?

H. L. Miller #3 - 229

What repercussions might you have received from the Army and the Air Force?

Adm. M.: The Air Force recognized that we had a very good program, but nobody in the Air Force seemed to be able to put an air force picture together like we put sea power. Neither did the Army, and they were very envious of our shop. They would really like to have seen it get disbanded. They accused us of an awful lot of things, you know, in selling the Navy. But we were open-handed about it, our cards were on the table, and we were out to sell. All these presentations had to be cleared by the Department of Defense, so we weren't dealing under the table. We had them cleared before we gave them.

Q: Was there any attempt on the part of the other services to join you, to emulate you, and to begin a 'sell' program of their own?

Adm. M.: We didn't see any. However, my career was almost short-lived in Op-09 Dog when Captain McCain put on a private sea power presentation for me. I told him that one of the sentences that he had in there - it went something like "the 1,500 mile missile that the Russians have pointed at these NATO bases" - well, nobody at that time knew that the Russians had a 1,500 mile missile, except our secret intelligence people. So I said, "You know, I think that's secret," and he told the officer responsible for the presentation to take it out, but nobody took it out. So Jack McCain was relieved, goes to sea, and I'm scheduled to put on the sea power presentation before the National Security Industrial Association in the Interior Department auditorium. The day before, the various media representatives in the Washington area wanted a copy of my presentation, so we put out twenty copies.

Well, the next day I put on the presentation and it was a resounding success, and as I finished a messenger came up to me and said, "Admiral Burke would like to have you in his office right away." I said, "What's the subject?" "Well," he said, "I don't know," so I called the office from the Interior Department auditorium and they said, "Don't you know the reason?" I said, "No." "Have you seen the afternoon paper?" I said, "No, I hadn't." It said in big headlines "Secretary of Defense Wilson (this was just around Sputnik time) says this, Miller Says That - a 1,500 mile Russian missile." Wilson said, no, I said the Russians have a 1,500 mile missile. Wow! I reported to Arleigh Burke's office and he said, "Have you seen the headlines?" I said, "Yes, I saw them," and he said, "How the hell did it get in there?" And I said, "Well, I pointed this out to Jack McCain and he told somebody to take it out. Nobody took it out and none of the correspondents noticed it except the Associated Press." He said, "Well, I've already told Chinfo to get you off the hook with the Department of Defense. So, go back and keep selling."

So, poor old Chinfo had to take the brunt of this attack from the Department of Defense for the next couple of weeks. I checked out of the running.

Q: You also deleted it from the presentation!

Adm. M.: Very fast.

Q: So, you came to the end of your tour of duty much later, and you had command of a carrier?

Adm. M.: Yes, Sir. The USS Hancock. That's the same carrier from which I flew with Air Group 6 in World War II. I took over command in the San Francisco Navy Yard at Hunter's Point. The Hancock had been there for about six months getting an awful lot of work done. It was a very fine ship, but we had a long way to go because the year before they had a pretty poor administrative and material inspection. They hadn't passed the operational readiness inspection and their under-way training inspection. So we had a long way to go. But when it was all over with, we won the E as the Number One carrier in the Pacific. So it all turned out nicely.

Q: Tell me what you did to effect this miracle in such a short time, because you were only in command for a year.

Adm. M.: First of all, anything you did was a plus because it was so bad from the start. There was only one way to go, and that was up. At the change of command, the crew looked like Cox's Army, their uniforms and shoes and everything else looked terrible. It was just a case of encouraging them to save a little money and get some clothes to look decent, get a haircut, and we published results of some of the operations that we did a good job in, and we boosted up

H. L. Miller #3 - 232

the competition, the morale, and what-not. Pretty soon we had a gung-ho bunch of guys who were really proud of their ship. So they started winning and they kept on winning. Quite a bunch.

Q: A lot of that must have been generated at the top and came down . . .

Adm. M.: Well, we had some good officers on there. Some of them were brand new and took a tremendous interest in getting that ship going, and some of the others who weren't interested were reaching the end of their tour. So we had some new people who were a bunch of tigers.

Q: Where did the Hancock operate?

Adm. M.: Our home port was Alameda and we operated up and down the coast from there to San Diego. We went down to San Diego for underway training, and after that we went back to Alameda and continued our operations prior to going to the Western Pacific. We operated off that stretch of shoreline from the San Francisco area to the Monterey area, except for fleet exercises, and then, we spread out all over the ocean.

Q: But you did become a unit of what - the Pacific Fleet?

Adm. M.: Yes, Sir. We became a unit of the Pacific Fleet, the Seventh Fleet, and in August of 1959 we left Alameda and proceeded to Pearl Harbor, where we had an operational readiness inspection which was successful. Whereupon we proceeded to the Western Pacific, put in at Guam, then to the Philippines, then to the Seventh Fleet and primarily to the carrier division commander, Admiral Red Welch, who was a very fine CarDiv commander. Most of the time we operated from the southern part of the Seventh Fleet's area, and the other carrier that was there, the USS Midway, operated from the northern part, around Japan. Several times we got together on joint exercises, and then we switched. They operated in the south for a while and we got to Japan over the New Year's period. We were at sea for Christmas.

Q: In building the morale, did you have any kind of educational program to supplement your efforts?

Adm. M.: We had a very comprehensive program of education, training, athletics, and other competions around the ship. We had a good air group, too, on board who helped out because they were good. All their outstanding operations reflected on the operations of the ship. So one helped the other. It all wor ked out nicely. We also had a lot of fun. Wherever we went we had fun.

Q: That's important to the morale.

Adm. M.: That's right. When we got to Hong Kong - I had known people in Hong Kong from my Philippine days, we had a reception aboard. One individual from the San Francisco area told me that at this reception be sure to have lots of celery because they just didn't get it out there. Well, we had a very wonderful reception and we had loads of celery, and all the American colony in Hong Kong ate every bit of it. And I was going to say, how was I to know that they wanted celery, except for that tip.

Q: Did you do anything to prepare the enlisted men who were new to the Far East, prepare them for any of the ports where they might have leave?

Adm. M.: Oh, yes, Sir, and say, for the Philippines, we scheduled trips to Baguio, which was about a five-hour ride by bus from Cubi Point. We also flew officers and sailors up there in our COD planes from Cubi Point. We reserved areas, cabins and rooms for them. We had a fine recreation program. At Baguio there's a beautiful golf course, there's baseball, and there's archery, there was all of the recreation plus good food and beautiful scenery. In addition, visiting various Filipino villages over there and buying some of the things in the town of Baguio was very educational and interesting.

At Subic Bay they have a very good golf course, and we had a round of beer parties for all hands on the ship. You can't get them all in one day, but in the course of about three beer parties you can take care of the whole crew, and this is what we did. They enjoyed that. We didn't have any trouble. They all behaved pretty doggone well.

Whenever we put into a port, we'd always send a message on ahead and say we wanted to sponsor a <u>Hancock</u> golf tournament. So we always had something cooking, and everybody enjoyed it. When we got to Hong Kong, we scheduled trips - or in Manila. Once we went up to

Manila. The Perle Mesta of Manila was Conching Sunico. Conching and I used to fight like cats and dogs when I was at Sangley Point. She really had elaborate parties. They were just beautiful, but she would always expect you to come to her parties, and when I was tired, I wasn't about to go to parties day and night, and she didn't like that a bit. But after that, she and I really got along and were darned good friends. So when we first put in to Subic Bay, I called her on the phone and said "Hi," and she said, "Now, when you come to Manila I want to have a party for as many officers as you want to bring, and I said, "Okay, will you get them dates?" Sure. So I told Conching we'd be in on a particular Saturday morning, we'd be there Saturday night, Sunday, Sunday night, and would leave on Monday morning. So, she said okay, Saturday night, and I was bringing twenty officers. So she got the dates and the food and the drinks for twenty officers. It just so happened that Friday we lost a pilot and we set up a sweep for him all through the South China Sea, and we had other ships from the Seventh Fleet helping, and all Saturday, so I didn't get to Manila, and she probably had chicken for the next two months to try to use up. We did get in on Sunday morning and I told her how sorry I was, but it was just too late to eat up all that chicken.

We actually scheduled tours there before we went to Manila and I also sent them across the bay at Sangley Point just to see that base. Later on, we did the same at Hong Kong, tours all over there. Sailors always get a tremendous kick out of Hong Kong. They just love that city. You can see everything in the world there, buy things, and all that, and they have a good golf course out of Hong Kong. It's right next to the border. It's the Royal Hong Kong Golf Course and a few years ago, most of the caddies were communist boys and they didn't give you very good service when they caddied.

In Japan there are a lot of places to go. We put in at Yokuska and sailors and officers spread out all over. A lot of them went over to Atsugi and played golf at our air station there. Some of them went to a beautiful little golf course outside of Yokuska, about twenty minutes away. It's just a straight mountain-top golf course. You're up on a hill and down another, all the time. There are so many things right close to Yokuska. You can go to some of these towns, go sightseeing in every one of them, buy things, and then Tokyo is a great big beautiful city with everything in the world going on. So they had plenty of recreation and plenty of tours and they loved it.

There was only one thing wrong with I think the second trip that we put in to Yokuska. They had some Japanese and Koreans that would come up to some of these sailors that were just about broke and tell them to go and buy golf clubs or golf bags at the PX, and they'd give them $20 extra for doing it. Some of them bit and some of them were caught, and when they were caught they were busted right bang like that to the next lower rate. Now, the Commander of the Seventh Fleet and everybody else knew about this and they didn't tell us about it, and I sent him a very nasty message. They were keeping it a great big secret, saying that the Navy investigative service was still investigating this, so I said, "What the hell do you have to investigate. It's been going on for months. You ought to tell the whole bloody fleet about it so that these kids won't get into trouble. Why don't you pick up those guys?" You see, the Koreans, stayed right outside this big recreation place for the enlisted men and when any of these sailors came out half boozed up, they would get them to buy golf clubs just like that. So Mr. Seventh Fleet and I at the time didn't get along very well.

Just before leaving San Francisco, the selection list came out and I found that I was on the selection list for admiral, and it was sort of a funny situation at that time because we looked around at the Pacific and nobody of the Pacific crowd had been selected except me. Then, just as we got in to Guam, the list came out for commander to captain, and my executive officer made captain, and we looked around at the Pacific and we couldn't find anybody else that made captain. At some of those places we weren't too well received, but as my exec said, "Why should we worry?"

Q: It meant that you were going to get a new command very shortly?

Adm. M.: Well, you can hold on to a carrier only one year, no matter what happens, and I was fortunate that they let me stay aboard and hold on to it the whole year, which pleased me no end because I had a good time on the Hancock and I hated to give that ship up. As a matter of fact, when we were in San Francisco just prior to going over to the Navy yard and getting some work done to the ship, I stayed on an extra two weeks because I liked it.

Q: This leads me to a question. Does command of a carrier add another dimension to a man's understanding of things?

Adm. M.: I think so. An understanding of all the operations that take place in the Navy. Additionally, you're back with the troops again. You're not sitting in an office in Washington totally oblivious to the fact that people are the most important asset that you have in the Navy. There you see the people. On the flight deck of that carrier, day after day, there are very dangerous operations and it's with fear and trembling when you get a new batch of sailors aboard that you have to break in on that flight deck. This is a continuous operation. This always happens. You tell your top men please lead them by the hand, don't let them get in trouble, just force-feed them this way, let them watch, see, and hope they learn. In a month's time, and this happened time after time after time, those kids just out of boot camp are running your bloody flight deck. They're great. They catch on. And all these operations around the clock, day after day. It's really hard to believe. Those are the kids that are running the Navy and they're doing a marvelous job, but you forget about that at that office in Washington, D. C. You come to the full realization of the capabilities of these kids when you look down on that carrier deck.

Q: Does being skipper of a carrier give you a new sense of power, too, when you've got such a tremendous weapon in command?

Adm. M.: Well, you really have. Let me see, with the carrier and the air group and everything aboard, I suspect we had a plant value of about 250 to 300 million dollars. You had a sense of accomplishment when you saw all these operations work day in and day out, and a happy crew. They did a good job. You went in to a port, everybody had a good time, you left everybody in that port with a happy feeling that here was a United States ship with a whole bunch of wonderful kids aboard. They left a powerful image wherever they went, so you did have a great sense of accomplishment that you don't have in some systems command or Op-Nav office or in the Joint Chiefs of Staff in Washington, D. C..

Q: Were you impressed with the striking power of this instrument of war?

Adm. M.: Yes. You have that whole bag of airplanes aboard that carrier. They can carry conventional bombs, they can carry A bombs, they carry bullets, they carry rockets, they carry missiles. You have quite a striking force. You can come right in close to an enemy shore and let them have quite a devastating punch.

Q: Every officer has one command which in many ways seems to exceed all others. Was this perhaps yours, the Hancock?

Adm. M.: That's a tough question to answer because I look back at my first fighter squadron, Fighter Squadron 23, and then Air Group Six that I had on the Hancock in WW II. I enjoyed those commands, and those of course were wartime commands. Following that, the Hancock, I probably would say this, that in peacetime situation I liked the Hancock better than any other command, but in wartime, I thought my greatest sense of accomplishment, the one I enjoyed most was putting the first nuclear-powered task force, the Enterprise and the Bainbridge into combat in Vietnam for the first time.

This is one last story on the Hancock. When we came back from our WesPac cruise in January of 1960 we sent our people ahead to be sure that we had a good reception awaiting us, and San Francisco turned out. All the wives and the sweethearts and the kids and everybody else were on the dock there waiting for us at Alameda, and just as we tied up we unfurled a great big banner that went from stem to stern, and it said, "You're all beautiful." The wives really loved that.

Q: You're a true public relations man, I can see.

H. L. Miller # 4 - 241

Interview No. 4 with Rear Admiral Henry L. Miller, U. S. Navy

Place: Patuxent Naval Air Test Center, Maryland

Date: Monday morning, 24 May 1971

Subject: Biography

By: John T. Mason, Jr.

Q: Admiral, this should be a great chapter considering the circumstances under which it's being delivered (this was actually recorded on the Admiral's barge as we cruised on the Chesapeake Bay.) You said you wanted to add something that happened during your command of the Hancock in November of 1959.

Adm. M.: Yes. There were 15 senior military leaders of 15 free nations of the Western Pacific and Southeast Asia who accepted invitations to witness a weapons demonstration conducted by the United States Military Forces under the command of Admiral Don Felt, who was then commander-in-chief, Pacific. Following a brief weekend stay at Baguio in the Philippines, where they all congregated, they embarked at Subic Bay on the aircraft carriers the Hancock and the Midway. It was a wonderful meeting. The following countries were involved: Australia, Cambodia, China, France, Indonesia, Japan, Korea, Laos, Malaya, New Zealand, Pakistan, Philippines, Thailand, United Kingdom, United States, and Vietnam.

Q: When you say China, you mean Nationalist China?

Adm. M.: Oh, yes, Nationalist China. As I said, they all gathered at Baguio, which is a

The United States Air Force runs the Camp John Hay Center there. All the leaders had their meetings initially in civilian clothes. They got to know each other and talked very freely. Remember, some of these military leaders from those countries never did speak to each other before that time. In Subic Bay they boarded the carriers and we headed for Okinawa. Enroute, both the Hancock and the Midway conducted air operations day and night, dropping bombs, strafing, formation flying, showing them what we could do.

At Okinawa the Army, the Air Force, and the Marines put on a combined show for these military leaders. Following that, they all left for their respective countries. For some of these leaders, it was the first meeting that they had face to face. They found out that they weren't really all bad guys. Indonesia attended for the first time, and I was fortunate in having those military leaders from Indonesia aboard the Hancock.

Q: Are any of them in prominence today?

Adm. M.: Oh, yes, several of those military leaders are prominent. There's General Thanom who is now the prime minister of Thailand, and he has been a very prominent leader all his life.

Q: I meant from Indonesia. Do they represent the present thinking in Indonesia?

Adm. M.: I do not know because I didn't keep up with those Indonesian military officers. They did not attain Number One ranking in

Indonesia. En route to Okinawa we ran into some very bad weather necessitating curtailment of some of the air operations, but this wasn't bad. It sort of turned out to be a blessing in disguise because the military people had to look at each other and talk to each other in the wardroom. They did get together. They played chess, they played checkers, they played bridge, and they really got to know each other much better than if we'd had the good weather.

Q: It closed in on them and they had to.

Adm. M.: They made some very lasting friendships on that particular cruise, and I know that they enjoyed every bit of it because the chairman of the joint chiefs in China offered to pay for a trip from the Hancock to Nationalist China for the escorts that were so nice to them during that short cruise. They all appreciated it, and later on one of the officers who was from Indonesia came halfway across Indonesia to see me when I was there in 1962 with General Maxwell Taylor. Additionally, when I went to Thailand with General Taylor, General Thanom paid more attention to me and I received more courtesies than General Taylor.

Q: Well, personality had something to do with that! But obviously this was a way of impressing them with our naval capacity, too, wasn't it?

Adm. M.: That's correct. We had more time to show them our naval weapons and our ways of doing business than the Army, the Air Force, or the Marine Corps. At that time, Admiral Hopwood was commander-in-chief of the Pacific Fleet and divided his time, as did Admiral Felt, between the Hancock and the Midway. While they were aboard we had them sit at different tables at each meal, so that they did get to know each other better, and naturally our officers on the Hancock went out of their way to ensure that those military leaders saw what they wanted to see and had a good time.

Q: Were there any security measures in effect?

Adm. M.: Yes, there were, but normally what you see around an aircraft carrier is mostly unclassified. So we weren't afraid of any security violations. We had one pretty good story. I think, as you recall, Admiral Hopwood looked a little bit like an oriental. He had a slit to his eyes, and our Catholic chaplain who went all-out to ensure that everybody was well taken care of, went from table to table and introduced himself, came to Admiral Hopwood's table, it was Admiral Hopwood's turn to sit at the head of the table for that particular meal, and he said, "Admiral, I am Father So-and-So. What country do you come from?" I nearly fired him when he told me the story!

Incidentally, that was the Catholic chaplain who got married about a year and a half ago and kept it quiet for almost a year before he confessed.

Q: Was this demonstration a usual thing with the Seventh Fleet, or was it a first time?

Adm. M.: They had started these weapons demonstrations I think two or three years before, and it was, in my opinion, a wonderful thing to do. It got all the leaders together and the future leaders together. It also showed them what we could do - what the United States could do, Army, Navy, Air Force, Marine Corps - and it brought people together. They communicated much better with each other. They found out that there are some pretty good people in every one of those countries, very outstanding leaders.

Q: If only for the public relations value, it seems to have been an awfully good idea. Who originated it?

Adm. M.: I believe Admiral Stump originated the idea when he became commander-in-chief, Pacific.

Q: Tell me about another milestone in your career, selection for flag rank, which occurred in July of 1959.

Adm. M.: When I was halfway through my tour as commanding officer of the Hancock, I was selected for rear admiral. It did not take effect until I reported as chief of staff to commander, Naval Air Force, Pacific Fleet. I reported in February of 1960 to that particular job. The boss man at AirPac at that time was Vice Admiral Ekstrom, the great Swede Ekstrom. He was a big, tall, powerful man. He was a wonderful person and an outstanding naval officer, and it was so nice working for him because we both had the same ideas, and you might say we spoke the same language along those lines. Additionally, both of our wives got along very well.

Q: Would you elaborate on that - you both had the same ideas and spoke the same language?

Adm. M.: Admiral Ekstrom was an action man. He got around the AirPac empire. He saw what was going on and he made changes right on the spot, if he saw this had to be done. He wanted to be sure that the Naval Air Force, Pacific Fleet, was a real ready outfit that could respond when the commander-in-chief said "go." My job there was only for a year's time and during that time we supplied logistic support, administration, and training for all our pilots and our ships, we had the aircraft carriers and we also had the seaplane tenders. Since then the seaplane has gone out of the Navy inventory. That was a very unique weapon that we had at the time. We looked after the people, we looked after the airplanes and the ships, and I think that we did just about the best job that we could in providing a ready naval force - naval aviation force - for the commander-in-chief, Pacific Fleet.

Q: Just as a footnote. You were saying that the seaplane went out shortly thereafter. Has its function been supplanted adequately by other means?

Adm. M.: Yes, Sir. The seaplane went out I believe in 1967, and the long-range patrol craft, the P-3, A, B, and C, put the seaplane out of business, because it has long legs, it can go great distances faster and longer than the seaplane. There may be remote areas where you'd like to have the big seaplane, but the P-3 airplane can more or less take care of that part of the business now.

Q: Tell me about some of the operations during the time you were chief of staff to Admiral Ekstrom.

Adm. M.: Well, there were extensive carrier operations that went on 365 days a year. We still supplied the aircraft carriers and the ships and the men for the Seventh Fleet. We tried to emphasize taking care of people. We got the personnel officers more actively involved, we got the chaplains, the public affairs officers, and the legal officers to do just a little bit more in taking care of the officer, the enlisted man, and their families.

Q: Could I wager that this was your inspiration?

Adm. M.: No, I think Admiral Ekstrom put a great deal of emphasis on people and taking care of people. He always did this and we all got behind it and pushed just a little bit harder. We had some very fine individuals on the staff who took an active interest in all the officers and men and families that we had.

We had a very outstanding maintenance officer, Rear Admiral Max Reynolds, who did such a tremendous job there that he'll leave his mark in naval aviation for ever. He came in one day after we'd had a great deal of difficulty with some of the airplanes coming aboard the carriers. They were landing slow, they were landing high, and we were having just too many aircraft accidents. He asked me what I thought of the idea of photographing the planes coming aboard and then showing that film to the pilots. I told him that I thought it was a great idea and why hadn't I thought about that ten years ago. Well, believe it or not, he proposed that to some of the other officers before talking to me and they threw out the idea. Admiral Reynolds used one of the carriers, he went aboard, he set up his camera along the center line underneath the flight deck. He bored a hole through the flight deck and glued that camera right up through the hole on the flight deck, along the glide slope and the center line of the ship. He got the pictures and he also put another camera on the landing signal platform, and another one on the starboard side of the ship around the air operations office. He took some marvelous pictures. He showed them to the pilots and he convinced them that they were coming aboard either too slow or too fast or too high, depending on what the picture showed.

Now, he further improved this by getting the Ampex people to bring their machines aboard, and they got all this on video tape with an instant play-back. Ampex tried this out aboard the Ranger. It worked beautifully, and with that, Admiral Reynolds bought the first installation to put aboard a carrier showing the pilots in the ready rooms their own pilots coming aboard, and they could all see what they were doing wrong. Now they call it the PLAT system, and I don't know what P-L-A-T stands for, but Admiral Max Reynolds was the officer who came up with the idea, expanded it, and probably saved the Navy and Naval Aviation millions and millions of dollars in airplanes and lives.

Q: There were some notable results, then, immediately?

Adm. M.: We had immediate results from photographing the pilots coming aboard. We didn't have to argue with them because most aviators think they're doing a great job coming aboard, and it's hard to convince some of them that they're doing something wrong. With the picture, it's very easy to convince the pilot immediately that he has to take some corrective action the next time he comes aboard.

Q: He convinces himself, as a matter of fact, doesn't he?

Adm. M.: He sure does. But I think that Admiral Reynolds deserves an awful lot of credit in naval aviation for just that one significant idea.

Q: Is that being used on all carriers now?

Adm. M.: Yes, Sir, that technique is used in every carrier that we have. We also had some other individuals there with great ideas, one of which was the antisubmarine classification and analysis center. They call it an ASCAC. This was a center where we analyzed the information that we were getting from our sonar pinging on a submarine. Our helicopters, our fixed-wing S-2 airplanes, and our destroyers all had the capability to detect a submarine that was under water. We were hard pressed at that time in developing the capability to receive the sounds that were reflected from the sonar against the hull of that submarine and determine whether or not it was really a submarine or a school of fish or seaweed, or something like that. We didn't have an immediate means to transmit those reflections, those sounds, to instruments that could analyze them. So we rigged our helicopters - it cost us about fifty dollars apiece - to transmit those sounds as soon as they were received aboard the helicopter back to the carrier to our ASCAC center. There, we put those sounds into various machines, various equipments, so that an individual could see and hear whether or not they were pinging on a submarine - and compare to other sounds that we had from reflections on a submarine. We could pretty well determine, through this analysis process, whether or not we had a submarine or a school of fish or seaweed, or an old sunken hull that was down in the water.

Additionally, we got the same capability into our fixed-wing S-2 aircraft. It took only eleven feet of cable to do this. Our destroyers had the capability but hadn't used it. All they needed to do was re-plug a couple of circuits and transmit those sounds over to the carrier. In this way we were able to tell within a few minutes' time whether or not we had an honest-to-god submarine under water. This was a very significant achievement. It hadn't been done before and today, ten years later, we still don't have a much better way of doing it than what we had at that time. We have refinements to it now. They're very good, they're very significant, but at this time is when you might say we re-invented the wheel as far as ASCAC is concerned.

Q: Well, Admiral, that need was apparent in World War II. Why was it so long in being accomplished?

Adm. M.: Probably because antisubmarine warfare received such a low priority in the Navy's stockpile of budgets and programs.

Q: But, as you describe it, it was largely an idea, rather than anything else. I mean the equipment wasn't that expensive.

Adm. M.: No. As a matter of interest, when I left the AirPac staff, I went to an ASW group and Admiral Ekstrom gave me eighty-five thousand dollars to make the installation aboard that particular aircraft carrier. In today's thinking and money, it was a very cheap way of acquiring a significant capability in antisubmarine warfare. In other words, if you didn't have that, it was pretty difficult out there on the water to find a submarine and track it.

Q: It was the idea and then training the personnel and giving them experience in order to analyze these various sounds.

Adm. M.: That's correct. The ASCAC not only gave you the capability to identify and track a submarine, but it was a splendid training device for pilots and air crewmen coming into that center and just seeing how all this stuff happened and what they could do out there in an airplane or a helicopter, or aboard a destroyer, in finding a submarine, identifying it, and tracking it.

Q: The analogy in the world of medicine in the increased ability to read x-rays!

Adm. M.: Yes, Sir.

Q: Those were certainly accomplishments in that time when you were Chief of Staff. Is there anything else that comes to mind?

Adm. M.: No, I think those were the two most significant happenings while I was chief of staff. We had many other improvements of much smaller scope that went into Naval Air Force, Pacific Fleet, but the PLAT system and the ASCAC were, I'd say, two of the most important ideas that came out of AirPac during that year, and certainly paid off tremendously to the rest of the Navy in all the years afterwards.

Q: Admiral, this tour of duty as chief of staff occurred during a change-over in the over-all command at the White House, a change of administration, and with the change in administration there was somewhat of a change in strategy, was there not, military strategy and defensive strategy? Was this apparent in the Pacific at that time or was it too soon?

Adm. M.: 1961 was when President Kennedy relieved the watch, so to speak as President of the United States. We didn't see any change in over-all strategy while I was at AirPac. All of this came later and it was very apparent, but at this stage of the game we did not know what policies President Kennedy was going to affix to the strategic picture as far as the United States was concerned and the rest of the world.

Q: Admiral, you said just a minute ago, off tape, that in 1960 General Eisenhower paid a visit to San Diego. Do you recall anything of interest during that visit?

Adm. M.: President Eisenhower always liked to visit military installations because he had such a great love for the military. He came to San Diego. We showed him our vast military structure around there, exhibits, fly-bys by airplanes. He was briefed on all aspects of our immense military complex in the San Diego area, and then he departed for a political rally at Chula Vista. Ike always had to combine his military visits with a little politics to keep the Republican flag flying.

Q: In the latter days of his administration that was true, but not at the beginning, was it?

Adm. M.: No, Sir, that's correct. But everybody was always glad to see President Eisenhower come. He was very popular with the military and with the great American public. Probably the most popular military leader of the last fifty or so years.

Q: Well, Sir, your interests and your accomplishments as chief of staff certainly pointed the direction for your next assignment.

Adm. M.: Well, since we were heavily involved in antisubmarine warfare, or trying to get heavily involved in antisubmarine warfare, I was very well pleased when I received my orders as Commander, Carrier Division 15, in the Pacific. This was an antisubmarine warfare billet. My flagship was the USS Bennington, and I knew that this would give me an opportunity to further develop the ASCAC concept. When Admiral Ekstrom gave me eighty-five thousand dollars to get an installation aboard the Bennington, I was very happy even though we did take laboratory equipment and worked it from the USS Bennington.

Another thing that we did when I had the carrier division was to talk to the submariners. The submariners had a lot of tricks up their sleeve on fooling the ASW people. We learned an awful lot from them and after we briefed them on our methods of detection and tracking, they learned an awful lot from us. But they gave us more than we gave them. They were smarter because the submarine business was their livelihood. During the time that I had that carrier division, I went aboard submarines several times, seeing what they were doing in keeping track of us and our operations. I would normally take a helicopter; they'd lower me down to the submarine, and I would cruise aboard the submarine for a few hours, finding out what was going on.

Q: It might be interesting, Sir, if you would pause for a moment and contrast the personality of the submariner with the naval aviator - the differences and the likenesses.

Adm. M.: The naval aviator and the submariner are pretty much alike. They are professionals in their particular field and, as I say, wonderful professionals. The submariner has a tremendous responsibility for that boat. The aviator has a tremendous responsibility for the airplane or groups of airplanes that he is commanding. They both have the same gung-ho spirit. They have an awful lot in common and, surprisingly enough, the submariner and the naval aviator get along very well together.

Q: You made it your business to know in detail the life of a submariner at this point?

Adm. M.: Yes, Sir. There's an old saying, "you should know your enemy" and in the antisubmarine warfare business the U-boat is the enemy and I tried my darnedest to find out as much as I possibly could of the ways that the submariners fought their boats and used all the tricks in trying to fool us.

Q: What particular insights did you gain as to their tactics?

Adm. M.: A good submariner is always thinking. He's always devising ways of fooling the people that are hunting him down, and he passes this information to all of his cohorts to ensure that the submarine force is on their toes twenty-four hours a day.

H. L. Miller #4 - 256

They're a smart, capable group of officers and a very dedicated group. The submarine force of the Navy is a tremendous credit to the Navy. I know they are without a doubt the best submarine force in the world.

Q: At this point in time, the Polaris was coming onto the scene, was it not?

Adm. M.: Yes, Sir.

Q: Would you talk about the scope of your activities when you were with Carrier Division 15, the antisubmarine hunter-killer task group? What were you objectives?

Adm. M.: Well, of course, in antisubmarine warfare our job was to kill as many U-boats as we possibly could in various exercises that we were on, and to learn the ASW game from A to Izard.

Our first encounter with our own submarines in an exercise took place en route from San Diego to San Francisco. We were a just newly organized carrier division staff and we had just got a new commanding officer for the USS Bennington, so we were sort of green at the game. And I can tell you that on that exercise the submariners murdered us twenty times over. It was a very poor showing by our carrier division, not only the airplanes but also our own destroyers. When we came back from that exercise and critique, we licked our wounds and started all over again to really go at this business and get it organized. In this the Antisubmarine Classification and Analysis Center played a very big part. It was so important that we get real time analysis that I didn't even want to leave the dock unless the ASCAC center was working.

Q: How big a staff did you have in this center, this ASCAC?

Adm. M.: The ASCAC Center was a very small staff of just three or four people, but they were experts in listening to sounds and in analyzing the graphs that came off of the equipment that we had. So the ASCAC began to play a greater and greater part in this overall business of finding the submarines, identifying them, and tracking them. Later on, when the time came for us to deploy to the Western Pacific, we had to go through an operational readiness exercise at Pearl Harbor. Maybe we were at a tremendous advantage at that stage of the game because the submarines had beaten us so badly before that I think perhaps their guard was down. So when we went out on that week's operations we killed three nuclear submarines and six conventionals, and I can assure you when we came back at the end of that week, the submariners were in a state of shock. They couldn't believe it. But it was the truth. We had given them the works, but good.

Q: You just pulled yourselves together and went at it.

Adm. M.: Yes, we'd pulled ourselves together, but we also got that ASCAC working to help us make real-time, or almost real-time, decisions.

Q: Did the Bureau in Washington show any great interest in ASCAC in the experimental stages of it? I mean, did they send representatives out?

Adm. M.: Surprisingly enough, Washington did very little to help us out. We did it on our own to the extent of running a seminar in San Diego, right at AirPac headquarters, inviting industry reps to participate and get their enthusiasm going to produce equipment that we could use. We were the ones, not Washington. Washington just didn't seem to have the picture.

Q: Is this unusual with a centralized authority like the Navy?

Adm. M.: No, it really isn't unusual because I believe that wherever you have a de-centralized establishment, you'll find a great many people all over the Navy who are coming up with ideas and implementing them on the spot, and maybe, later on, Washington hears about it and gets interested. It appears that Washington is so doggone busy taking care of their day-to-day paper work that they don't have the people who can do this implementing.

Q: But it takes, doesn't it, a tremendous amount of initiative on the part of the local commander to do this kind of thing, and isn't it more or less in defiance of Navy Regs?

Adm. M.: No, not necessarily. I think the Navy, by and large, encourage innovation, ideas, as long as you come up with the results and don't plague Washington too much.

Q: This must have been very encouraging to have done an about-face and won such a victory over the submarines. What did it lead to?

Adm. M.: Well, that was the first week, and the next week we had to do an impossible problem. The submariners sent out two boats that would transit from a given area outside of Pearl Harbor to the island of Hawaii. They would take one week's time to do this, and naturally they'd do very slowly on the bottom. A submarine squadron commander told me that it was absolutely impossible for us to get one of those submarines. Of course, we didn't take that as the gospel truth. He rode with us for two days and then flew back to Pearl. On the last day we detected and identified one of the submarines and we surfaced that submarine. He didn't have enough juice left in his batteries to light a cigarette. And, to add further insult to injury, I sent the destroyer squadron commander, Captain Frank Romanick, over in a boat with a camera, photographer, everything else, to take the formal surrender. I don't think the U-boat sailors will ever forgive me!

Q: Tell me, your startling success with these exercises, was it influenced in part by your own intimate knowledge of the submarine? I mean the effort you made to learn about the submarine and about the submariner, the insight you gleaned from this. Were they in part employed in this victory?

Adm. M.: That helps, but I had a good staff. I had an operations officer on that staff who knew the antisubmarine warfare business. He was a tenacious guy and one of those individuals who never gave up. He wasgoing to find that submarine on that last day if he had to dive over the side and go searching for it.

Q: You were going to tell me something about your joint operations with some of the SEATO nations and with Japan, too.

Adm. M.: When we deployed to the Western Pacific, our first stop was Yokosuka. We had an exercise planned with the Japanese Navy, with their destroyers actively participating with our destroyers within the task group, and their land-based patrol squadrons also as active participants. I remember we took as our guests a couple of Japanese admirals who rode the flagship with me and watched the whole operation as we went along. We had operations day and night just like a regular U. S. wartime practice. The Japanese did an outstanding job. They were on their toes. They were so enthusiastic, so anxious to do a good job, that I imagine most of their troops stayed up day and night to ensure that no mistakes would be made.

We had our critique in Sasebo. We started out at Yokosuka, went all the way around on active participation in ASW, and then we ended up in Sasebo with a big critique. All the U. S. and Japanese were there. Believe it or not, this was not a put-up job. We awarded the prize ASW plaque for that exercise to one of the Japanese destroyer skippers. They just performed like they'd been in the business a million years, outstanding and very agressive. We got the biggest kick out of that exercise working with the Japanese.

Q: Wasn't this unusual since their Navy had been so depleted? You'd almost think they'd lack experience in handling ships.

Adm. M.: The Japanese didn't have at that time the moneys that they have today for a Navy. What they had they used and used expertly. They trained every minute of the time that they were out on the water to ensure that they got a maximum out of every operation.

They're good ship-handlers. The Japanese have always been good ship-handlers. They've been good leaders and good technicians. Remember, at the start of World War II they were terrific, very aggressive, and they haven't lost that. They haven't lost their expertise. They're still gung-ho and they want to win just like we do.

Q: What about some of the other Far Eastern navies?

Adm. M.: We went from Japan down to the Philippines where we based out of the Naval Station at Sangley Point and the Naval Station at Subic Bay. There we joined up with the Australian task force that was at that time commanded by Rear Admiral Alan McNichol, who later became the Chief of Naval Operations of the Australian Navy. We got together preliminary to a SEATO exercise and laid out the roles and procedures and what we were going to do. Alan was placed in charge of the operation by Admiral Felt, who was then Commander-in-Chief, Pacific, and had you might say the primary influence in SEATO at that time.

Q: This was an innovation in itself, was it not?

Adm. M.: That's correct, because the Americans just don't want any foreigner ever in charge of their particular military operations.

Q: Why is this?

Adm. M.: It's because the USA, I believe, has the most experienced Admirals and Generals in the world, and whenever American equipment and lives are involved, they want to be doggone sure that an American is in charge. As far as our operations there were concerned, I had most of the airplanes under my direct command and I had all the American sailors and officers in my ships.

Q: Does this American attitude not cause problems at times when we deal with allied navies and armies and so forth?

Adm. M.: Yes, it does. Naturally, some of our allies feel that they're just as competent militarily speaking as we are, but we want to have command of our own forces. It worked out very well in that SEATO exercise. They called it Sea Devil. It was the largest SEATO maritime exercise in 1962. All nine member nations participated. It gave the task group an opportunity to exercise with every facet of its antisubmarine warfare capability.

Q: That was the main thrust, was it, antisubmarine warfare?

Adm. M.: Yes. We had strikes, attack strikes, by one of the British carriers that participated, but the primary effort by the Australian Navy and the American Navy plus the other ships that were there from Pakistan, Thailand, and the Philippines was in antisubmarine warfare. This was the big part of the exercise. We had pre-exercise visitors to our flagship and to the Australian flagship which was the <u>Melbourne</u>, an aircraft carrier. These representatives were from all the nations participating, and it was a simulated SEATO exercise wherein all the partners came to the aid of a nation that was a neighboring nation and was being attacked. In this case it was Laos, or I should say, weeks later it was Laos, when the Communists started marching in that country.

The Sea Devil exercise was designed with many goals in mind - joint operations, to see how we all did it, see how we worked as a team on different destroyers, different carriers, the teamwork involved, the coordination that was absolutely necessary day and night to get ships from different nations to do this job, and, you might say the success of the operation resulted from the meeting of many minds - the people on the ships, the planes, the staffs, everybody cooperated. They showed a tremendous sense of coordination and cooperation - a marvelous sense of humor of all activities, too. It was a great exercise and we all enjoyed it.

Q: Did the potential enemy have observers thereabouts?

Adm. M.: We didn't see any, but we had a lot of fun during it. We had a competition one day. One of the Australian destroyers was going to start from scratch and come alongside and refuel from the

Bennington, my flagship, while one of my U. S. destroyers was going to start at the same time and refuel from the Australian carrier, the Melbourne. That was Admiral McNichols' flagship. They both made a dash for their respective ships, and the Australian was hooked up alongside my flagship and did a marvelous job. I was waiting for the American destroyer to come up with a signal saying that he'd made it all right, but there was some delay. Then Admiral McNichol told me later that the American destroyer came alongside. They were fast, efficient, did a nice hooking-up job. Then they were very cautious about sending over the first container via high line. Just when it got halfway over, they pulled a string and it took the top off of it, and at the same time they pulled another string and the sign came down between two of the stacks and it said, "We knew you were coming, so we baked you a cake." They sent over a great big cake with HMS Melbourne on it. Alan McNichol will never forget that as long as he lives. He thought it was a great thing.

Q: I take it by this time that some of the allied navies, the Royal Navy and the Australian Navy, had mastered the technique of refueling at sea?

Adm. M.: Yes, and we even had HMS Ark Royal, the British carrier, that participated in the exercise, but they really didn't get involved in the twenty-four-hour-a-day business, like the ASW forces were. And then, too, to really climax the whole affair, we had the critique in Manila. Naturally all the ambassadors of those countries were involved. We had parties, and I arranged with the Filipinos for the Wac Wac Golf and Country Club for special privileges for all officers of the whole task force. So, along with a very trying exercise day and night, we also had a lot of fun.

Q: And this critique, when it was accomplished, was it done in the presence of ambassadors? Was it more or less a public critique?

Adm. M.: No. The critique was mainly for the principal staff officers and any other ships' officers of the task force - all the destroyers, the carriers, and whatnot. They could send as many officers as they wanted and they did. We had a tremendous gathering there. The critique was held on the Australian carrier, the Melbourne.

Q: I take it that a thoroughgoing report was made then to the Navy Department in Washington on the results of this exercise?

Adm. M.: Oh, yes, Sir, and every exercise in which we participate with any foreign countries like that, we make a comprehensive report, not only to our own navy, but to the Commander-in-Chief, Pacific, who has control of all Army, Navy, Air Force, Marine forces in the

Pacific. They were all very pleased with the results of the operation and the wonderful coordination and cooperation that they heard about from that exercise. Mind you, we had quite a few press aboard, including quite a number of civilian media representatives from Australia. These all rode with us throughout the exercise, and made their reports direct to their home papers, without censorship.

Q: The mechanics of such an operation are fairly extensive, the logistics and all the rest of it. How long a time was it in preparation?

Adm. M.: As far as we were concerned - and I'm not talking for Admiral McNichol getting out his operation order, but just from my task force and the carrier division - it was a relatively short period of time that we took to get ready for the entire operation. We were pretty well geared to swing into anything in a very short space of time.

Q: This is something of a commentary, is it not, on the rate of our growth in the post World War II era? We came of age, did we not, as a nation, in terms of our fighting forces?

Adm. M.: Yes, we did, and we came to the realization that if anything happens, you can't take two or three months to prepare for it.

You have to get going today and work out your operation order en route to the target and be ready to go when you get there. So, right now, you might say we're many, many times more responsive to any situation that happens around the world than we ever were.

Q: So we're in a kind of a semi state of readiness all the time?

Adm. M.: Yes, we are. I think wherever our forces deploy from the shores of the USA, they're pretty much ready to do combat immediately.

Q: There was a rather amusing episode which occurred in between this operation - not the SEATO operation, but the antisubmarine warfare operation that you conducted with our own submarines - would you tell me that? It was something that emanated from Hawaii, I think, did it not?

Adm. M.: When we all got to Hawaii, Vice Admiral Thach, who was then Commander, ASWPac, had a big party for us at Ford Island. The submariners were there, the destroyer people, the carrier people, the staff people, and all of his staff plus others from Commander-in-Chief, Pacific Fleet staff. It was a very wonderful evening but we had big things to do the following week, so I left when...

Q: The big things being a continuation of the exercise?

Adm. M.: Yes, that's right. We had to start in the next week and find U-boats and we were pretty confident that we would be able to do it. Just as I was leaving I paid my respects to Admiral and Mrs. Thach, and Mrs. Thach said, "Well, now, Hank, will you people have anything to do with, say, covering certain forces or sending ships to various places in the Pacific Ocean when Jackie Kennedy goes to India and makes that trip?" Are you going to have anything to do with it, with the flagship?" I said, "Well, this is being held very closely," but Jackie is going to India aboard my flagship, the <u>Bennington</u>." of course, this was quite a surprise to Mrs. Thach. Admiral Thach knew it was a big lie but he wasn't giving it away. So, with that, Mrs. Thach said, "Who are you taking with her?" Don't you need a military wife?" I said, "That's up to the White House. They're giving the orders and all we're doing is providing the space and facilities and all that. They would have to decide whether or not a military wife was going." I thought it would be a good idea, and, of course, Mrs. Thach wanted to go.

Then she said, "What are you going to do about a hairdresser?" I said, "Well, of course, we knew that we couldn't supply everything, but we sent one of my barbers aboard ship to beauty school.

H. L. Miller #4 - 270

He's the best barber and I think he'll do a wonderful job."

Q: Did you say this without hesitation?

Adm. M.: Yes. Everything just sort of came to me in flashes and I rattled it all out. But, you know, she's a pretty smart woman and she said, "What's this man going to do in the meantime? He has to practice on people every day." I said, "Madeleine, we took care of that, too. Nobody knows this, but the White House gave us a mannequin of Jackie. We didn't have any money to buy a wig for the barber to practice on so we dyed an old swab black, and every day he puts that wig on the mannequin's head and does all the necessary work to keep his hand in." Whereupon I waved goodnight and said, "I have to get going and really be on the job tomorrow morning."

She believed it, but I think her husband probably told her the real story the next day. I thought nothing more about it because my mind was principally concerned with the ASW exercises we were going to have that week with that bunch of expert U-boat sailors of Submarine Force, Pacific Fleet. As I mentioned before, we got nine U-boats - killed nine U-boats - that week. We came into Pearl Harbor and Captain Bob McNitt, who had the destroyer squadron and who is now a rear admiral, had a party for us all - the carrier people, the flyers, the staff, the destroyer people, were all triumphant because they'd really kicked the hell out of the submarine force, and those poor submarine sailors were over there in a corner licking their wounds. But, when I walked in, the wives weren't talking submarines and how many we got, they wanted to know when I was going to take Jackie to India. Of course, it came as a shock to me because I'd forgotten all about that. And then I was in a cold sweat, because this story was all around Pearl Harbor and Honolulu. The wives wanted to know every detail of it, and I was wondering when I was going to get a call from the White House or from the Department of Defense or the Secretary of the Navy putting me on the report for spreading that story!

Q: Your sins caught you up!

Adm. M.: That's one time I wanted to get out of Pearl Harbor in a hurry.

Q: That's a good story. Tell me about your relief.

Adm. M.: My relief was Rear Admiral Joe Tibbitts, a classmate and a very good friend of mine. A tremendous guy. We were going to be in Hong Kong for about a week, so I wrote my brother who was with USIA in Dacca, East Pakistan. I asked him to fly up and visit us in Hong Kong. I got an immediate reply saying that he was back at the old stand in Dacca but his wife, Luree, and the three kids were still in Seattle and they would be in Hong Kong about that time. Whereupon I wrote Luree and gave her our schedule and said if she could hurry it up she would get a unique United States reception and tour in Hong Kong during that week. Luree responded. I met her and the kids at the airport, got them squared away at the hotel, and the man there at the hotel counted us, three children that all required beds, two adults, and wondered how five of us were going to get into two double beds! I couldn't convince him until I told him that this lady was my sister-in-law and I was living aboard ship. That night we went to the airport and met Admiral and Mrs. Tibbitts, got them squared away, and for the rest of the week we toured Hong Kong, we went shopping, and we had a great time. They had lunch and dinner in the Flag Mess aboard ship and were invited out by my friends in Hong Kong. When they got back to Dacca, they told brother Bill that he had joined the wrong outfit!

Then came the final turnover of command and a big reception, that was given for Admiral Tibbitts and myself. Well, all these young flyers were looking at this old man called Miller and wondering where he picked up this nice young chick of a wife. They really gave me many a bad eye until I told the aide to be sure that all subsequent introductions were not Mrs. Miller and

Admiral Miller, it was "Mrs. Miller, the sister-in-law of Admiral Miller." That cleared up an awful lot of thinking and doubts at that particular reception.

From there, I hopped a plane and went to Japan to transfer to another plane to Honolulu and back to San Diego, where my family was. On the plane leaving Japan, I asked a gentleman in the plane if the seat alongside of him was still open. He said, yes, so I sat down. I told him my name and he said his name was Madden. I looked at him again and I said, "You know, you were my squad leader at the Naval Academy back in 1930 and 1931." And he was, and I hand't seen him since 1931, but he was still the same guy.

When we got to Pearl Harbor, we were only there for a short time. I had sent word ahead to the destroyer wives that I would be glad to meet with them at the airport and tell them about the wonderful job their husbands were doing out there in my task force. Another reason I wanted to meet with them was to tell them not to fly to Japan to meet their husbands because those destroyers were leaving Hong Kong and going south to the crisis that was then taking place in Laos. They'd be heading south, not north to Japan. The wives did meet me. I told them this was happening, but please don't broadcast it to the newspapers. A couple of them did go and by the time they got there, the situation in Laos was pretty well stabilized and they sent the whole task group up to Japan, where they were supposed to go in the first place. It was a very nice meeting with a wonderful bunch of wives. I was well taken care of on that journey back to San Diego. After Honolulu, I went commercial to San Francisco where a Navy plane met me to take me to San Diego before midnight - which was important. At San Francisco, the Airport security patrol picked me up, got my baggage, and whisked me to the waiting Navy plane to get me to my wife and family for our 23rd wedding anniversary before the midnight deadline!

Q: Now, Admiral, we're coming to an extremely interesting phase of your career, when you went to CinPac as chief of staff for plans. What was the date of that?

Adm. M.: I reported to CinCPac in, I think, June of 1962. Yes.

Q: Tell me about the scope of your activities as chief of staff.

Adm. M.: Well, the boss at that time at CinCPac was Admiral Don Felt. He was tough, he knew his stuff, he was dictatorial, he and I clashed many times, but we sure did make a lot of history during the two years and two months that I was on that staff.

My job was Assistant Chief of Staff for Plans, CinCPac. I

was in charge of all the long-range plans, strategic plans, and all the contingency plans for the Pacific, Asia, Southeast Asia, South Asia, and general direction to SEATO planning, all SEATO meetings, and the agendas for those meetings.

Q: I think at this point it might be well to ask you, and have you clarify, what were the sources and the feed-in of information to you in order to enable you to function in that capacity?

Adm. M.: First of all, before any plans could be put together, we had to have the necessary intelligence so that we could proceed with courses of action to attain a specific objective that we had in mind for a particular plan. Then we built the number of forces, Army, Navy, Marine Corps, Air Force - U. S. Forces - that we needed to implement that particular plan. And we included allied forces, if they were available, and allied facilities. Then we laid out our courses of action to implement those plans and attain the objective that we planned initially. Basically, that's the way we went about building a particular plan for a specific contingency.

Q: This implies, then, a fairly knowledgeable staff to begin with, doesn't it?

Adm. M.: Absolutely. In the planning business, one had to get the thinkers with ideas. Innovation was a primary part of this whole business. We had to have the thinkers, we had to have the "idea" people, and we did. During the time that I was there we had some very fine Army, Navy, Air Force, and Marine Corps planners. They're a different breed from the operators. The planners have to think, they have to look into the future, but they also have to be practical. If you can't implement a plan, it's no good. You have to come down to earth and say these are the forces that I have, that's all I have, and now I've got to do this particular job. How am I going to do it.

Q: That particular breed is hard to come by, isn't he?

Adm. M.: Yes, but we have quite a few in the armed forces today who are what I called darned good planners. They know their business and they do a marvelous job.

Q: Incidentally, are they being recognized today in the Navy as a special group, and can they advance up the ladder by remaining in that group? Or do they have to go out and get diversified experience?

Adm. M.: Normally, planners are the top people in the armed services today. Naturally, from time to time, they have to get away from the planning and go to an operating job that gives them more experience. They have to get down to the practical side of the business, and that's what you learn in operations - what you can do with these particular weapons, weapons systems, these men, these ships, these tanks, these airplanes. Planners who do not get back into operations normally go off into the wild blue yonder and do too much impossible planning. You can't do that and succeed.

Q: Naturally, in this capacity, then, Admiral, as officer in charge of plans, you had access to anything from the United States government, from any of the departments, State, CIA, and what-have-you.

Adm. M.: We had control of the forces that were assigned to us by the Joint Chiefs of Staff in the Pacific. That didn't include all the forces in the Pacific, just those that were assigned by the Joint Chiefs. Now, in the Pacific area, there's the commander-in-chief of the Pacific Fleet, the commander-in-chief of U. S. Air Forces, Pacific, the commander-in-chief of the U. S. Army, Pacific, and there's the commanding general of the Fleet Marine Force, Pacific. They all, in operations there, report to the Commander-in-Chief, Pacific, who is the over-all commander. Remember, the commander of all the forces in Vietnam, who later on was General

Westmoreland, now General Abrams, is under Commander-in-Chief, Pacific.

Q: Was it not a difficult task, with all these sources for your basic information, to sift this information and select that which you thought was right information and draw your plans accordingly?

Adm. M.: Well, we had an assistant chief of staff for intelligence who had a very competent group. We had excellent intelligence information, and, of course, he could get and tap other sources back in Washington for any additional information we wanted... Normally, we had good intelligence from which to produce our plans.

Q: That was somewhat of a tangent, but I wanted to establish the base for your planning. Now, if you'll go on and tell me about the activities and general scope of them.

Adm. M.: The job of assistant chief of staff for plans certainly covered an awful lot of waterfront. But, first of all, I'll go through the countries that we were concerned with and the plans and staffs that we had control of.

The first was Japan. Through the Commander, U. S. Forces Japan, we talked to the Japanese Defense Forces in all of their planning for the defense of Japan. Naturally, the defense of Japan, as far as the Japanese were concerned, was strictly an

American responsibility, but we helped them to pick their air defense system that they wanted to put all round the country. The Military Assistance Advisory Group that we had in Japan came under my immediate supervision. Also the military aid for Japan.

The next country was Taiwan. The Taiwan Defense Command came under my planning, also the Military Assistance Advisory Group in Taiwan.

Following that was Korea. Liaison with the U. N. command in Korea was my responsibility, also the Military Assistance Advisory Group there came under my immediate supervision.

The next area there was Okinawa. The staff there was under a Lieutenant General of the United States Army. He was called the CinCPac Rep (for representation), Okinawa.

The next was the Philippines. The U. S. and the Philippines have a defense treaty that came under my shop, also the Military Advisory Group, Philippines, was under my office.

Going from there to Hong Kong we have a U. S. - United Kingdom defense plan. This was also in my area. We maintained liaison with the American consul general in Hong Kong.

Following that was Vietnam. All the plans for Vietnam got their approval and their scrutiny from my particular office, and the Military Assistance Advisory Group there came under me.

Next was Thailand. SEATO headquarters are in Thailand and we had lots of business with them. The Military Assistance Advisory Group in Bangkok came under me. Also Commander U. S. Forces, Thailand (Comus Mac Thai).

Later, in 1964, we did some preliminary planning between Thailand and the U. S. This never did come to fruition. We didn't pursue it that hard because of the Vietnam War.

As far as Pakistan was concerned, my area of interest was in the SEATO planning, of which Pakistan is a member.

Then comes Laos. Laos had a Military Assistance Advisory Group and a big military aid program from us. They also had an economic aid program.

Finally, Cambodia. When Sihanouk was there we had a Military Assistance Advisory Group. The head of the MAAG was Brigadier General Tony Scherer, who had a very good communications with Sihanouk. Why? Because he played soccer and basketball against the national team of which Sihanouk was a member. So he had great communications and rapport with Sihanouk. The Ambassador was very ineffective because he just couldn't seem to communicate with Sihanouk. In addition to all this, my office had close liaison with the officials of the Aid program, economic aid to all these countries. In other words, when we had finished with our proposed allocation of military aid funds to these nations, we would ask the economic aid people please to come out and check with us to see if we were on the right track, economically speaking and militarily speaking. Then CIA in the Pacific used to come and check with our shop and keep us posted as to their activities in these countries.

We had a very close working relationship with all American activities in every Asian country. In short, when any new ambassador from these countries would come through Pearl Harbor, they would check with CinCPac headquarters every time, going and coming. All the ambassadors received briefings at CinCPac headquarters. We had a State Department representative as a member of the staff of the Commander-in-Chief, Pacific, headquarters. This was a great help and provided wonderful cooperation, coordination, and communication between all elements.

Q: It was a great example of this integration of effort!

Adm. M.: Yes, Sir. We knew every ambassador in the Pacific. Whenever we went on a trip, we checked in with the U. S. military in that particular country, with the ambassador, and then with the foreign military in that country. We always kept everybody cut in.

Q: As a part of your education for this new job - and it seems to have been most fortunate that it happened at the outset -

General Maxwell Taylor was making a tour of the Far East, was he not, in preparation for his role as Chairman of the Joint Chiefs of Staff?

Adm. M.: Yes, Sir. Just before General Taylor was recalled to active duty, President Kennedy was making him the chairman of the Joint Chiefs of Staff, he came to the Pacific to get the briefings, the orientation again, and get cut in. He told Admiral Felt he would be glad to take one of CinCPac's staff along. Whereupon, it was suggested by an Air Force General on CinCPac's staff that I go with Maxwell Taylor.

I was very fortunate in having the opportunity to make that trip because it was a wonderful indoctrination for me. Our first stop in the Presidential Jet was Wake Island, where we had time to get a swim, take a look around, then proceed on to Japan.

In Japan we received briefings from the American Embassy and also from the Military Assistance Advisory Group and the commander of the Seventh Fleet, who was then Vice Admiral Schoech, but Admiral Schoech was in the hospital and we received the briefings from the staff. At the reception in Japan there were so many there that I can't tell you who we met. That was, I think perhaps the biggest number of people that we had in one locale at one time during that trip. After we received the Navy and the MAAG briefings and the

United States Air Force briefings in Japan, we took time out to get a wonderful Japanese dinner, and it was surprising to me going to some of these shopping places prior to that dinner that there were a great many people who recognized and said hello to General Taylor because of his previous tour, many years ago, in Japan as an intelligence student.

Q: Was he a Japanese-language student?

Adm. M.: Yes, Sir, he was. Following that, we went to Korea where we received the United Nations briefings, the MAAG briefings there, and the briefings from the Korean military staff. We also took a trip to one of the Army camps in the DMZ, met the people there, and were given briefings on the present situation along the DMZ. Then, the last night, we had a state dinner with President Park - they pronounce that Pak. He's still in power and, believe it or not, at that time there were some Americans believing that he could possibly be a Communist planted down there by North Korea. He was a very pleasant individual, very intense, very dedicated, and I thought he was a pretty competent guy.

From Korea we went across the water again to Taiwan. In Taiwan we checked in with the Taiwan Defense Command there, it was Vice Admiral Charlie Melson. We received briefings there. We also had extensive briefings and demonstrations by the United States Air

Force part of the Taiwan Defense command. We saw their antiaircraft defense system. We thought they were really in pretty good shape. Then we received a ride in one of the Chinese planes over to the island of Quemoy. We went through all the defenses there, were given a fire-power demonstration, and returned later on that afternoon to Taiwan. I might add that one of the other members of our party with Maxwell Taylor was later Ambassador Bill Sullivan. He was Ambassador to Laos. Bill at that time was in the State Department in Asian Affairs.

Our last day was spent in final briefings. We were given very detailed briefings by several of the commands there and by the Chinese. And, finally, the last night was a state dinner with General and Mrs. Chiang Kai-shek. A very wonderful affair, lots of food, wonderful Chinese food, but, as usual, I got a bug from it.

We left Taiwan the next day and proceeded to Okinawa, where we had lunch with Commander-in-Chief, Pacific, Representative, a Lieutenant General in the U. S. Army. We were briefed by his staff, very extensive briefings on the way that we would use Okinawa in case of an attack, the strategic importance of that particular area. Then, off we went to Hong Kong. That bug I received the night before was still working, so when we got to Hong Kong and we had the entire floor very closely guarded at one of the hotels there on the Kowloon side, begged off from going out to dinner because I wanted to take all the medicine in the world to kill my bug. It was the most restful night I had on the whole trip. I was by myself and I didn't have to attend briefings, I didn't have to go to late dinners, or to drink all those drinks.

Following Hong Kong, we proceeded to Saigon where we were briefed by the Military Assistance Advisory Group, which was then headed by General Harkens of the U. S. Army. General Harkens was with Maxwell Taylor in Korea and also at West Point. They apparently were very good friends and had worked together in the United States Army many times. I liked General Harkens. He was a very straightforward man. We received the briefing from the Americans and from the Vietnamese. We went on a helicopter ride to a couple of the areas. They wanted to show us their strategic hamlets and what they were doing about it. Additionally, we met with the U. S. Ambassador, Fritz Nolting, who was a wonderful guy. He had great communication and rapport with the Vietnamese.

As you know, the man who was running Vietnam at that time was President Diem. He was a very controversial individual. He was a Dictator and since he was a Dictator there were many people in America who figured that he should be put out of office and a democratic organization take over. Well, you can't say that a dictator is bad for any country. When a country has to be run, if it's difficult, maybe a dictator is the guy to do it. But we could sense that the good old USA didn't like to see a dictator in there who was labeled as the president and who ran the country single-handedly.

Q: It takes preparation for democracy, doesn't it?

Adm. M.: That's correct, and they weren't ready for any democracy. Diem had control. He knew what he wanted to do, he had the area under pretty good security and protection. Personally, I think he was doing a good job. He was always behind the eight ball on his sister-in-law, Madame Nhu, but, so be it. Diem still did a wonderful job. We had dinner with him. Of course, I was still a little bit sickly from Taiwan, but I enjoyed the dinner, enjoyed meeting him, several members of his staff, and the Vietnam military people.

After Vietnam we hopped across the border to Cambodia and a meeting with Sihanouk and the present head of Cambodia, General Lon Nol. Before I left CinCPac, Admiral Felt told me to give his very best regards to General Lon Nol. They were good friends. But be sure and tell General Lon Nol that we didn't like the situation there in the northeast section of Cambodia, where Communists or North Vietnamese or Viet Minh were operating with the full knowledge of the Cambodian government.

So at the first luncheon it happened that I was sitting right alongside of General Lon Nol, and I told him that Admiral Felt really had a great deal of respect and admiration for him, but this was one message that he wanted me to pass on to General Lon Nol. Well, General Lon Nol told me that if they found any of those Viet Minh or North Vietnamese or Communists up in the northeast section, they'd kill them and/or cut their heads off. It was a very nice luncheon. We were briefed later by the Cambodian military and given very fine briefings by our own Military Assistance Advisory Group there. It was interesting - I had a very brief talk in Pnom-Penh, the capital, with Mr. Sol Brown, who is a retired warrant officer from the United States Navy and who worked for me at one time at Sangley Point in the Philippines. Sol was Sihanouk's public words officer. He was building all the bridges and the roads around Cambodia, and doing a very fine job of it, too. Naturally, he had one of these cute little Cambodian girls who used to keep house for him, bring his shoes in, and keep the bed warm.

The Military Assistance Advisory Group was commanded by Brigadier General Scherer. Maybe we should have left him there for three or four more years, because as soon as he left, Sihanouk started taking measures to kick us out - the MAAG and also the ambassador. The last night we went to a very elaborate state dinner at the palace. It was a little bit unusual because Indonesia had their delegation there at the same time. Their delegation was headed by Hartuni, who was Sukarno's second wife. They were going on from Cambodia to Peking where they were having meetings with the Chinese in Peking. Well, the first part of the evening was a late-afternoon reception. All the ambassadors from other countries were there and their wives. We met quite a bunch.

From there we went to dinner, and it was an elaborate dinner. The table was almost as long as the State of California. Sihanouk was very clever. He always wants all the attention in the world. He sait in the middle of the table and he would command everybody's attention and shout in both directions. It was quite a show. He should have been in Holly wood. But what was very interesting was the fact that the Palace and all the buildings around it had all electric lights lit and there were thousands and thousands of them. Of course, that was taking most of the juice from the town so the city of Pnom-Penh was practically dark but the Palace was well lighted.

After the dinner we went to the Cambodian opera. Sihanouk's daughter, who was a good-looking girl, was the star in the opera, but I can assure you that dragged on 'til about one o'clock in the

H. L. Miller #4 - 289

morning and it was boring. We had a very difficult time trying to stay awake. It was significant that when the opera was over and Sihanouk got up and left, he came over to Maxwell Taylor and me, shook our hands, but he didn't do that to the Indonesian delegation or anybody else.

Well, the next morning the rest of the party asked me how the dinner was, the opera, and all that, and what did we do afterwards. So, with a little of the devil in me, I said, well, they knew Hartuni was there from Indonesia, so I told them that Hartuni and I went out on the town and that she was a darned fine girl and I can see how Sukarno really appreciated her. They got inquisitive as the devil and they said, where did you go? I said we took in every night club in Pnom-Penh. Of course, there are no night clubs in Pnom-Penh, but they didn't know it. They said, tell us more, and I said, "I've got to go pack. I've got to make that plane. I'll tell you later on when I get aboard."

Q: You had another international incident in the making!

Adm. M.: They thought that Hartuni and I really took in Pnom-Penh. Of course, I didn't see her after the opera.

Q: Tell me, General Lon Nol at the luncheon by his remarks to you must have indicated that he was covering this issue under the table. Was he?

Adm. M.: First of all, I think he knew that there were Viet Minh and/or North Vietnamese who were sort of using the northeastern part of Cambodia as a camping place for forays into Vietnam.

Q: A privileged sanctuary?

Adm. M.: Yes, but I think he wanted me to be sure to convey the impression to Admiral Felt that he, Lon Nol as an individual - he was secretary of defense then, you might say the head of the armed forces in Cambodia - would take immediate action to rectify this. He wanted to maintain Admiral Felt's friendship. He liked Admiral Felt. This was a good thing to have, to have that rapport between military leaders in all those countries. That's one thing about Felt. Those Asian leaders really respected and admired him, just like they did Admiral Felix Stump before him. They thought the world of Admiral Stump, and Admiral Felt kept that going.

After Cambodia we went into Thailand and their prime minister was General Thanom. He replaced Sarit, who had died just shortly before that from a kidney-liver ailment. Sarit was worth about 150 million dollars when he died. He made most of it through the opium and dope that was brought in there from Laos and sold from Thailand to various other countries, also probably from a lot of the military aid that was given there and economic aid and, believe it or not, from a pig farm that was right outside of Bangkok.

In Bangkok we received briefings from SEATO headquarters, from the Thailand armed forces, from our own Military Assistance Advisory Groups, and from the embassy. It was a very busy, busy period. I certainly enjoyed meeting all those people, particularly seeing General Thanom again. He had been my guest aboard the <u>Hancock</u>. As a matter of fact, it was sort of embarrassing because being the Prime Minister he was supposed to take care of General Taylor, but he sort of let General Taylor go and he was taking care of me. I kept telling him that I was the Number Two guy and he'd better go back there and take care of Number One, but he wasn't about to do that. He was going to show me that Thailand was pretty hospitable too. The head of the defense establishment there was Air Marshal Dawee and he's quite a guy. He was an actor at one time. He's quite a good flyer and quite a personable gent.

Well, Dawee during World War II took the navigation course at the United States Naval Academy, so he feels that he is an alumnus of the Naval Academy. He loves the U. S. Naval Academy. When he comes to the United States he always goes down to the Naval Academy and takes a look. But it's quite a chore because in Washington they say, no, you can't go down to the Naval Academy today, you have to give us some time because we lay out the plush-carpet treatment. This is what you rate for your position in Thailand. He says, "All I want to do is go down to the Naval Academy and see my beloved Naval Academy." They say, no, you can't do that. So, after all those arguments, I just go. I get a taxicab and say take me to the Naval Academy. I go down to the Naval Academy and I park the taxicab out at the gate and say, you stay there until I return. And I walk all over the Naval Academy. I love it."

Well, they were very nice and hospitable to us. We received all the briefings in the world and we also were entertained royally.

From there we went to Indonesia. This was a very unusual time in Indonesia. Sukarno, of course, was still in power. Nasution, who was formerly the chief of the Army in Indonesia, was now the chairman of their joint chiefs of staff. Sukarno wanted to eliminate Nasution many times. He was a fine, steadfast, honest, dedicated individual. They always tried to eliminate him but he, somehow, always came back and survived.

Q: Yet he was essentially a non-political character, wasn't he?

Adm. M.: That's right. He always survived. We didn't see Sukarno. The American Ambassador was, I think, Ambassador Green. He was back in Washington on a selection board for foreign service officers, so we had his deputy who was a former newspaperman, and this deputy was one of those individuals representing the United States who would always give the farm away. Nothing was too good for Indonesia, and he wasn't thinking, you know, about what he was going to do for the good old USA. The first meeting that we had at the embassy, the first night we arrived, he gave us a briefing, a rundown on what was happening in Indonesia. Our Military Assistance Advisory Group was headed by a colonel and he gave us a rundown on what was happening. The deputy ambassador, you might say, then came out with the statement to General Taylor saying, well, here's the situation and this is the way we see it. Now we want you to dump General Nasution.

Well, we were sort of shocked. We couldn't believe that we'd arrived in a foreign country and have some U. S. representative say "dump the nation's top military leader." The next thing that happened, the colonel who was head of the Military Assistance Advisory Group - an Army colonel - was saying practically the same thing. It was pretty hard to believe that our own people, a military man and a civilian, would come out with that and advocate it, but this is what happened. In the next couple of days we had all the briefings and we had private meetings with General Nasution. I liked him. We met with others. We were given detailed briefings, the dissident elements, where they were, how they were hunting them down, all that.

And also what they were doing with the military aid that we gave them. It was surprising. As you recall back in that time, 1962, September, the chief of the Air Force in Indonesia was suspect. He was, of course, flying Russian airplanes. Russia had supplied Indonesia with three billion dollars in ships, planes, tanks, guns, all that. Some of it was practically worthless. They couldn't keep the ships going. It was sort of tragic when you saw that with all of that they still had very little capability to do anything. They couldn't keep anything working. But our own colonel, United States Air Force colonel, who was on the Military Assistance Advisory Group staff was telling us to give everything to the Indonesian Air Force. The Indonesian Air Force General was supposedly a great one and all this sort of stuff. It was a tragic situation. One of the jobs that I was asked to do going down there was to look at the living conditions of our MAAG people, enlisted and officers. So on the last afternoon I got into a sport shirt and a pair of slacks and made a detailed inspection of the houses of the Army, Navy, Air Force, Marine Corps officers and enlisted down there. It was a horrible mess. The students were trying to study in lights that would blind you. There just wasn't any light in the rooms. Utilities would go out. Toilets would get clogged up. It was a very depressing situation, and naturally I wrote every detail of this up so that we could get money to rehabilitate those facilties and even though it belonged to the Indonesians I just thought it was absolutely essential that we provide decent living conditions for our people. Nobody would live like that - no American with a half-decent salary would live like that.

Q: And morale must have been pretty low, wasn't it?

Adm. M.: Oh, yes. I told them I would do something about it, that helped, and I did. We enjoyed that trip to Indonesia. One of the highlights was getting into a couple of Russian helicopters. I'd never do it again, but I didn't want to insult the Indonesians by saying I wouldn't ride in those two really shaky helicopters. They weren't fit to fly, but I didn't want to tell General Taylor. He didn't know anything about flying and I thought, well, if he doesn't get killed I guess it's all right. They took us up to a village that had been given aid by our military assistance program and our economic program. They wanted us to see this village that was certainly an example, so we went up and they had along with the tour a sort of celebration - there were dances and then came the luncheon. All the women in this village had gotten together and prepared this luncheon, and I tell you, whether you were hungry or not, you had to eat some of it. Well, we walked into this tent and there was all the food, big chunks of rice, hot food, hot, hot food, but everything covered with great big flies. It almost turned my stomach, but I said I've got to do something about it. At least they had beer. I knew I probably couldn't get bugs from that, so I drank beer. Then, I looked at that great big mound of rice covered with big flies. I took my spoon and I bored a hole right into the middle of it and got some rice that was not under flies. Then General Taylor said, "Here, have some of this," to all of us, "it's real good hot stuff." He was used to hot food from when he served in Mexico for a while, but I'll tell you I took a couple of bites and it was so hot I gagged until the tears just poured down. It was impossible, just impossible for me to eat it. But I ate some of the rest of the food and got out of there alive. General Taylor ate that as though it was just a Sunday brunch. Then - he was very gracious - he thanked all the women for going to all the trouble preparing this delicious luncheon. Boy, it was a tough one for me to swallow!

I enjoyed that trip to Indonesia. I did some shopping, bought some batik and other things. I got a big kick out of it. From there we made our last stop in Manila. We were supposed to have a short meeting with, perhaps, the president but it didn't turn out that way. We stopped at the International Airport there and some of our own people met us from U. S. Naval Forces, Philippines, and from the embassy. I listened to them for a little bit. We had about an hour to kill, and it just happened that Mariles Romulo, General Romulo's daughter-in-law, was right in the next building and I had a very nice meeting with her and a Philippine Air Force General who was there and whom I'd known from previous tours.

We got into the airplane and headed for Guam where we made a short stop to refuel, and then back to Pearl Harbor.

Q: That was a pretty strenuous tour, wasn't it? How was General Maxwell Taylor as a traveling companion?

Adm. M.: Maxie Taylor is a very nice man. He's very astute, but he's sort of hard to talk to. He's not very warm. He's not very friendly, he's very reserved, very reserved. However, in Japan, you know, all those people who remembered him as a young officer ccame up and said "Hello, you're General Taylor, how are you?" and he was very nice and friendly. But, in the main, if he doesn't know you well, he's pretty cool.

Adm. M.: Just to set the stage for the year 1962 and later of the events that took place in Vietnam, I want to give you some of the facts of life in the CinCPac area in 1962.

Let's look at the USSR. The Soviets had both medium-range ballistic-missile sites and intercontinental ballistic missiles. They also had surface-to-air missile sites, about one hundred of them. This was in the USSR. They had more nuclear submarines than ever before. They were better quality submarines. They also had guided-missile sites. And, to further point the finger at the Pacific command, the Soveits were making ICBM test firings in the Pacific area. In other words, the impact area was in the Pacific and we were watching this.

Let's look at China. There was no change in 1962 in the Chinese Navy. It was just a very poor navy, nothing much to it. The Chinese - this is the ChiCom - Air Force was a poor air force. They had Russian MIGs but Russia was not giving them the spare parts that they needed.

Now, for the U. S. forces. The Army had about 100,000 people of all types in the Pacific. They had about 10,000 in the Army Logistics Support Group in Thailand. The Air Force had a goodly number of people in the Pacific. In 1962 they upped their numbers about 3,500. The Navy and Marine Corps had the biggest number of people in the Pacific area - about 150,000. And when we talk of the mainland southeast Asia, let's see the countries that are involved.

There's Laos, the Republic of Vietnam, North Vietnam, Thailand, Cambodia, Burma, Malaya, and Singapore. That's mainland Southeast Asia. Our other allies were the Australians, the New Zealanders, the British, the Pakistani, the Filipinos, the Republic of China, South Korea, and the French.

H. L. Miller #4 - 299

Now, of all the planning that we did at CinCPac, we had another small part of our staff at SAC headquarters in Omaha, Nebraska. This was the Commander-in-Chief, Pacific, Rep (representative) there with a small group of people doing nuclear planning with the SAC group. We also had an Air Force lieutenant general who was commander of U. S. Forces in Japan. He had a staff. They had some joint planning with the Japanese forces. CinCPac was also responsible for the Trust Territories of the Pacific. There was very little attention paid to the Trust Territories because we had such limited resources to put into that area.

Q: The Trust area - did that include Okinawa?

Adm. M.: No, the Trust Territories did not include Okinawa. You might say they are from Guam to Okinawa. And then CinCPac was also responsible for the two research and development groups that the DDR and E office of SecDef set up in Saigon and Bangkok. This was to test out weapons and weapon systems in the hot, humid climate of Southeast Asia.

Q: Talking about test areas, what about the Christmas Island test center and Polaris missiles?

Adm. M.: We had Johnson Island in the Pacific as a test station for range instrumentation for the Polaris missiles for Polaris firings - and for other tests of missiles. Also Kwajalein which is a big missile-test center.

Q: Were extra security measures taken around those areas?

Adm. M.: We really didn't have to worry about that because they were so isolated that with the groups aboard they had plenty of security.

One of the other things that we did at CinCPac, and we were the only big U. S. military command in the world doing it, was war-gaming. In other words, we took a plan, we tested it. We war-gamed to see under those particular circumstances how many forces would be left after a battle, how many would be killed, what other resources that we had would be demolished. Also what resources that we had would remain. And we, at that time, were the only U. S. military command in the world doing that sort of thing.

Q: Did you have any cooperation, or did you work in conjunction with the Naval War College in this area?

Adm. M.: No, Sir. We had our own war-gaming group and we were probably far ahead of most agencies in that business.

Now, in 1962 we had what was called the De Soto patrol. It consisted of a destroyer or two that would patrol the China coast - the Red China coast - and along the Korean coast. It would stay outside the 12 mile limit, checking on the radars and any other intelligence that they could gather from the ChiCom and the North Koreans. This was from April on. We ran those patrols at odd times. There was no regular schedule. In December of 1962, we sent a destroyer, the Agerholm, around Thailand and into the Gulf of Tonkin to 21° North. It was interesting that the Agerholm was followed by three ChiCom naval units, but they didn't do anything.

In May of 1962 CinCPac sent Army, Navy, Air Force, and Marine Corps units to Thailand when Nam Tha in Laos fell to the Communists. There was a Marine Battalion Landing Team that was put in Thailand. Marine helos went to Udorn, and about 20 Marine A-4 aircraft went to Udorn. Also, CinCPac sent a small staff labeled Task Force 116 to Thailand to take charge in case any contingency broke out.

Q: Is that the operation I have a note on taking place on the 12th and the 16th of May when the President had ordered a task force of U. S. Seventh Fleet ships with 1,800 Marines to move toward the Indochinese peninsula to back up his diplomatic efforts to save Laos?

Adm. M.: Yes, and at the time they sent the heavy attack carrier, the Hancock, in that direction steaming south with their bag of airplanes in case help was needed. Additionally, the Bennington - I had just turned over command of the antisubmarine warfare task group, the USS Bennington and the destroyers, to Rear Admiral Tibbitts. This was done in Hong Kong in May, and they had orders to proceed south toward the Indochina coast, instead of going up to a nice rendezvous in Japan. Also, in October of 1962, to further complicate the picture, there was the Cuban crisis, and CinCPac sent a Marine Battalion Landing Team via ship from the Pacific to the Panama Canal to the area around Cuba.

Q: Was this in advance of the President's announcement of the quarantine?

Adm. M.: I forget the date, so I'm not too sure of that. However, that Battalion Landing Team returned to the Pacific in December of 1962.

Q: After the quarantine had been lifted?

Adm. M.: Yes.

Q: May I ask this. In connection with the sending of that force, the White House at that point was ordering ships about, and was this an order that came from the White House or did it come from the CNO?

Adm. M.: No, Sir, this came from the Joint Chiefs of Staff. We were fortunate that we weren't in that confusion, where the President and the Secretary of Defense were ordering ships and units all over at quite a helter-skelter pace.

The next item of importance. On the 23rd of July 1962 we had the first of a series of Secretary of Defense conferences at Hawaii. These conferences were established to review plans that CinCPac had for various contingencies and to continuously review the military assistance program, specifically for Vietnam and Thailand, but also including the military assistance to other countries. I don't think that I included Burma in my last statement, but Burma was the recipient of military assistance from the United States.

Q: That was in the days before General Win?

Adm. M.: With General Win, too, we still gave them military assistance - guns, bullets, and all that - but it wasn't labeled as such. Also, and I'll touch on it later, on the 8th of October after I made the Western Pacific trip with General Maxwell Taylor, we had another Secretary of Defense meeting at CinCPac headquarters.

Q: Secretary McNamara was present at both of those meeting?

Adm. M.: Oh, yes, Sir.

Q: Was it the first time that you had met him, in July?

Adm. M.: Yes, Sir, that was the first time I met Secretary McNamara. We had all the commands represented, but I'll touch on all that later.

Q: There's one other event of some significance, I would imagine. On the 13th of October, Admiral Moorer took over the Seventh Fleet.

Adm. M.: Yes, Sir, that was soon after the Secretary of Defense conference. I should say, too, that in all of our CinCPac planning we had many plans in coordination with the State Department on the evacuation of U. S. nationals from these countries in case something happened. Those are well-established plans all over the world.

INDEX

for

SERIES OF INTERVIEWS WITH

REAR ADMIRAL H. L. MILLER, U. S. NAVY (Retired)

USS AGERHOLM - DD: on patrol in Thai waters, 1962, 301

Aircraft Carriers - Weapons system: comments, 140-141

Air Group #6: Miller given command when he leaves the CV PRINCETON, 84-85; assigned to the USS HANCOCK, 85.

Air Operations Instructions (US F-4): summation of best procedures, formation, advice to come out of WW II, 102 ff; subsequent revisions cover jets, 105

Alaskan Survey: Navy Department sends Miller to Fairbanks, etc. (1946) for a survey of human resources, 106-108

Angled Deck - Aircraft Carriers: 188

HMS ARK ROYAL - CV: participates in SEATO Exercise (1962), 265-266

ASCAS - Anti SS classification and Analysis Center: used effectively with CV's to detect a SS and distinguish from other underwater sounds, 249-250; same technique used with S-2 aircraft, 250-251; Adm. Ekstrom makes funds available to install ASCAS equipment on flagship BENNINGTON, 254; success of the equipment in exercises, 257-259; Washington shows little interest, 258.

Atoms for Peace: 184

B-17 raids: Gen. LeMay changes tactics and follows the Navy in low level bombing of Japanese mainland targets, 94-95

Baguio, Philippines: 203, 241-242

Bandung Conference: 193

Bangkok: Miller sets up Commissary - Px for U. S. Military in 1955, 200

Basic Research vs Applied Research: 131-132

USS BENNINGTON: Flagship of CarDiv 15, 254

Bigelow, LCdr. Neff: fighter sweep leader whom Miller orders to shoot down attacking Japanese "gently", 92

Blackburn, Capt. John T. (Tommy): carries message back to Washington for Miller, 75-76

Blandy, ADM Wm. Henry P.: Cinc, Atlantic Fleet (1948) when Miller ordered to his staff, 134, 143, 146-147, 150

Bombs - Walleye and other types: 67-68

British Sea Power: remarks on its decline, 170-172

Brown, Sol: retired warrent officer of the USN - serves as Public Works Officer for Sihanour (1962), 287

Burke, Adm. Arleigh A.: his efforts in support of sea power and the navy, 139; Miller assigned (1953) to his Op. 60, 178-179, 185-187; visit to the Philippines with Adms. Felt and Libby, 208-9; Miller called back to Washington in 1957, first to serve as aide to Burke and then as Ass't. Director, Progress Analysis Group - CNO, 210 ff.; Burke heartily approved of Progress Analysis project to sell seapower to the American public, 210-211; annoyed with Legislative Liaison Branch - assigns task of appearing before Johnson sub-committee to Progress Analysis group, 220; pleased with the PR work of the Progress Analysis Group, 227; reaction to Op. 09 dog statement on Russian missile capability, 230

Car Div 15: Miller becomes Commander of this Anti SS Hunter-Killer Task Group (1961), 253-254; objectives of the Command, 256-257

CARNEY, Adm. Robert B.: 187

Catapults (1939): 28-29

CincPac Staff: Miller serves as Assistant Chief of Staff for Plans from June, 1962 to September, 1964, 274; what is entailed in such Plans, 275-78; views on military planners, 276-277; countries of cognizance, 278-281; resume of the International Picture (1962) as it pertained to the CincPac area, 297-299; wargaming, 300; DeSoto patrol, 300-301.

Clifton, RADM Joe (Jumping Joe): 17, 26-27

Commander, Fleet Air, Philippines: Miller given this assignment, September, 1955, 196

Composite Squadron #7: 155-162; attendance at bomb school in Albuquerque, 155-156; all-weather flying at Corpus Christi, 157; security, 158-160

Compton, Dr. Karl Taylor: President of M.I.T., 113-114.

Connolly, the Hon. John: fighter director officer in Pacific during last days of war (1945), 91

Cruse, Capt. Andrew Wm. (Bat): senior navy man on Eniwetok, 74

Cubi Point: In construction, 1955 - 196; 203-204

Damage Control: efforts by Damage Control Officer (LtCdr. Slacks) on USS HANCOCK saved the ship when attacked by kamikaze, 96-97. Damage control - comments, 96-97

Dawee - Thai Air Marshal: 291-292

de Florez, RADM luis: 113; his role in basic research, 113, 116, 124-126

Dennison, Adm. Robert Lee: 186-187

De Soto Patrol: 300-301

Diem - Ngo Dinh: President of South Viet Nam, 285-286

Doolittle, Gen. James H.: 30 ff

Doolittle Flyers - Tokyo Raid (1942): Miller assigned from Pensacola for their training, 30-35; Elimination of Lt. Bates, 36-38; preparations on board the USS HORNET, 40-41, 45; Japanese fishing boats sighted, 41-42, Adm. Halsey gives order to launch, 42; morale building effort, 45; annual reunion, 45-46; casualties of the raid, 46; comments on preparation of pilots, mental attitude, etc., 53-54; aftermath - Miller called to Washington for briefing of Adm. King, 50, and SecNav, 48-52

Doyle, ADM Austin K.: 22, 27, 51

Drew's prep school: 5

Dudley, RADM Paul Lee: skipper of the LEYTE, (1951), 163

Duncan, Adm. Donald B. (Wu): 35; chief planner for Tokyo raid, 35, 51

Eglin Field: Miller ordered there in Feb., 1942, 31-33

Ekstrom, VADM Clarence E.: (Swede) C.O., Naval Air Force, PacFlt (1959), 245; Miller serves (1960) as his Chief of Staff, 245; his objectives in the job, 246.

Empress Augusta Bay: November, 1943 - carrier operations against Rabaul to save the U. S. landings at Empress Augusta Bay, 62-64

Eniwetok: 73

Espiritu Santo: Task Force with CV PRINCETON calls in before attack on Palau, 75

Felt, Admiral H. D.: 241, 244; places Australian Admiral in command of SEATO exercise, 262-267, 290

Flatley, VADM James H., Jr.: air officer for Adm. Mitscher on LEXINGTON, 83; ordered air group commanders to stay out of air battles, 83-84

USS FRANKLIN: flagship of Adm. Bogan, 88; heavily damaged in Japanese attack, 89

Gallery, RADM Dan V.: takes over command of USS HANCOCK after signing of the Japanese surrender agreement, 101

Gates, The Hon, Thomas: SecNav (1957), prepares with help of Op 09 dog testimony to be given before Johnson subcommittee, 220-221

Gliders: 17

USS HANCOCK: Miller with air group #6 boards her at Ulithi (Feb. 1945), 85; attack on Okinawa, 85-86; airgroup sinks the YAMAMOTO, 88; takes over Task Group schedule from damaged USS FRANKLIN, 89; search for camouflaged Japanese planes on mainland, 90; prohibited target cities, 90; final air engagements before surrender, 91-93; account of kamikaze attack on the CV, 95-96; RADM Gallery takes command immediately after surrender, 101; Miller given command in San Francisco (Jan. 1959). 231; builds morale on board, 232, 236-237; joins the 7th fleet, 232-233; visit to Hong King, 233-236, lessons learned from duty on carrier, 238; return to San Francisco, 240; with MIDWAY embarked SEATO leaders for weapons demonstration, 241-242

Harkins, Gen. Paul D.: heads MAAG in Saigon, 1962 - 285

Harlow, The Hon. Bryce: White House liaison with Congress - 1958 - 221

Hartuni: wife of Sukarno (Indonesia) - she headed delegation to Cambodia and Peking (1962), 288-289

Hayward, VADM John T.: organizes the navy's A-bomb squadrons, 155, 158-159, 161

Hilger, Jack: Executive Officer to Gen. Doolittle, 32-37

Hoover, ADM John: Skipper of the USS LEXINGTON, 25

Hopwood, Adm. Herbert G.: CincPacFlt, 1959, 244

USS HORNET: Army flyers put aboard carrier for Tokyo raid,

37-40, 42

Hydraulic Fluid - non-flammable: developed at the N.R.L., 126-127

Industrial College of the Armed Forces (ICAF): 172-177

Japan: Japanese participation in Joint Naval Operations, 260-261; CincPac planners had cognizance over all planning involving Japan, 278-279; first stop on tour with Gen. Maxwell Taylor in 1962, 282-283

Kamikaze attacks: on TICONDEROGA at Ulithi, 86-87; latter day kamikaze attacks, 98-99

Keleher, RADM T. J.: influence on the career of Adm. Miller, 14-15

Kennedy, The Hon, John F.: 252

Kwajalein: base of operations against Eniwetok, 73-74

Kyoto: U. S. airmen prohibited from bombing, 90

Lacson - Mayor of Manila: 196

Laos: President Kennedy sends TF of Fleet and Marines to Indochinese waters to support diplomatic efforts to save Laos from communists, 301-302

USS LEXINGTON: Fighting Squadron #3 of the SARATOGA transfers to the LEXINGTON, 24-25

USS LEYTE: Miller becomes Executive Officer, 162-163; tour of duty with 6th Fleet, 163-164; visits to various ports, 164-169

Livingood, Alaska: 10

MAAG - Indonesia: Miller makes a survey of living conditions, 294-295

Magsaysay, Ramón: President of the Philippines, 1956, 205-206

Massive Retaliation - Doctrine: 181-183

McCain, Adm. John S.: In 1957 served as Director of the Progress Analysis Group (Op 09 dog) in CNO, 210-211; goes to sea as C.O. of the USS ALBANY, 215; Miller takes over, 216; his presentation of the message on seapower, 217; incident involving statement on Russian missile capability, 229-230

McNichol, RADM Alan (Australian): placed in command SEATO Exercise SEA DEVIL (1962) by CincPac, 262-267

Meade, Dr. Grant: Professor at Old Dominion College, Norfolk - helped with preparation of the Public Information Manual for the Atlantic Fleet, 143-144

HMAS MELBOURNE: flagship of Adm. McNichol for the SEATO Exercise (1962), 264; final critique held on board, 266

Miller, RADM George: helped the efforts of the Progress Analysis Group, 223

Miller, RADM Henry L.: data on early life, 1-7; Naval Academy days, 6 - 13; exposure to Naval Aviation, 13-15; marraige, 24-25; flag rank, (1945), 245

Miller, Wm. and his wife, Luree: brother of Adm. Miller - USIA in Dacca, Pakistan (1962) - incident involving

Luree and the change of command in Hong Kong, 272-273

Mitscher, Adm. Marc A.: skipper of the USS HORNET, 38-39; gives Miller permission to remain on USS PRINCETON for Palau operation, 75

Murder board: a dry run on prepared testimony before a Congressional Committee, 220

Nasution - Indonesian General: Chairman of the Indonesian JCS (1962), 292; U. S. State Department reps wanted to depose him, 293

National Science Foundation: Congress establishes and Dr. Allan Waterman of ONR becomes first head, 129

Nauru: planes from CV PRINCETON make attack on island installations, 65

Naval Air Bases; Philippines: Miller named Commander (Sept. 1955), 196

Naval Aviation: 14-15; training at Pensacola, 16-19

Naval Aviators and Submariners: Characteristics, 255

Naval Ordnance Test Station - Inyokern: 127-128

Navy Oil Reserves - Alaska: 109-111

Navy Plane Types (1939): Grumman Biplane, Brewster F-2A-1 and 2; Grumman F-4F-4, F-6F, and the Vought F-4U, 27-28

Navy - Public Relations: 141-42; first Public Information Manual for the Atlantic Fleet, 143-146; need for naval officers able to present the navy's point of view, 148-150

Night Flying - training in: 19-21

Nol, Gen. Lon: Cambodian General — Adm. Felt sends him message, 286-287, 289-90

Nolting, The Hon. Frederick E., Jr.: U. S. Ambassador in Saigon (1962), 285

Oceanography: 128-129

Okinawa: 85-87; post WW II base constructed there, 190-191; SEATO Weapons Demonstration held there in 1959, 242

ONR (Office of Naval Research): 112; established in 1946 for basic research, 112-114; various scientists who served in ONR (late 1940's), 133-134

Parris Island Marine Corps Field: see also entry under Willow Grove; 57-58; trainers installed by Luis de Florez, 126-127

Pensacola: see Naval Aviation — also, 29; Miller returns as Instructor (1940), 29-30

Philippines: three principal bases there, 191

Point Barrow, Alaska: location of the Navy Arctic Research Lab, 110-111

Pomeroy-Hawaiian Construction Co.: 204-205

Prince Sihanouk: maintained good rapport with Brig. Gen. Tony Scherer, head of MAAG in Cambodia — but not with U. S. Ambassador, 280, 286-290

USS PRINCETON — CVL: fitting out, 58-59; in the Pacific, 59-60; first war mission — August 1943, 60; in the South Pacific with the LEXINGTON, 62; attack on Rabaul, 62-63;

Miller gets his first Japanese fighter, 64; attack on Japanese installations at Nauru, 65-66; comments on bombing techniques over Pacific Island fortifications, 66-67; air crew trains on Hawaii while PRINCETON repairs at Bremerton, 69-70; air strikes on the Marshall Islands, 72-73; battle for Eniwetok, 73-74; Mitscher gives permission to Miller to remain on board for operation against Palau, 75; lessons learned from various operations, 77-80, 82-83, 87-88

Progress Analysis Group (Op 09 dog): Miller becomes assistant director under (1957) Capt. John S. McCain, 210-231; one part of job - sell seapower, 210-211; operations and logistics section studied various aspects of Navy, 211 ff.; study of manpower, 212; presentations made with vugrafs, 214; in 1958 a new presentation of seapower, 215-216; why seapower program failed to get long-range results, 218-219; Adm. Burke assigns group task of appearing before Johnson sub-committee, 219-220; Group has representative sit in on Congressional hearings - then makes immediate summary for CNO, SEC NAV, etc., 221; opposition to efforts of Group within Navy, 223; sponsors movies on various subjects - actual filming of Lebanon landings, 225; efforts to build program of Navy League and Naval Reserve, 226-227; attitude of other military services to Op 09 dog, 228-229;

incident involving statement on Russian missile capabilities, 229-230

Public Information Officer - Cinc Atl Fleet (1948-50): Miller ordered to staff of Adm. Blandy, 134; weekly cruises for benefit of Congress established - to education Congressmen and other VIPs on subject of aircraft carriers, 135-136; seminars at the Type Commands, 136-137; selection of VIP's and media reps, 138; writing of Public Information Manual for the Atlantic Fleet, 143-146; contact with editors of weekly newspapers, 151-152, connection of program with recruitment, 153-154

Read, RADM Albert C. (Putty): Skipper of the USS SARATOGA, 22-23, 30

Rees, Dr. Mina: mathematician in ONR, 133-134

REGULUS I and II: 189-190

Revell, Dr. Roger: 128

Reynolds, RADM Max: Inventor of the PLAT system to photograph plane landings on CV's, 247-248

Riddle, LtCdr. Meredith C.: damage control expert, 97, 167

Romulo, General Carlos: Ambassador to the United States - 1955, 199-200

Saigon: Miller sets up Commissary-Px for U. S. Military in 1955, 200

Sangley Point Naval Station: Miller becomes CO, August 1955, 194 ff; importance of good relations with Mayor of

Manila and other local officials, 197-198; Filipino contracts for construction work, 204-205; entertaining the Papal Nuncio, 207-208

USS SARATOGA: Fighting Squadron #3 aboard, 18, 21, 23-24, 26

Sarit Thanarat - Thai Field Marshal: 290-291

SS SAVANNAH: Eisenhower gives approval for building the first nuclear-powered merchant ship, 184

Scherer, Brig. Gen. Tony: MAAG head in Cambodia (1962), 287

Seaplanes: their demise - comments; 246-247

SEATO: 192, 194; Joint group in Bangkok does the intial planning, 194, Joint Naval Operations, 260-261; Japanese participation, 261-262; Australian Admiral in command of operation based on the Philippines, 262

SecDef Conferences: at Pearl Harbor - July, 1962 and October 1962, 303-304

Spruance, ADM Raymond: 197, 199

Strategic Plans Division, Office of CNO: Miller assigned in 1953 - aids in developing a new look for the Eisenhower Administration, 179-181; NATO planning, 179; Far East planning, 185-186, 190-191; SEATO planning, 192-194

Stump, ADM Felix: Commander Naval Air Force, Atlantic Fleet (1948), 136; supported the Public Information program in the Atlantic Fleet, 136-137, 245

Sunico, Conching: Manila hostess, 235

Tarawa: 65; bombing of targets, 68; difficulties of landing

force, 68-69

Taylor, General Maxwell: makes a tour of Far East (1962) before taking over as Chairman of the JCS, 282 ff; takes Miller with him, 282 ff; Japan, 282-283; Korea, 283; Taiwan, 283-284; Okinawa, 284; Hong Kong, 284-285; Saigon, 285-286; Cambodia, 286-290; Thailand, 290-292; Indonesia, 292-296; Taylor as a travelling companion, 297

USS TEXAS - BB: Miller's first tour of duty (1934), p. 13-14, 16

THACH, ADM John S. Commander ASWPac - throws party at Ford Island, 268-269; Miller tells a tall tale to Mrs. Thach, 269-271

Thanon Kittikachorn - Thai General and Premier, 1957: 242-243, 290

Tibbitts, RADM Joe: relief of Miller in Command of CarDiv 15, 271-272

Tokyo Raid - 1942: see entries under Doolittle Flyers

Truk: air attack by planes from PRINCETON, 76

Turner, Roscoe: suggests a Tokyo raid to Jimmy Doolittle, 44

Twitchell, Captain: Supply Corps officer in Op 09 dog who worked with Miller in operations and logistics planning and projections, 213-214

Umiat, Alaska: navy oil deposits in this area, 108

Vagnozzi, Cardinal: Papal Nuncio in the Philippines, 1956 207-208

HMS VICTORIOUS: target of the last kamikaze attack as WW II ended, 99; comments on effectiveness of the British carrier task group operating with the U. S. Fleet, 99-100

Viet Nam: Plans for Viet Nam are the cognizance of Assistant Chief of Staff for Plans, CincPac, 279-280; 285-286

Wagner, Capt. Edwin Otto: head of air branch, ONR - 1946, 129; 132-133

War Techniques - Atlantic vs Pacific: 79-80

Waterman, Dr. Allan: Instrumental in getting Congress to set up the National Science Foundation, 129

Willow Grove training: Miller ordered to commission a fighting squadron - destined for USS PRINCETON, 52; 55-56; transfer to Marine Corps Field at Parris Island, 56-57; Luis de Florez helps with trainers, 126-127

Wright, Adm. Jerauld: 104-105

In Reply Refer
to No.

CV8/A16-3

Serial 0015

U.S.S. HORNET (CV-8)

SECRET
DECLASSIFIED

April 28, 1942

OF10/Ld

Care of Postmaster,
New York, New York.
San Francisco,
California.

From: Commanding Officer.
To :   Commander-in-Chief, U.S. Pacific Fleet.
Via :   Commander Carriers, Pacific Fleet.

Subject: Report of Action, April 18, 1942, with notable events prior and subsequent thereto.

Reference: (a) U.S. Navy Regulations, 1920, Article 712.

1. In compliance with reference (a), the following report of action is submitted:

(a) On 1 April, 1942, while HORNET was moored at the U.S. Naval Air Station, Alameda pier, sixteen Army B-25 bombers were hoisted to the flight deck and there parked. Under the command of Lieut. Colonel James H. Doolittle, U.S. Army, the B-25 Detachment consisted of seventy officers and one hundred thirty enlisted men. Lieutenant H. L. Miller, U.S. Navy, attached to the detachment as carrier take-off instructor also reported aboard for temporary duty, intending to return to Alameda after a demonstration take-off for the benefit of doubting Army pilots. The idea was abandoned when all planes were spotted for take-off and it was found that sixteen bombers could be comfortably accommodated, leaving a take-off run of 467 feet for the first plane. The advantage of having an extra plane for attack outweighed the desirability of demonstrating a proper take-off.

(b) At 1000, April 2, 1942, Task Force Eighteen, consisting of HORNET, NASHVILLE, VINCENNES, CIMARRON and Desdiv 22, stood out of San Francisco in a fog which reduced visibility to about 1000 yards. Once clear of the swept channel a northwesterly course was set. Air coverage was provided by Commander Western Sea Frontier until late afternoon. Navy blimp L-6 delivered two boxes of navigator's domes for the B-25s. Vessels of the Task Force were notified

CV8/A16-3
Serial 0015
DECLASSIFIED
OF10/Ld

April 28, 1942

Subject: Report of Action, April 18, 1942, with notable events prior and subsequent thereto.

---

of the mission by semaphore message late in the afternoon, and the crew of this vessel were informed by loudspeaker. Cheers from every section of the ship greeted the announcement and morale reached a new high, there to remain until after the attack was launched and the ship well clear of combat areas.

(c) On 6 April a strange type of numeral code was heard on 3095 kcs, strong signal (type of code: 69457 R 73296 R 47261 R). Japanese broadcast stations were continually monitored in order to establish program continuity. Any departure from their usual arrangement while HORNET was in the combat zone could have been construed as a warning of danger.

(d) Weather conditions were generally bad throughout the voyage. Heavy seas and high winds, coupled with rain and squalls, reduced the danger of being sighted but prevented cruiser aircraft from conducting flight operations. At times speed of the force was reduced to prevent structural damage to the CIMARRON. Destroyers fueled on 8 April.

(e) On April 9 instructions were received to delay rendezvous with Task Force 16 until 13 April. Reversed course and slowed to comply. Attempted to fuel HORNET from CIMARRON but had to defer the operation because of heavy seas. CIMARRON lost two men overboard in the attempt; one was recovered by life ring and heaving line, the other by MEREDITH. A man previously lost overboard from VINCENNES was also recovered by MEREDITH in a prompt and efficient manner. On 10 April CIMARRON fueled both cruisers. On 11 April set course 255° true for rendezvous with Task Force 16. On 12 April fueled HORNET and topped off cruisers and destroyers. CIMARRON efficiently fueled two destroyers simultaneously under adverse weather conditions. At 1630 LCT 12 April, radar transmissions were detected from 230°, distant 130 miles. Contact was made with Task Force 16 at daylight 13 April. From 2 April until junction with Task Force 16 no contacts of any kind were made.

(f) Various minor difficulties were experienced with the B-25s from departure until launching. Generator failures, spark plug changes, leaky gas tanks, brake trouble, and engine trouble culminated in the removal of one engine to the HORNET shops where it was repaired, then reinstalled. Planes could not be spotted for take-off until after final fueling because their wings overhung the ship's side. The high winds encountered

- 2 -

CV8/A16-3
Serial. 0015
SECRET

OF10/Ld

April 28, 1942

Subject: Report of Action, April 18, 1942, with notable events prior and subsequent thereto.

---

caused vibrations in all control surfaces. Constant surveillance and rigid inspections were required to make certain the planes were properly secured to the flight deck.

(g)   B-25s were spotted for take-off on 16 April. The last plane hung far out over the stern ramp in a precarious position. The leading plane had 467 feet of clear deck for take-off.

(h)   On 18 April at 0800 orders were received to launch aircraft. Army crews, who had expected to take-off late in the afternoon, had to be rounded up and last minute instructions. Engines were warmed up, HORNET turned into the wind and at 0825 the first plane, Lieut. Colonel Doolittle, USA, pilot, left the deck.

(i)   With only one exception, take-offs were dangerous and improperly executed. Apparently, full back stabilizer was used by the first few pilots. As each plane neared the bow, with more than required speed, the pilot would pull up and climb in a dangerous near-stall, struggle wildly to nose down, then fight the controls for several miles trying to gain real flying speed and more than a hundred feet altitude. Lieutenant Miller, USN, held up a blackboard of final instructions for the pilots, but few obeyed. That the take-off could be made easily when properly executed was shown when a B-25 made a straight run down the deck, lifted gently in an easy climb and gained altitude with no trouble.

(j)   Plane handling on the flight deck was expeditious and well done. One plane handler lost an arm by backing into a B-25 propeller. A high wind of over forty knots and heavy swells caused HORNET to pitch violently, occasionally taking green seas over the bow and wetting the flight deck. The over-all time for launching sixteen bombers was 59 minutes. Average interval, 3.9 minutes.

- 3 -

CV8/A16-3
Serial 0015
DECLASSIFIED / SECRET

OF10/LA

April 28, 1942

Subject: Report of Action, April 18, 1942, with notable events prior and subsequent thereto.

(k) From April 13 to April 16, little of note occurred; weather continued to be heavy and squally, with generally poor visibility, which of course contributed to the success of the mission. ENTERPRISE maintained air patrol. Steaming on westerly courses.

(l) On April 17 all heavy ships were topped off and oilers and destroyers were detached. After fueling, cruisers and carriers continued their westerly advance at various high speeds (20 - 25 knots). 2000 position April 17: Lat:36°-33'N; Long. 157°-54'E. At 0310 April 18 made radar contact on unknown object, distance 3100 yards abeam. At 0313 course was changed by TBS to 350° T. At 0411 the ship was called to General Quarters and course was again changed to west. At 0507 course was changed into wind for launching of ENTERPRISE planes. At 0522 changed course to 270° T. At 0633 changed course to 220° T. At 0738 sighted enemy patrol craft of about 150 tons bearing 220°, distance 20,000 yards. At 0748 changed course to 270° T. At 0755 NASHVILLE opened fire on patrol vessel which was also bombed and strafed by ENTERPRISE planes. The vessel was still afloat when out of sight astern; NASHVILLE remained behind to destroy it. 0800 Position, April 18: Lat. 35°-26' N.; Long. 153°-27'E. At 0800 received orders from Comtaskfor 16 to launch bombers. At 0803 changed course into wind and prepared to launch; steaming at 22 knots, course 310° T. Crews manning planes and numerous lashings being removed from planes consumed several minutes. At 0825 launched first B-25 (Lieut. Colonel Doolittle pilot). Second plane launched 7 minutes later. Launchings have been previously discussed. Last bomber launched at 0920, after which HORNET reversed course to 090° T. and joined disposition. At 1100 word was received that enemy aircraft contact had been made by Japanese at 0830 (-10 time) in our approximate position at that time. At 1107 NASHVILLE rejoined. HORNET aircraft being made ready for launching. At 1115 launched 8 VF. At 1410 small enemy craft sighted 15,000 yards on port beam. NASHVILLE proceeded and destroyed this vessel. At 1425 an ENTERPRISE VSB crashed dead ahead of this ship while flight operations were being conducted. NASHVILLE recovered plane personnel. At 1445 Japanese language and English language broadcast announced the raid on Japan. No enemy aircraft sighted at any time. General Quarters stations were manned throughout the day.

- 4 -

CV8/A16-3
Serial 0015
DECLASSIFIED

OF10/Ld

April 28, 1942

Subject: Report of Action, April 18, 1942, with notable events prior and subsequent thereto.

    (m) The remainder of return trip was uneventful except for the loss of one VSB - both occupants were seen to sink - one with the plane and one unconscious alongside the plane. Entered Pearl Harbor morning April 25.

    2. The Commanding Officer desires to state that the morale of the crew was exceptionally fine. All officers and men performed their duties in a completely satisfactory manner. No individual was outstanding or deserving of special commendation, and there is no reason for censure. Morale was somewhat lowered after danger of enemy air attack had diminished; a majority of the officers and men were quite surprised that no further action against enemy bases was contemplated, and were obviously disappointed. It is believed that attacks should be made as frequently as possible on raiding missions to keep morale and "action exhilaration" in a high state.

    3. Submarines used in conjunction with such an attack would be highly valuable. They could cover the retreat of the attacking force and could possibly eliminate the patrol vessels in the track of the attacking force, permitting the latter to reach a more favorable launching point without being discovered.

                                                    M. A. MITSCHER.

A16-3

UNITED STATES PACIFIC FLEET
FLAGSHIP OF COMMANDER CARRIERS

Serial 0024

Pearl Harbor, T. H.,
29 APR 1942

DECLASSIFIED

S-E-C-R-E-T

1st endorsement to
CO HORNET Serial 0018
of April 28, 1942.

From: Commander Task Force SIXTEEN.
To: Commander-in-Chief, U. S. Pacific Fleet.

Subject: Report of Action, April 18, 1942, with notable events prior and subsequent thereto.

1. The Task Force Commander considers that the successful transportation and launching of the Army bombers under the continuous adverse weather conditions which prevailed reflects great credit to the Commanding Officer, HORNET, Lieutenant Colonel Doolittle, and the Army personnel involved.

2. The radar contact at 0210, April 18, distance 21,000 yards abeam, mentioned in paragraph 1(1) of the basic report, is at considerable variance with presumably the same contact as reported by ENTERPRISE radar. At the time the ENTERPRISE was one mile astern of the HORNET, course 265 true. At 0210 the ENTERPRISE radar reported contact on two surface vessels bearing 255 true distance 21,000 yards. The contact was plotted to a minimum range of 12,000 yards, and disappeared from the screen at 27,000 yards, bearing 321 true.

W. F. HALSEY

Copy to:
CO HORNET.

SECRET
Declassified

U.S. NAVAL AIR STATION
Pensacola, Florida.
May 7, 1942.

copy to
R.Adm. Switzer
Com Nav Phil.

From: Lieutenant Henry L. Miller, U.S. Navy
To: Captain D. B. Duncan, U.S. Navy.
Subject: Temporary additional duty assignment, report on.

1. On March 1, 1942, I was assigned to temporary additional duty to perform the following mission: To train Army pilots in carrier takeoff procedure employing B-25 aircraft at Eglin Field, Florida.

2. The narrative of events and operations subsequent to March 1st follows herewith: On March 4, 1942 I reported to the B-25 at Eglin Field for the above duty.

Prior to formulating take-off procedure a study of characteristics and performance of the B-25B airplane and engine was made. Initial take-off procedure was based on the assumption that a maximum number of planes would be taken on board the carrier and that maximum allowable distance for take-off would be three hundred fifty (350) feet in a forty (40) knot wind with the plane loaded to 31,000 pounds, 2000 pounds over designed maximum load. A field was set aside for the exclusive use of the B-25 detachment. Runways were painted with a yellow stripe so that pilots could practice holding left wheel on the yellow line throughout the run. Flags were set at 250 feet, 400 feet, 450 feet, 500 feet, 550 feet, 600 feet, 650 feet and 700 feet.

On the first day with load of about 27,000 pounds, Captain Jones took the plane off at (50) miles per hour using the following procedure:

indicated air speed.

      Flaps - Full down 45°
      Stabilizer - 3/4 tail heavy.
      Feet on brakes - brakes held on.
      Co-pilot opened throttles to 44".
      Pilot released brakes simultaneously, eased back on yoke to get nose wheel light; then, as plane gathered speed, the pilot kept easing back on yoke until the tail skag was about two (2) feet off the runway, at which point he held it until the plane flew off.

      Immediately after take-off, the pilot pushed the nose over and rolled the stabilizer forward. He had to keep both hands on the yoke and fly the plane. The co-pilot worked the landing gear, throttles, and engine revolutions, after which the pilot bled the flaps up gradually.

The distance was not measured on this run.

(1)

Declassified

SECRET.

May 7, 1942.

Subject: Temp. Add. duty report, Lt. H. L. Miller

The above procedure was what was finally decided upon after experimenting with different flap settings, stabilizer settings and power settings.

To obtain the data which is recorded below, one man took stop watch time for 250' and time of take-off; one man measured distance of take-off; one man, myself, stood behind the pilot and took the airspeed on take-off. I also watched the pilot's technique so that constructive criticism could be given. Captain Jones and 2nd Lieut. Gray acted as instructors in showing the pilots exactly what to do. From the beginning, it was necessary to make the pilots constantly check the ball in the center and to insist on smooth flying throughout the takeoff:

Preliminary Training.

This was given merely for all pilots to get the correct procedure in mind. Also to obtain our best performance data. [Results are tabulated in Annex Afirm.]

Intermediate Training.

This training was given to ease the pilots into correct procedure with a greater load. [Results are tabulated in Annex Baker.]

Final Training.

This training was given to demonstrate to the pilots the procedure with the plane loaded for the mission assigned. [Results are tabulated in Annex Cast.] *On the last flight, last take-off (Lt Bates) we crashed. No one hurt. Plane did not burn. Reason Take-off was in a skid and emergency power not applied.*

On several occasions when only one or two planes were used, brakes heated up fast. A turn was made around the field with the landing gear down to remedy this situation.

The following details cut take-off distance considerably:

1. Nose wheel straight.
2. Release of brakes simultaneously.
3. Same amount of power on both engines: i.e. 44".
4. Getting nose wheel light initially.
5. Not dragging tail skag on the runway.
6. All pilots got considerable practice in takeoffs with wind as much as 90° to the runway. As each pilot progressed in take-off procedure, additional obstacles were placed in his way so that he would be able to take care of any

Declassified

SECRET.

May 7, 1942.

Subject: Temp. Add. Duty Report, Lt. H. L. Miller

---

situation which might arise on the "Big Day".

All pilots, with the exception of a few conservatives, caught on quickly. Doolittle, Gray and Jones were particularly outstanding. It was found that constant practice had to be given because pilots were prone to switch back to the conventional take-off.

Practice was given at Eglin Field, Florida, and at Willows, Calif., which is eighty-five (85) miles north of Sacramento, Calif.

Prior to going on board, lectures were given to officers and men on Carrier Deck Procedure, Safety Precautions, Naval Customs and Traditions, and Living Aboard Ship.

When the unit finally got aboard ship, it was found that with sixteen (16) planes, a take-off distance of four hundred sixty (460) feet was available. An extra plane was taken aboard, which was the sixteenth plane, for Lt. Joyce and myself to fly off on a demonstration run. However, when it was found that four hundred (460) feet were available, all sixteen (16) planes were taken on the trip.

Prior to the day of attack, all B-25-B's were dispersed along the deck.

On the day of attack the only change to the original take-off procedure was to keep the nose down (nose wheel still light) until the plane was past the island (stack and bridge); then, normal procedure was used. However, due to high wind across the deck, stabilizer was put in neutral after the first three (3) planes took off.

The first plane off (Doolittle) made a nice take-off. Second plane kept his nose in the up position too long and nearly stalled the plane. After the third plane took off pilots were shown via blackboard at the starting line to put the stabilizer in neutral. Succeeding take-offs were all good except one in which pilot did not have his flaps down. Either that or they worked up. He got away with it. Flaps on three (3) other planes were up, but ground crew caught it before take-off. Flight deck crew also straightened nose wheel before take-off.

Only casualty prior to take-off was a cracked nose glass in one plane caused by the rudder of another. Neither plane was held up. One sailor got an arm cut off by a propeller. It is believed that towing planes out of spot with tractor

Declassified

~~SECRET~~

Subject: Temp Add. Duty Report, Lt. H. L. Miller   May 7, 1942

would get them out with less risk to both planes and men when a forty (40) knot wind is blowing over the deck. It is

Take-offs were made under the most trying conditions. The ship was pitching badly. Fly One Officer released plane when ship was on down roll and between heavy pitches. There were intermittent rain squalls during the entire launching operation. Pilots held the left wheel on a white line which was painted on the deck. They did a mighty good job of it.

3. Recommendations for Future Operations with same type airplane:

1. Nose wheel pins, to keep nose wheel locked straight while plane is coming out of the spot aboard ship, should be left in place <u>until plane is out of spot</u>. [Pins were made for this purpose but were not used because the Army Engineer Officer ordered them taken out before we could stop it.]

2. A capable Engineer officer should be assigned to keep a constant check on the planes while aboard ship. The officer assigned for that duty on the ship should see that the planes are in all respects ready for flight operations. For the attack one plane (Capt. Jones) took off with a leaky bomb bay tank. He was given an additional fifty (50) gallons of gasoline in tin cans. Two planes (Lt. Lawson and Lt. Smith) took off with 24-volt generator out so that turret would have to be operated by battery. The right engine of one plane (Lt. Smith) was overhauled aboard ship. One plane (Lt. Watson) required a change of plugs on rear bank right engine just prior to take-off.

3. Spare batteries should be provided to be used while regular plane batteries are being charged. Spare generators should be taken along. Two (2) spare sets of plugs per engine should be provided. [One hundred (100) more gallons of gasoline per plane should be provided.]

4. A Finance Officer should be assigned to the detachment for regular payment of funds to the officers and men. This will maintain better security of the mission. Too many people wanted to know why the crews were supposed to be paid all over the country. The men were paid by the Navy aboard ship.

5. Greater secrecy should be maintained in the organization and administration for the assigned mission. [Too many civilian and Army personnel knew what was being done, or seemed to know. Too much loose talk was heard from time to time.] Overhaul and repair bases wanted to know too much.

Declassified

SECRET
Subject: Temp. Add. Duty report, Lt. H. L. Miller

May 7, 1942.

6. [More experienced Navigators should be assigned for such an exacting assignment.]

4. *Conclusions:*

a. 7. During the time aboard ship officers and men of both Services lived and worked together with commendable cooperation and unity of purpose. The Commanding Officer and personnel of the U.S.S. HORNET did everything possible to provide for the health and welfare of the combat crews and to insure the success of the mission. The Navy had the greatest respect and admiration for the Army combat crews who reciprocated this feeling. [However it is recommended that naval aircraft Carrier Pilots be assigned to future tasks of this nature.]

b. 8. Take-off procedure for forty (40) knots of wind down the deck:

    (a) Flaps full down - 45°.
    (b) Stabilizer in neutral.
    (c) Nose wheel straight.
    (d) Left wheel on white line.
    (e) Pilot hold brakes, then open throttle to 44". Co-pilot lock throttles in this position.
    (f) Pilot hold yoke to get nose wheel light on deck.
    (g) Pilot release brakes simultaneously and keep nose wheel light on deck until past the island. Then ease yoke back to get the nose up slowly until the tail skag is about two (2) feet off the deck. Hold this attitude until the plane flies off.
    (h) Immediately after take-off, pilot push nose down and adjust stabilizer. Co-pilot pull up landing gear, adjust throttles and engine revolutions, after which pilot bleeds up flaps. Pilot must fly the plane constantly while making take-off. Co-pilot handle throttles, etc.

[4. Note: Two or three sets of hoisting gear for B-25 airplane are on the HORNET. In addition, two sets are at the Sacramento Air Depot.]

[H. L. MILLER.]

c. 9. B-25B airplane, 31,000 lbs. can take off in 250' in a 40 kt. wind, using 44" M.P. On day of attack average run was about 350'. *Naturally every pilot was conservative.*

6. 10. [Another recommendation:] Planes should be out of check and overhaul two days before going aboard. Some of the planes on this mission got out of the Sacramento Air Depot on the day they were hoisted aboard; consequently a good test hop was impossible.

H. L. MILLER.

It was an exemplary performance by an outstanding group of American boys who gave their all to fight a war. At the hour of take-off, every officer and enlisted man aboard the Hornet would

Pilot	MP	Flap	Load	Wind	A.S.	Remarks	Time	Dist.
York	30" then 44"	35°	appx. 26,000#	cross 45° 20 mph	70 mph	Did not come back fast enough on yoke. Strong cross wind. 30" released brakes then slow getting up to 44".		492'
"	"	"	"	"	75 – 80	Hard to get nose up. Did not have stabilizer back far enough. Strong cross wind.		552'
Hilger	"	30°	"	"	79	Touched again after take-off. Slow getting up to 44".		550'
"	"	"	"	"	74 – 78	Let nose drop after take-off. Slow getting up to 44".		appx. 560'
Joyce	40" then 44"	"	4 men fwd, 1 man aft, 6 100# bombs De-Icers	1 mph	75	Too long on ground with nose wheel. Released at 40" while still easing throttle on to 44".		750'
Gray	44"	35°	appx. 26,000#	7 mph	78	Jerky. Pilot swerved on take-off and was slow catching it.		804'
"	"	"	"	6 mph	70	Pretty good.		610'
"	"	"	"	"	"	Had to catch a turn of nose wheel with brakes at start		545'
Beth	"	"	"	5 mph	"	Excellent take off		495'
"	"	"	"	3 mph	78	Seemed okay.		640'
"	"	"	"	"	70	Good.		636'
Hallmark	"	45°	"	"	"	Seemed to hold it on ground a hair too long.		600'
"	"	"	"	"	75	Pilot started slow but rapidly got the dope on this procedure. Poor start.		775'
"	"	"	"	"	"	Little slow getting nose up.		610'
"	"	"	"	"	70	Good procedure.		554'
McElroy	30" then 44"	35°	"	1 mph	80–85	Pilot had trouble easing up to 44" and keeping nose straight		990'
"	40" then 44"	"	"	"	74	Pilot had trouble easing up to 44" and flying plane at same time		800'
"	"	40°	"	"	70	Pilot had 45" left engine and 41" right Plane was cocked around on take-off.		500'
Watson	"	"	"	3 mph	80	After release of brakes, pilot let nose drop.		665'
"	40" then 44"	"	"	"	65	Held nose on ground too long. Pilot had trouble easing both throttles to 44" evenly.		602'

Subj: Temp. Add. Duty, Lt. W. [illegible] Nov 7, 1942

Results of Preliminary Training (cont'd)

Pilot	M.P.	Flap	Load	Wind	A.S.	Remarks	Dist.
Watson	44"	40°	appx 26,000#	3 mph	62 mph	Released brakes and yanked up nose too high at start.	570'
			Note: Pilots seemed to have a great deal of difficulty trying to fly the plane smoothly when they used 30% or 40", released brakes, then opened throttles to 44". Hence, it was decided to start out initially with 44" manifold pressure. Col. Doolittle agreed that this was sound procedure.					
Holstrom	44"	45°	appx 26,000#	1-2 mph or none	75 - 80	Pilot was practicing by himself at beginning. His distances were 940'-910'-944'. When given procedure he readily got it and distance was cut to 810'; then to 510'	810'
"	"	"	"	3 mph	75	Held nose down a little too long.	510'
Daniel	"	"	"	8 mph	"	Distances for take-off before instruction were 820'-931'-918'. This plane did not seem up to par. Pilot had a hard time gathering speed.	754'
"	"	"	"	"	"		552'
Joyce	"	"	"	11 mph	"	Did not get nose up soon enough or high enough.	560'
"	"	"	"	"	"	Did not get nose up soon enough.	550'
Farrow	"	"	"	none	75	Poor start. Nose wheel not straight. Touched twice.	690'
"	"	"	"	3 mph	"	Ran too far forward on nose, then yanked back.	663'
"	"	"	"	"	"	Tail wheel hit deck.	
Steward	"	"	"	"	"	Tail down too much but procedure improved. Am not including his data. He did not go with group.	600'
Hite	"	"	"	1-2 mph or none	74	Could not keep nose straight. Lost time and distance on takeoff.	678'
"	"	"	"	1-2 mph	70	Good procedure.	575'
Hirman	"	"	"	14 mph	70	Jerky. Tried to shove nose down too much.	445'
"	"	"	"	12 mph	65	Procedure Okay.	431'
"	"	"	"	"	75	Held on too long.	441'
"	"	"	"	13 mph	70	Tail was a hair too low.	430'
"	"	"	"	15 mph	75	Take off was made between gusts of wind.	450'
Smith	"	"	"	12 mph	70-	Tail off deck exact amount. Good procedure.	439'
"	"	"	"	13 mph	75	Could get nose up one second earlier.	
"	"	"	"	"	"	Excellent. This pilot has the news! Wind helps get weight off nose wheel.	365'
"	"	"	"	"	"	Excellent.	295'
"	"	"	"	12 mph	"	Excellent.	294'

- 2 -

Subj: Temp. Add. Duty Report, Lt.H.L.Miller

Pilot	M.P.	Flap	Load	Wind	A.S.	Remarks.	Dist.
Hoover	44"	45°	appx. 26,000#	14 mph 20°-30° cross	70- 75	Good Wind. Good procedure for first time up.	312'
"	"	"	"	"	"	Seemed good take-off. Wind died down during this period. Pilot stated he could not get power out of engine. Dragged tail skag on deck.	530'
"	"	"	"	15 mph 20°-30° crosswind	"	Dragged tail skag on deck.	470'
"	"	"	"	"	"	Seemed Okay.	440'
Bates	"	"	"	"	"	Good procedure	450'
"	"	"	"	"	"	Okay.	450'
"	"	"	"	"	"	Nose down too long.	480'
"	"	"	"	16 mph 20°-30° crosswind	"	Nose down too long.	530'
"	"	"	"	"	"	"	500'
Bower	"	"	"	12-15 mph	"	Got tail down too far. Dragged tail skag on runway.	470'
"	"	"	"	"	"	Same	470'
"	"	"	"	"	"	Nose down just a bit too long.	450'
"	"	"	"	"	"	Nose down too long, then yanked back.	430'
"	"	"	"	"	"	Nose down too long.	500'
"	"	"	"	"	"	Nose down too long, then yanked back, and dragged tail skag on runway.	430'
Lawson	"	"	"	"	"	Nose down too long.	460'
"	"	"	"	"	"	Nose down all way.	560'
"	"	"	"	"	"	Nose still down too long.	450'
"	"	"	"	"	"	Okay procedure.	410'

- 3 -

Subject: Temp. Add. Duty report, Lt. H. L. Miller   7 May 1942.

Results of INTERMEDIATE TRAINING.

Annex BAKER

Pilot	M.P.	Flap	Load	Wind	A.S.	Remarks	Dist.
Jones	44"	45°	6 100# bombs. 2 men aft, 4 fwd. Full gas	30° cross 7 mph	75 mph	Poor start. Plane got cocked around on take-off. Nose was held down a little too long. Plane left ground as soon as nose came up.	535'
"	"	"	same except 5 men fwd	60° cross 7 mph	"	Good start. Radio man on toilet seat. One man on high turret.	550'
"	"	"	"	"	78	Poor start. Nose wheel cocked around.	600'
"	"	"	4 500# bombs 2 men aft, 4 fwd, full gas	45° cross 9 mph	80	Nose would not come up. Poor start.	750'
"	"	"	Same, but 2 men by toilet	"	73	Easier getting nose up. Poor start and touched brakes once along run.	700'
Smith	"	"	4 500# bombs. 2 men aft, 5 fwd, full gas	60° cross 10 mph	75-80	Pilot stated it was harder to get speed up with this weight. Difficult to keep plane straight in cross wind.	700'
"	"	"	"	"	"	Same	700'
Farrow	"	"	Same except 4 men fwd	45° cross 9 mph	75	No ammunition. Farrow made about six landings previous to this. Data was not recorded: Lt. Miller was not there.	688'
"	"	"	4 500# bombs. 3 men aft, 5 fwd, gas full less 100	"	80	Pilot did not get his nose up in time. Farrow flies plane smoothly though. He seems to have the news.	705'
McElroy	20"	"	Same except 120 after release gal short	Slight cross 11 mph	75-80	Slow coming back on yoke. Could have got plane offsooner.	685'
"	"	lease down 45°	"	Slight cross 9 mph	75	Did not hold it off when he had nose in take off position.	720'
"	"	"	"	Slight cross 10 mph	74	Seemed like a pretty good take-off.	668'

Note: Full gas equals bomb bay plus wing tanks.

-1-

Results of INTERMEDIATE TRAINING (cont'd)

Pilot	M.P.	Flap	Load	Wind	A.S.	Remarks	Dist.
Gray	44"	20° then 45°	4-500# bombs 5 men fwd, 3 aft, Full gas less 120 gal	Slight cross 10 mph	80 mph	Gray and co-pilot Hinman said 45° flap at start was better. Co-pilot might push flap handle wrong way after start of run. Flaps got all way down at 450 ft.	618'
"	"	30°	"	Slight cross 12 mph	76	Wind seemed to be picking up. Pilot dragged tail skag on mat.	710'
Hinman	"	45°	Same except less 200 gal.	Slight cross 13 mph	75	Nose down too long.	650'

Note: Full gas equals bomb bay plus wing tanks.

It was found that all pilots readily caught on to heavier load take-offs, and because time was at a premium, final training with full load was begun.

Doolittle, Jones, Greening, York, Hilger and Gray made additional preliminary and intermediate test take-offs which were not recorded. All pilots made short take-offs from time to time just to keep in practice.

- 2 -

Subject: Temp. Add. Duty report, Lt. D. L. Miller.

Results of FINAL TRAINING

Annex CAST

Pilot	M.P.	Flap	Load	Wind	A.S.	Remarks	Stabilizer	T.O. Time	Dist.
Hoover	44"	35°	Full gas 5 men fwd 1 aft, 4 500# bombs 800# ammunition	14 mph	70 mph	Poor start. Pilot cocked plane tailheavy around. Lost time and distance.	tailheavy 3/4		750'
"	"	"		13 mph	"	Same	1/2		740'
"	"	45°		14 mph	65	Seemed like a good takeoff. 45° cross wind, gusty.	tailheavy full		720'
"	"	30°		"	72	Cocked plane around on takeoff this and next run.	same		660'
"	"	40°		"	68	Lost time and distance. Wind seemed lighter for this takeoff.	same		750'
"	"	35°		15 mph	75	Pilot said both of the runs felt tailheavy to him 60° crosswind.	same		700'
"	"	45°		14 mph	68	60° crosswind	same		750'
Daniel	"	35°	Same except 3 men fwd, 1 aft	90° cross 14 mph	78	Plane flew pilot all over mat due to crosswind of 90°	same		750
"	"	45°		90°cross 15 mph	65	Could have pulled back a little sooner.	same		680'
Watson	"	35°	Same except 2 aft	90°cross 17 mph	60	Dragged tail skag on deck for 30°	same		750'
"	"	45°		90°cross 14 mph	55	Just touched tail skag lightly once	same		660'
Greening	"	"	Full gas 3 men fwd, 1 320# ballast. 4 500# bombs	7 mph appx.	80	Held nose down much too long. Did not haul yoke back enough.		14 sec.	990'
"	"	"		8 mph	75-76	Got yoke back but took a running start. Said brakes wouldn't hold.		13 sec.	800'
"	"	"		9 mph	74	Better. Put stab. back farther to 3/4ths.		14 sec.	830'
Hinman	"	"		11 mph	75-80	Good start. Nose up too much. Dragged tail on runway.		14 sec.	750'
"	"	"		"	74	Good start. Was off in 650' but did not hold it.		12½ sec.	720' MPH 250'
Holstrom	"	"	Same except 4 men fwd	9 mph	70	Held nose up then released. Good start, rough procedure.		12½ sec.	680' 55mph
"	"	"		11 mph	68	Good start. Handled nicely.		10½ sec.	640' 55
Beth	"	"	same	"	75	Did not get nose up quite soon enough. Rough technique.		12½ sec.	700' 5
"	"	"	same	"	69	Good start, good procedure. Perfect take-off.		11½ sec.	630' 50
Hite	"	"	Same	"	70	Good start, good takeoff.		11½ sec	680' 50
"	"	"	"	12 mph	74	Good start. Tail down too much.		11 sec	635' 52

Note: Full gas equals bomb bay and wing tanks.

Pilot	M.P.	Flap	Load	Wind	A.S.	Remarks	ToO.Time	Dist
Gray	44"	45°	Full gas 4-500# bombs.	15°-20° cross	74 mph	Dragged tail skag. Poor start	17 sec.	785'
Bower	"	"	"	"	"	Poor start. Dragged tail skag	15	770'
"	"	"	"	8-10 mph wind & rain	80	Poor start. Jerky. Touch tail skag	16	810'
Lawson	"	"	4 men forward 1300# ballast		74	Jerky. Poor start. Pulled and pushed yoke.	14	715'
"	"	"	"		"	Cross wind. Left wheel off at 575'. Jerky coming back onyoke.	15	740'
"	"	"	"		"	Won't get nose up. Nose wheel cocked on take-off	15	740'
Bates	"	"	"		"	Won't get nose up.	13	640'
"	"	"	"		75	Won't get nose up. Could have been off in 500'	12	600'
Smith	"	"	"		76	Nose down a hair too long	12½	640
"	"	"	"		73	Nose down too long. Yanked it off, dragged tail skag and wheels were off 150' before tail	14	740'
"	"	"	"		75	Got lots of speed then yanked it off, dragged tail skag and lost speed	15	750'
Hallmark	"	"	"		77	Did not seem to gain speed on this run even tho nose was down. Nose cocked around for take-off.	14½	750'
"	"	"	"		74	Lots of rain. Wind died down, did not get nose up enough for takeoff. Nose cocked around	14	700'
Hirman	"	"	Full gas 4-500# bombs	None	70	Lost time and distance on straightening out after release of brakes. Shows what an initial wind will do to help straighten out.		995
"	"	"	3 men fwd 750# ballast	cross 30° 708 mph	70	Same. And tail not down.dragged last 100'		900
"	"	"	Same except 4 men fwd	cross 20° 10 mph	70	Same. And tail okay 12'		850
Doolittle	"	"	"		75	Brakes slipped slightly. Lost time and distance getting straight. Left engine came back to 42". Nose up then pushed down.		950'
"	45"	"	"		"	Better procedure, but can still get tail down a little more.Nose was late coming up.		850'
"	46"	"	"		"	Bad start. Jerky procedure.		870'
"	45"	"	"		"	Nose up and down twice on takeoff.		810'
"	"	"	"		"	Bad start. Nose wheel cocked. Used brakes to staighten out		850'
"	"	"	"		78	Bad start.		900'

Subject: Temp. Add. Duty Report, Lt. H. L. Miller, May 7, 1942

Results of FINAL TRAINING (cont'd)

Annex CAST

Pilot	M.P.	Flap	Load	Wind	A.S.	Remarks	Dist.
Gray	44"	45°	4 500# bombs, 800# ballast. 5 men fwd. full gas	45° cross 9 mph	75 mph	Had trouble holding brakes. Pilot said nose would not come up without stabilizer back at least 3/4ths.	710'
"	"	"			80	Pilot did not have trouble keeping left wheel on yellow line, which was painted on runway. Tail skag hit on runway last 100'.	750'
"	"	"			70	Nose cocked around on take-off. Good procedure but pilot eased nose up too fast. Wind died down about 5 mph for this run.	710'
Holstrom	"	"		70° cross 10 mph	74	Good procedure. A little trouble keeping straight due to crosswind and nose wheel cocked.	850'
"	"	"		20° cross 10mph	78	Better run, but pilot lost distance by hitting tail on deck.	750'
Joyce	"	"		12 mph	80	Did not get the nose up soon enough. Cool air, therefore much better prop efficiency and lift.	750'
"	"	"		"	74	Same remarks as above.	685'
Smith	"	"		"	74	Did not get nose up soon enough. Poor start.	816'
"	"	"		10° cross 8 mph	78	Did not get nose up soon enough.	770'
"	"	"		2-3 mph	65	Hit tail on runway but used better procedure. Runway very wet. No tendency of tires to slip on runway.	750'
Daniel	"	"		15° cross 12 mph	70	Could not get nose soon enough due to loading of plane.	720
"	"	"			75	Did not get nose up soon enough. Veered off yellow line. Poor start. Lots of rain.	820'
"	"	"		45° cross 8 mph	65	Kept plane in straight line. Touched wheels twice after take-off.	700'

Pilot	M.P.	Flap	Load	Wind	A.S.	Remarks	Air Temp.	Dist.
Gray	44"	45°	Full gas plus crawlway tank. 4 men fwd, 1 man aft.	20° across 5 mph	76 mph	Good start. Tail just right. Got plane off then settled back.	60° F	950'
"	"	"	4 500# bombs.		"	Good start. Good procedure.		850'
Bates	"	"	900# ballast aft.	7 mph	75–80 mph	Jerky procedure. Good start. Still jerky procedure but much better. Pilot has improved greatly on technique.	63°	800'
"	"	"	100# ballast fwd.	5 mph				850
"						Good procedure. Plane crashed after takeoff due to pilot taking off in a skid with right wind down, and holding nose up too long after takeoff. No casualties.		850

Note: It was found that DeIcers made no appreciable difference in takeoff. Additional takeoffs were made at Willows, Calif. with light load for several of the pilots, so that their procedure would be refreshed.

Note: The whole-hearted cooperation of all pilots contributed materially to the ease with which the procedure was learned.

- 4 -

STORY OF "FIGHTING TWENTY-THREE"

Fighting Squadron TWENTY-THREE (VF-23) was commissioned on November 16, 1942, at what was then the Naval Reserve Aviation Base, Willow Grove, Pa. The Commanding Officer was Lieutenant Henry L. Miller, USN, and the Executive Officer was Lieutenant Harold N. Funk, USN.

It was to be a twelve (12) plane fighter squadron with a complement of twenty (20) pilots, and three (3) A-V(S) officers. The initial planes which were assigned to the squadron were F4F-4's. The squadron was part of Air Group TWENTY THREE, with its ultimate destination, CVL-23, the U.S.S. PRINCETON, a converted 10,000 ton cruiser, then under construction at the New York Shipbuilding Company, Camden, New Jersey. The Commanding Officer of the Air Group, at the time, was Lieut. Comdr. George B. Chafee, a TBF pilot.

The original complement, as finally completed in December 1942, consisted of the following officers:

- Lieut. Henry L. Miller
- Lieut. Harold N. Funk
- Lieut. Samuel J. R. Froelick
- Lieut. Claude C. Schmidt
- Lieut. Charles M. Kenyon, A-V(S)
- Lt(jg) Richard J. Hefler, A-V(S)
- Lt(jg) James R.O. Rickard, A-V(S)
- Lt(jg) James A. Smith, III
- Lt(jg) Leon W. Haynes
- Ens. Oscar H. Cantrell
- Ens. Albert W. Robbins
- Ens. Richard P. Selman
- Ens. Robert Jefferson Young
- Ens. John J. Redmon
- Ens. Leslie H. Kerr
- Ens. Walter John Kirschke
- Ens. Joe M. Hebb
- Ens. James W. Syme
- Ens. Jack D. Madison
- Ens. Jack M. Aboll
- Ens. Robert S. Tyner
- Ens. David H. Olin
- Ens. William G. Buckelew

The enlisted personnel of the squadron totalled eighty-seven men; the leading chief was William Carlin, ACMM, a veteran of the United States Navy of almost continuous standing since the First World War.

The facilities at Willow Grove were all incomplete; the only building which was complete was the Officers Quarters. The rooms were very comfortable with each officer occupying a room. Along with the condition of the grounds, the terrible weather prevented the commencement of any training program, so that operations were held to a minimum.

War Diary of Fighting Twenty-Three

November 16, 1942. Lieut. Henry L. Miller, USN, assumed command and posted the watch. Officers aboard. Lieut. Harold N. Funk, USN, Executive Officer.

November 17 - Routine inspection of squadron area.

November 18 - Routine inspection of squadron area.

November 19 - Ens. Leslie H. Kerr reported for duty.
November 20-22 - No activity.
November 23 - Ens. Albert W. Robbins reported for duty.
November 24 - No activity.
November 25 - Ens. Joe M. Hebb and Ens. Jack D. Madison reported for duty.

- 1 -

CONFIDENTIAL

November 26 - Lt(jg) Leon W. Haynes, and Ens. Robert J. Young reported for duty.
November 27 - Ens. Robert S. Tyner and Ens. James W. Syme reported for duty.
   Operations during this period of time merely consisted of flying around the area for purposes of familiarization. This was done in an SNJ.
November 28 - Ens. David H. Olin reported for duty.
November 29-30 - There was no activity to speak of; occasional flights in the SNJ, and getting the squadron personnel in order were the main jobs.
December 1 - Lt(jg) James A. Smith reported for duty.
December 2 - Lt. Samuel J. R. Froelick reported for duty.
December 3-6 - There were occasional flights when the weather permitted; otherwise activity was held to a minimum.
December 7 - Ens. John J. Redmon reported for duty.
December 8-16 inc. - the temperature was down to 20° F. Ceiling was zero, and the area surrounding the field was also closed in.
December 17 - Lieut. Miller and Lieut. Funk returned from Norfolk with two new F4F-4's. We had our first fighter planes; now the question was, will it ever clear up so as to be able to fly them.
December 18 - Lieut. Miller departed for Parris Island, Marine Air Station, S.C. He had heard about a good training base there, and no one was using it.
December 19 - Lieut. Claude C. Schmidt reported for duty.
December 20 - Temperature was down to 10° F.
December 21 - Lieut. Miller returned from Parris Island. He accidentally had run into a friend was was Commanding Officer of the Air Station down there, so the chances of moving the squadron down began to brighten up.
December 22 - Ensign Walter J. Kirschke reported for duty.
December 23 - It was getting warmer, temperature was up to 32° F.; however everything was closed in around the field.
December 24 - Ensign Richard P. Sulman and Ens. Oscar H. Cantrell reported for duty
December 25 - A Merry Christmas to ALL.
December 26 - Day after Christmas - - what can you expect? Right!
December 27 - Rain, fog and smoke. There was a pilots' conference, and it was understood we would move to Parris Island in a few days.
December 28 - Lieut. Charles M. Kenyon and Lt(jg) James R.O. Rickard reported for duty.
December 29 - Lt(jg) Richard J. Hefler and Ens. Jack M. Abell reported for duty.
December 30 - There was the usual rain and fog, with a ceiling of 100 feet.
December 31 - The squadron received two more F4F-4's from Norfolk. Ensigns Webb and Kerr flew them in.

January 1, 1943 - A HAPPY NEW YEAR TO ALL.

January 2 - Lieut. Pincetich flew Lt(jg) Smith and Ensigns Syme and Kirschke to Norfolk for the purpose of picking up new F4F-4's for the squadron.
January 3 - Ens. Syme and Young left Norfolk for Willow Grove. Ens. Young was our Navigation Officer, but for some reason or other, Syme convinced Young that he (Syme) could fly that course blindfolded - (he really knew the way). Well, today the squadron had its first forced landing case. Syme was lost, so landed in a cornfield in Virginia, and was surrounded by friendly natives. Young had gone a little farther and made an airfield in Charlotteville, Va.
   Also on this eventful day, Lt(jg) Hefler, who was indoctrinated as an Intelligence Officer, was ordered to proceed to Parris Island with the colored boys, and establish a BOQ. His experience in such matters was nil, but he left in spite of it all.
January 4 - Lieut. Funk departed for Charlotteville to rescue our lost Ensigns.
January 5 - Ensigns Young and Syme returned home in the SNJ-4; and Lt(jg) Haynes departed for Parris Island.
January 6 - 1000 - all of the squadron planes departed for Parris Island, arriving at 1700.
January 7 - Flight operations commenced. The facilities were ideal, the weather was exceptional for flying, and there were no other squadrons present.
   So the long grind commenced. Hefler turned out to be an exceptional BOQ manager, with the able assistance of Lewis, our first class officers cook, so that when we all arrived, each had his private room, and a dinner-de-luxe.
January 8 - Friday - We must have brought the rain with us, since due to the weather flight operations were held up; however, the vans with our material arrived so all hands were kept busy.

CONFIDENTIAL

January 9 - Saturday - Our first Saturday at the Marine Base. The rain continued, so we were all busy unpacking and prodding Hefler to get us an "in" to the nurses' quarters. It seems that he met one of the nurses on the train, and had already fixed himself up for dates. The procedure was to attend the movie, then go to the officers' club, so we were informed. As to how the squadron would fit into the picture remained to be seen.

January 10-31 inclusive - Ground school was established, much to the disgust of all pilots, with a long comprehensive schedule worked out in detail to acquaint our boys with all types of ships, aircraft and fighter direction procedure. Kenyon was picking up the fine points of making out a schedule and realizing the problems of getting a flight off on time.

Occasional rains would periodically hold up operations. Whereupon the enlisted personnel would deluge the personnel office with requests for leave to visit their aged parents, or an ailing cousin.

Lieut. Curtis, the signal officer on the PRINCETON, arrived in order to conduct field carrier landing practice. The first of a series of trips to Norfolk to pick up parts was made by Ensign Madison. The proposed overnight trip turned out to be a lengthy one, due to the flying conditions in the North. Ensign Abell ran into a little difficulty in a soft-ball game, and sprained his ankle, so he hobbled around the office for a week.

Lieut. John J. Becker, who was to be in charge of the V-4 Division aboard the PRINCETON arrived; he was to see that all planes were always ready to fly, no matter how many crack-ups they had.

February - found the squadron well established at Parris Island. The boys had become well acquainted with the various marine regulations and marines, - and the nurses. The squadron had a Captain's Inspection on the sixth; all hands were at their best, so that the Captain was well pleased.

The operations schedule was running true to form, gunnery runs were being conducted every day, and carrier landings on returning to the field. The USS PRINCETON was to be commissioned on the 25th; most of the boys wanted to see the ceremony, - or was it Philadelphia? - However only the Captain and Lieut. Kenyon went up; since operations had to continue at Page Field.

March - turned out to be a tragic month for the squadron. On the 15th, Ensigns Robbins and Selman were killed when the SNJ they were flying crashed at Hilton Head Island, south of Page Field. A week later, on the 23rd, Ensign Young was killed when his F4F-4 landed on the water, turned over, and trapped him in the cockpit.

On the first part of the month all the pilots proceeded to Norfolk and qualified on carrier landings, then went on to Philadelphia to qualify for catapult shots, and take in the City.

On March 1st, Lieut. Miller was promoted to Lieutenant Commander. Also the story broke about Doolittle's bombing of Tokyo, i.e., the means used; whereupon Lieut. Comdr. Miller gave us a detailed story, since he had trained the pilots on carrier takeoffs, and went on the HORNET with them on their historical trip.

Later in the month, the Charleston radar station had eight of our planes placed on an alert status, since unidentified planes were reported off the Coast.

April - The Air Group Commander, Lieut. Comdr. George B. Chafee received orders to report as Air Officer on the USS CABOT. Lieut. Comdr. Henry L. Miller, as senior officer present, became the Air Group Commander.

Night flying and night carrier landings were being held. However, the planes kept the marines awake, and frightened the ladies at the O. Club, so the General ordered that the carrier landings cease, which somewhat curtailed our night operations. Fortunately, however, most of the night flying schedule had been completed by that time.

In spite of occasional differences of opinion between the marines and the Air Group, we gave the marines a party at the VOQ to show our appreciation for the use of their facilities. As to the complete success of the party, no doubt remained in anyone's mind, and memories of that memorable occasion still linger and are frequently referred to.

The Commander in Chief of the United States Army and Navy visited the Marine Base on April the 14th. All planes of the Air Group were flown in parade formation, as President Franklin D. Roosevelt inspected the balance of the officers and enlisted personnel of the squadron.

- 3 -

CONFIDENTIAL

April - continued -

From the middle of the month, until April 26, the squadron experienced a series of crash landings. First it was Ensign Kirschke who was forced down in a swamp on Hunting Island; then Ensign Tyner was forced down on the beach on Hunting Island; and within two days Ensign Buckelew and Ensign Madison had the unfortunate experiences of making respective forced landings in swamps. Fortunately none of the pilots were injured.

To add to all the excitement of this month, Ensign Jack Abell decided to get married. The wedding was held at the Marine Base Chapel, on the 12th, with Lt(jg) Smith, III, as best man. The bride was Mildred Marie Fariss of Roanoke, Virginia, a little girl that Jack had been after for years, and finally won.

May - Since most of the training schedule had been completed by this time, the squadron was working on polishing up the rough edges and working with the Scouts and Torpedo planes on group tactics.

On May 1st, Ensign Madison decided that he should be a married man, so took as his bride the former Helen Harrell of Moultrie, Georgia. Ensign Cantrell was best man, and the ceremony was performed at the Marine Base Chapel. One week later Ensign Tyner decided that he was not to be outdone by Abell and Madison, so took as his bride the former Jeannie Tyson of Lansdale, Pennsylvania. Bob had met her during our short stay at Willow Grove. Ensign Syme was best man, but did not succeed in getting more than one drink of champagne into Bob, who is an abstainer. However, you can be assured that a good time was had by all.

On the 18th we received our orders to leave Parris Island, and proceed to Pungo, an auxiliary field near Norfolk, Virginia. Pungo turned out to be quite a spot. We lived in quonset huts for the few days that the squadron was based there, and dined in an annex of the general mess. Fortunately Virginia Beach was but a few miles away. The boys became acquainted with a Navy Nurses Rest Home, so made frequent trips to the Beach in the Pungo milk wagon.

During our sojourn at Pungo the squadron qualified aboard the USS PRINCETON, while she was in the Chesapeake Bay, before docking at Pier 7 in Norfolk on the 25th. The planes were flown to Norfolk and hoisted aboard the carrier on the 27th, and at 1500 on the 28th the ship was under way for her shakedown cruise in the Gulf of Paria, Trinidad. However just before leaving, Lieut. Froelick was ordered to the hospital, so was detached from us.

We arrived in the British West Indies on June 1, 1943, entered the Gulf of Paria, and anchored at the Port of Spain, Trinidad. The following day was the start of a gruelling training period which set records in carrier landings for a shakedown cruise. The squadrons completed 1242 landings, day and night. The cruises in the Gulf of Paria were not without incidents however, since on the 2nd day three of our pilots lost themselves and landed at Carupano, Venezuela. Neither of the three, Ensigns Abell, Buckelew, or Tyner, knew or understood Spanish, but through some means, as yet unknown to us, explained where they came from, and were able to communicate to the squadron that they were safe and having a fine time.

On June 6th Ensign Cantrell was lost during a routine flight, and was not found. It is difficult to say what might have happened, so it is best not to venture an opinion.

Liberty was something we did not experience much of while in Trinidad. We were granted one liberty per week, between 1100 and 1800. Consequently whoever was fortunate to be on the liberty section was ready to disembark at 1100 sharp, and head directly to Maqueripe Beach Club, where one could swim and visit their bar or to Port-au-Spain and the Queens Park Hotel Bar, where the Planters punches were 24 per and delicious.

On the 29th of June we left the B.W.I. to return to Philadelphia. Every one was in high spirits in spite of the fact that all were tired from the strenuous exercises of the cruise, and looked forward to seeing the States again, and getting a few days leave.

July 3 - The USS PRINCETON was 150 miles at sea when it launched the Air Group which flew to Willow Grove and landed at 0900. The Air Station had certainly changed, since our departure in January. There were trees, lawns, paved streets, etc, instead of the mud and slush which we experienced earlier in the year.

CONFIDENTIAL

July 3 - continued -

Half of the officers and enlisted personnel were granted six days leave, and upon their return the balance were to leave. No sooner had the planes landed than all those departing had disappeared, headed toward all parts of the United States, - Florida, California, Washington, and even Boston; New York was kept in reserve as the place to visit, after returning from leave, every night upon the squadron being secured.

New F6F-3's were turned over to the squadron, and all planes were made ready to go aboard. The pilots had checked out in the F6F-3 while on the shakedown cruise, at Edinburgh Field, Trinidad. The new droppable belly tanks were tried out and found to be satisfactory.

Three new fighter pilots reported to the squadron: Ensigns Howard, Coyer, and Hill; and Ensign Parent, a gunnery officer, was also assigned to the squadron.

On July 1, in a wave of promotions, all of the former ensigns in the squadron were made junior grade lieutenants, so our new ensigns were alone in their particular rank.

July 20 - By 1400 all squadron personnel had to be aboard; to say the least it was a difficult task breaking away from New York, its cafes' night life, music, and beautiful girls. How Lieutenants Tolman and Rickard made it still remains a mystery. Lieut. Hefler, the romantic one, left his beloved Isolde with tears in her eyes and a milk shake in her hand. But we all made it in spite of Lieut. Hubbard's efforts to get the above gentlemen on the inebriated side during their sojourns in the Big City. At 0500 the 21st, the ship was under way, destination unknown.

Later in the day it was learned that we were to go to Panama. Ground School was held daily for all pilots, and combat air patrols were flown by the squadron, alternating the duty with the USS BELLEAU WOOD, who was with us.

We passed through the Panama Canal on July 26th. It was not too warm and all hands enjoyed themselves watching the procedure of taking us through the locks and passing through the canals and lakes. That evening we were granted liberty in Panama. The old hands who had been there previously made certain that all the known places were visited. So much happened during the liberties there that to attempt to correlate all events is an impossibility. However the high lights were: the famous drink known as the "Blue Moon", which consisted of a one-ounce jigger of orangeade - as we later discovered - and which cost one good American dollar; the famous girls who frequented the local bars would order these while you got high on imitation whiskey. Then there was the famous Chinese girl, known as Lilly Wong at Refugios Place. Lt(jg) Symu was taken aback with her Indian dancing, and decided that she was the only one for him, and it was to be done the hard way, without the famous Blue Moons! Did he succeed? As yet no one knows, and Symu won't talk!

On the 28th the PRINCETON, BELLEAU WOOD, and LEXINGTON received orders to depart from Panama, and as we later found out, to proceed direct to Pearl Harbor. The members of the squadrons who were unfortunate enough to hail from California expressed their views of deep disgust in their bad (?) luck of not being able to see their native state, if only for one day.

As we left Panama, Lieut.(jg) Olin suffered an appendix attack, and was operated on that afternoon. That evening Harry felt better and was glad it was over with and out.

Mail was received, and everyone was happy, that is, until the official mail was opened, wherein one particular letter inquired about and gently suggested that our former F4F's were "missing parts". Thereupon Lt(jg) Korr, our material officer, exclaimed in exasperation: "The monkey-wrenches be damned, let them buy others!"

By this time strict censorship had been invoked, so as a result, cries of murder, mayhem, and mutiny were being cast at the squadron censors, in spite of all out efforts towards explanations that it was not proper to tell your wife and/or sweetheart where you were, or where you were going, even though she'd love to be in Honolulu with you.

CONFIDENTIAL

During the long direct trip to Pearl Harbor, Lt. Comdr. Fuoss and Lieut. Chamberlin conducted fighter-director classes, and combat air patrols were alternated between our ship as the duty carrier, the LEXINGTON and the BELLEAU WOOD. Whenever the B.W. would launch her group a few seconds sooner than ours, the Air Officer would immediately conduct a session, to put it mildly, and the next day we would shatter all existing records, and thus maintain the reputation as the Peerless P.

On the 7th it was learned that the Air Groups from the three carriers would attack various targets on the Island of Oahu, in order to determine the alertness of the Army's defense. After the extended cruise from Panama, this was welcome news, since we would be ashore again. Consequently all were preparing for the dawn launchings on the 9th. The simulated attacks were successfully carried out, with no interceptions by Army fighters, and our planes landed at Barber's Point, at 0900. This Naval Air Station had recently been completed, consisted of 26,000 acres, runways thousands of feet in length; transportation was available, beds with Simmons Mattresses, and an Officers Club classified as very favorable, except for the little matter that other Air Groups were already in possession, and it was a bit difficult getting by them to the bar.

The Army Interceptor Command immediately placed the squadron under its jurisdiction, and every morning at 0300 one of our divisions was on an alert call, and generally scrambled. This continued for a period of three weeks, which gave the boys an opportunity to see beautiful Hawaiian sunrises.

Confusion and rumors were the order of the day for the next three weeks. Every day ComAirPac would incite new stories on the future of the Air Group. However between rumors, operations were carried on with fuel consumption tests and gunnery hops being stressed; occasional liberties were granted in order to give the boys an opportunity to give Honolulu the once-over. Waikiki was out of bounds, due to the dengue fever epidemic.

On the 21st we were informed that we were practically on our way to war so visit the medicos and get your tetanus shots. This we did with reluctance in spite of the fact that we should be accustomed to them by now. But for some reason or another the needles seem to get duller and duller. The enlisted personnel were taken to Ford Island, Pearl Harbor, to go aboard.

For this cruise the USS PRINCETON was to carry the Flag; Rear Admiral Radford and his staff were going aboard. As a result rooms and offices were being confiscated right and left; everything was in a state of last minute turmoil.

Our SBD dive bombers were to be left behind, along with three of our boys who were in the Naval Hospital at Aiea Heights. Lt(jg) Olin, and Lt(jg) Buckelew were to have their tonsils out; and Ensign Parent developed a case of yellow jaundice. Twelve fighter planes and pilots from Fighting SIX, Butch O'Hare's squadron, were to be attached on temporary duty with our squadron. When the planes were hoisted aboard on the 23rd, there were 24 F6F-3's and 9 TBF's aboard the PRINCETON when she left Pearl Harbor on the 25th at 0930 for a mission of war. Our Fighting SIX pilots were: Lt. Crews, Lt(jg) Loesch, Lt(jg) Trimble, Lt(jg) Altemus; Lt(jg) Odenbrett; Lt(jg) Palmer, Lt(jg) Coleman; and Ensigns Nyquist, Godson, Robbins, Philippe, Davis, and Roberts.

Later in the day the pilots were called into a conference, and our mission explained. We were to supply air coverage, along with the USS BELLEAU WOOD during the occupation of Baker Island, until the airfield was constructed. Never having heard of Baker Island, the Intelligence Officers, Hallowell, Hefler and Hubbard (in alphabetical order) immediately broke out maps, charts, slides, etc, and informed us that the island's only occupants were the beautiful Gooney birds, and guano; that it was 1235 miles SW of Pearl, at Lat. 0°12' N., Long. 178°30' W., a few miles from the Equator, and we would be there at least a month. What would the heat be like? Japanese planes were reported to be patrolling that area, so the pilots were happy and anxious for a Tallyho.

CONFIDENTIAL

On the 26th, Combat air patrols and fighter direction were the exercises for the day. The USS PRINCETON was the duty carrier, so we launched four of our planes. When the planes were recovered, Lt(jg) Loesch, who was in Fox-1 (The Imp), made a bad landing and went over the port side. Lt. Cdr. Miller, the Air Group Commander, has as yet not recovered from the loss of his famous Imp. After seven days of routine patrolling and proceeding at a slow speed, we left the convoy which proceeded on to Baker; while we remained off, and provided air protection. At 2357 or 1157 P.M., on the 31st, we crossed the Equator. This was the first of a series of crossings during our stay in that area. When we finally left we had crossed 34 times. The Crossing Ceremonies were belayed until later, when we had left the danger area.

On September 1st, at 0602, the first CAP was launched over the Baker Islandings. The patrol returned without incident. At 1200 we launched Dixie Loesch's division of Ens. Nyquist, Lt(jg) Coleman, and Ensign Robbins, for a CAP over the landings. At 1314 a Jap float plane bomber, known as Emily, was intercepted by Loesch and Nyquist, and was destroyed in ten seconds. The boys only made one run each and the Japs hit the water.

The PRINCETON was refueled on the 2nd, while the BELLEAU WOOD was the duty carrier, and carried on its patrols without incident. On the third of September we sent out our routine patrols. At 1201 Lt. "Sandy" Crews took off with a six-plane flight: Ens. "Junior" Godson, Lt(jg) "Jock" Odenbrett, Ens. Roberts, Lt(jg) Coleman, and Ens. Philippe. While over Baker another Jap bomber was intercepted by Coleman and Philippe, and after a mad running fight, the boys made the Japs hit the water and crash. The PRINCETON had two to its credit, and the BELLEAU WOOD had none.

It looked as though the Japs were very regular and prompt about arriving over the same area on odd days at 1300. Consequently everyone wanted that particular hop, and the BELLEAU WOOD squadron was claiming favoritism was being given the PRINCETON group. Whereupon the Admiral allowed the BELLEAU WOOD boys the patrols over Baker. As luck would have it, on the 6th, Lieut. Funk and Lt(jg) Korr were patrolling miles away from the Baker patrol, when, lo and behold, a Jap plane approached from a different direction; and number THREE Jap hit the water in short order.

Lieut. Comdr. Hatcher flew to Canton Island and brought us mail, - Happy Day. It certainly broke the monotony, and gave us news; Lt. Funk received orders to report to San Diego and assume command of a fighter squadron. He was addressed as Lieutenant Commander, so everyone was congratulating him and wishing him luck. However, rumor had it that before returning to Pearl we would attack Tarawa, a Jap held island, in the Gilbert Islands; so Mr. Funk was reluctant to leave immediately. Since he wanted to be in on that attack, his orders were temporarily forgotten. To add to all the excitement, Ensign Davis, on the 8th of September, in an early morning takeoff, failed to get his plane, Fox-3, airborne, hit the water just off the bow of the carrier, and caught fire. Davis escaped miraculously and was picked up by a destroyer. His face and hands were burned, but he was glad to be aboard, and was up and around upon arrival at Pearl.

On the 11th, it was definitely learned that we would attack Tarawa. On the 17th we crossed the 180th Meridian of longitude. This placed us in the four quadrants of the earth, in the short space of time of four months.

D-Day was the 18th of September. At the last minute it was decided that Makin Island was also to be attacked. Lieut. "Sandy" Crews and his wingman, Ensign "Junior" Godson volunteered to escort the TBF's. They were launched at 0330 and carried out a successful attack, strafing and setting four float planes afire. The Tarawa attack was launched at 0430, and successfully carried out; the boys evaded terrific AA fire and enjoyed strafing Japs who were jumping into fox holes all over the place. Later in the day, Lt(jg) Haynes took off for a CAP with his division consisting of Lt(jg) Altemus, Lt(jg) Madison, and Lt(jg) Syme. At 1513 (3.15 P.M.) a Jap torpedo plane was intercepted by the boys, and it was only a matter of seconds before the plane was shot down by Syme and Madison. The Fighting 23 boys had shot down every enemy plane they had met, and as yet Fighting 24 on the BELLEAU WOOD had none to its credit. So you can imagine their consternation.

- 7 -

CONFIDENTIAL

With a successful attack behind us, and all the boys present, the Task Force Commander sent us the following message: "Congratulations to all hands. Your alertness to meet the enemy in any way he chose to fight was one of the many highlights of the day. It was well done."

The Force was headed back to Pearl Harbor, and a much needed rest. King Neptune and his Royal Court came aboard on the 21st; the events leading up to Neptune's appearance were hectic, to put it mildly, in spite of the fact that the Pollywogs (those miserable creatures who had never entered into the Royal Domain before) outnumbered the shellbacks ten to one. For days before Neptune's appearance you would see Pollywogs with various assortments of haircuts about the ship. The Shellbacks would catch an unwary pollywog and give him the royal trimming. But the worm was to turn!

On the evening of the 20th the loudspeaker blared forth for Lieut. Kenyon to man Fox-1 on the flight deck. That only had one meaning; Chuck was to get a haircut! To the astonishment of the Shellbacks, Chuck remained in the Ready Room, along with a room full of rarin'-to-go pollywog pilots, officers, and enlisted men. They invited the honorable Shellbacks to come forth and see what they could do about it. The result was a terrific melee; chairs, dishes, backpacks, chartboards, shillalas, and Shellbacks were reeling and flying back and forth across the room. Shellbacks would be dragged into the room (in such number as could be most efficiently and adequately indoctrinated), worked over a bit, and bound up. Schmidt was standing on a cruise box inside the door, and as a Shellback would enter, he was tapped on the noggin with a shillala; whereupon Kirschke, who made Illinois a winning football team, and Webb, our man from Texas, would toss him to waiting pollywogs. Fortunately for the Shellbacks, the Admiral happened by and ordered peace and quiet restored, - until the official initiation the next day.

Later that evening we were all duly served with our subpoenas, listing individual offenses which had been committed during one's sojourn with the ship or squadron, and also notified what you were expected to wear and perform in the presence of Neptunus Rex. Costumes varied from the Queen of the May as depicted by Lt. Cdr. Hatcher, to Winter Flight gear, baby dresses; Hubbard was the Chicago Real Estate shark selling the Stevens Hotel to an unsuspecting civilian; some wore a gas mask and towel; others had binoculars made from rolls of that certain kind of paper; the Air Officer wore diapers; Symo was the most gorgeous blond girl we had seen in ages; Madison, a Texas cowhand; Marsh organized a band consisting of himself, Scott and Fratus, and led the parade of Pollywogs; Pincetich had a drill team dressed as wooden soldiers; then came the Queen of the May with her court, consisting of Lieut. Funk, Schmidt, and the TBF pilots, Lt(jg) Norris, and Ens. Cox, who danced around their queen madly and hilariously. Neptunus Rex was well pleased with the performance and accepted all new hands into his Royal Domain after we had run the gauntlet of going through a long double line of paddles manned by eagerly waiting shellbacks.

When the Task Force neared Pearl on the 22nd, the Air Groups were flown to Ford Island. Half of the squadron, Schmidt, Haynes, Symo, Webb, Kirschke, Kerr, and Madison were sent to the Chris Holmes Rest Home, which is run by Commander Air Force Pacific, for squadrons returning from combat operations and located on Waikiki. It is a beautiful residence located on the seashore, and walking distance from the Royal Hawaiian. The management furnished the boys with beautiful bedrooms, palatable meals, anything to drink, and later in the afternoon Mrs. Gault, the hostess, would invite girls for dinner and a movie. Due to the blackout at 9.00 P.M., the girls would be escorted home before the curfew. The first group remained there until the 27th, when they were replaced by Mr. Miller, Smith, Abell and Tyner. Hefler, Rickard and Kenyon took the cure on the 29th. Lieut. Funk was detached upon our arrival at Pearl, and took the first available air transportation to California.

During this time, Olin, Buckelew, Hill, Howard and Coyer were hard at work, flying a daily schedule with field carrier landings and gunnery being stressed.

CONFIDENTIAL

On October 1st, the long overdue ALNAV made its appearance. Haynes and Hefler finally were Lieutenants; to make matters worse for them, it happened that the Air Group was giving the Scouts a party. They had been officially detached from us and were headed South. The drinks however were not free (for the remaining Air Group) so everyone sought out the new Lieutenants; the result was an expensive day for the boys.

On the 8th, seven new Ensigns reported to the squadron. They had just arrived at Pearl from training, and needed combat training. During these few days, night operations were being conducted at Kaneohe; it was contemplated to move the squadron to Kaneohe in order to train our new pilots.

October 10th was a quiet, beautiful Sunday morning at Pearl Harbor. Plans were being made to move to Kaneohe. It was 0800 when Rickard answered what he believed was a call from a sweet young thing he met at Waikiki. It was the Air Officer; he wanted the Air Group Commander immediately; something was in the air; everything had broken down south and we were on the move. Lt. Cdr. Miller reported to the ship immediately, and shortly thereafter planes and pilots returned to Ford Island from Kaneohe. The seven new Ensigns were transferred to Fighting One in exchange for twelve of their experienced pilots; two were full lieutenants, Bascomb Montgomery, and Richard O'Connell; one (jg) Crockett, and seven Ensigns, Vaden, James, Matlock, Healy, McWilliams, Hahn, Boyd, Pupillo, and Muhlfold.

Everyone was assigned something to do, so that by 2400 that day the non-flying personnel and equipment were aboard the PRINCETON, ready to leave. Lt. Smith, our Engineering Officer, performed miracles in getting the planes in condition; he was all over the field with his skivvy shirt showing, personally supervising every detail on all the planes.

On October 11th we left Pearl. The PRINCETON was headed toward the South Pacific. As we left the harbor, the Task Force that attacked Wake Island was preparing to enter. Unfortunately through no fault of ours, we had missed that job, but we were headed into something bigger, and we would get the South Pacific Duty over with also. Later in the afternoon the new pilots were qualified in carrier landings, along with Ensign Howard, Hill and Coyer, our three Ensigns who had been joy riding since leaving Philadelphia, because they were not qualified.

We crossed the Equator for the 35th time, on October 15th, and held the traditional crossing ceremonies the following day. Buckelew, Olin, Parent, and our new pilots were the center of attraction, and suffered more than the original bunch who were in the majority at that time, and had demanded (and received) leniency. Sunday, October 17th, we crossed the International Date Line, and the next day was Tuesday. Monday was a lost day, but we were paid for it anyway. On October 22nd, Ensign Howard had a barrier crash and broke his ankle. He was taken ashore when we arrived at Espiritu Santo in the New Hebrides on the 24th of October. Here we were given two new pilots from VF-12: Ensigns Mooney and Darby.

While at Espiritu some of the new pilots were flying at Bomber Three, others were aboard and sending all excess gear home under orders of the First Lieutenant, before leaving Espiritu on October 29th. During a combat air patrol on the 31st, Syms experienced engine trouble while hunting out an unidentified plane, and was forced to make a water landing. A destroyer was immediately sent out; it found him enjoying himself sampling all the nicknacks in his back pack.

On November 1st, we were ordered to attack Buka, and Bougainville (Bonis Field) in the northern Solomons. We attacked on the first, and again on the 2nd of November. In the pre-dawn take-offs of the 1st, Lieut.(jg) Olin failed to get airborne and went off the bow into the drink. Harry yelled like hell as he passed the carrier, and was picked up by a destroyer in a few minutes.

- 9 -

CONFIDENTIAL

During the same takeoffs, Lt(jg) Tynor had engine trouble and had to make a water landing. Fortunately a destroyer saw him and picked him up. During the attacks of the second day, Ensign Keener, a pilot from Fighting TWELVE but temporarily attached to us, was lost during a strafing run, and has not been heard from.

November 3rd, we received the following message: "Admiral Halsey has congratulated the Task Force on the strikes on Buka and says Well Done, and that as a result that Buka is not now contributing to Jap War Effort."

The Force had retired and was awaiting further orders. The evening of November 4th everyone was about to enjoy a movie, when the Air Officer was summoned; then the Intelligence Officers; and later word was passed to man torpedo elevators. Something was in the air, but they went ahead with the movie; after which all squadron officers were told to meet in the Ready Room. No one could believe their eyes and ears. Rabaul was to be attacked in the morning! It was to be an all-out, repeat all-out, attack on everything the Japs had in the harbor. This was the Big Time Lieut. Comdr. Miller had so often spoken of, but little did anyone realize it would hit the boys in such a sudden manner without any preparation. To put it mildly, everyone's nerves were on edge, and everyone was only too anxious to get any information the Intelligence Officers could dig up on the Jap bastion of the South Pacific.

After consultations and many changes, Lt. Kenyon produced the flight schedule for the attack on Rabaul, November 5th, 1943, - a day never to be forgotten by our pilots. Lt. Cdr. Miller led the squadron, and had in his division, Lt(jg) Syme, Lt(jg) Kirschke, and Ens. James. Lt. Claude Schmidt led the second division with Ens. Coyer, Lt(jg) Abell, and Ens. Pupillo. Lt. Smith led the third division with Lt(jg) Olin, Lt(jg) Webb, and Ens. Hill. Lt. Bascomb Montgomery had the fourth division with Lt(jg) Buckelow, Lt(jg) Madison, and Ensign Massey. Lt. Dick O'Connell was in the fifth division with Lt(jg) Kerr, and Lt(jg) Crockett. This was the order in which the boys took off from the PRINCETON at 0900 November 5th.

Rabaul, located on the northern tip of New Britain Island was protecting a good portion of the enemy's fleet which had been gathering there for a major Jap strike. As our planes approached, the harbor was protected by an umbrella of terrific anti-aircraft fire, the like of which our boys had never experienced before, and hope never to see again. Japanese fighter planes swarmed the sky, Zekes, Tonys, Haps, everything the enemy could make airborne. Our bombers dove with deadly accuracy, while our fighters filled the sky with falling Jap planes. Hell had liberally broken loose, and planes filled every inch of the sky.

At 1250, as the first planes appeared over the carrier everyone was anxiously scanning the sky, counting planes, while others remained below to pick up radio reports on returning planes. As the first planes landed, reports looked bad, some had it that one complete division had been lost; but as the minutes passed, more and more planes were coming aboard. On the final count it was learned that Lieutenants Smith and O'Connell, and Lt(jg) Madison were missing. Reports on Smittie and O'Connell were meagre; no one could accurately account for what had happened to them. Jack Madison had started after a couple of Zeros, and reports indicate that he probably got them, but while after them, one got behind him and made his plane fall. When the boys left Rabaul, the place was an inferno. Cruisers and destroyers were hit, some sunk, while Jap planes were scattered all over the place, total wrecks.

CONFIDENTIAL

The official tabulation for the raid was:

	Definite	Probables	Damaged
Miller, Lt.Cdr.	Tony		Tony
Syme, Lt(jg)	—		Zeke
Schmidt, Lt.			Tony
Olin, Lt(jg)	Zeke		
Webb, Lt(jg)		Zeke	
Hill, Ens.	Zeke		Zeke; Betty
Montgomery, Lt.	1 Zeke / 2 Tonys		
Buckelew, Lt(jg)	Zeke		Zeke
Madison, Lt(jg)		Tony	
Massey, Ens.	Zeke; Tony		
Kerr, Lt(jg)			Betty
Crockett, Lt(jg)	Zeke		
Totals	8 VF	2 VF	6 VF / 2 MB

Tony)
Zeke) – Jap Zero fighter planes.

Betty – Jap medium bomber.

That evening the ship's flight surgeons broke out the brandy and the boys with nerves still on edge talked on into the night. The next day congratulatory messages were pouring in from all directions.

Admiral Halsey sent us a Well Done, that the PRINCETON and SARATOGA had performed a magnificent job. General MacArthur sent the following: Every Officer and man working with Admirals Sherman and Merrill deserves commendation. From the Commander of our Task Force to the PRINCETON: Msg Capt. Henderson. I am proud of the performance of your ship and Air Group on this whole trip. Both have demonstrated their ability to be full participating partners in the best combat team in the world. Adm. Sherman. From the Commander of our Cruiser Division: Please extend to the Air Groups from all hands our congratulations and great admiration for the outstanding job they have done, and the punishment they have dealt out to the Japs. We are proud to be with you. From General Arnold: The Army Air Forces congratulate the Navy for the magnificent day attacks by the carrier aircraft on Jap ships in Rabaul November 5th. The pilots established a record that other airmen will find difficult to equal. Please extend my congratulations to all concerned.

As the messages poured in, too much attention was not paid them, since the pilots were still tired as hell from the terrific ordeal, and everyone's thoughts were with our one and only Smittie, "Black Jack" Madison, and Dick O'Connell, who had failed to return. Everyone was missing these boys; they were the type that every squadron wants and is proud to have. We will never forget them.

Lt(jg) Crockett, who had been assigned the job of protecting the Air Group Commander of the SARATOGA, was reported doing well in Sick Bay. During the attack he and the Air Group Commander had been jumped by numerous Jap planes. Crockett's plane was riddled with bullet holes; 180 were counted on the port side only. He had been wounded, but still remained with the Commander, and shot down a Jap plane during the fight. To this day Crockett does not remember landing on the carrier after the attack; he was in such a weakened condition. The following message was received from the SARATOGA Group Commander: "Group Commander sends to Fighter pilot Number Three x Your courage, determination and loyalty will be a lasting inspiration to me x H H CALDWELL."

CONFIDENTIAL

Lieut. Schmidt's division performed the outstanding feat of protecting and bringing safely home 18 dive bombers from the SARATOGA. He had picked up the SARA planes upon the completion of their attack, and protected them from twenty Jap fighter planes that were attacking the bombers as they left Rabaul. Our boys claim they strained their eyes and were mighty happy to see their carrier and realize they were finally home.

On November 8th, we arrived at Espiritu Santo again. However, few were permitted to go ashore, since we were merely to take on supplies and leave again. We left again on November 9th. Our objective was to attack Rabaul again! Preparations were thoroughly made, and all details of the raid minutely gone over again and again. Here we borrowed a division from Fighting TWELVE. They were Lt(jg) Parker, Hughes, Russell, and Caldwell.

On November 11th, Armistice Day, Rabaul was again attacked! Our planes took off at 0545. Lt. Comdr. Miller was again leading the Air Group, and had in his division Lt(jg) Syme, Lt(jg) Webb, and Ens. Hill. Lt. Schmidt led the second division, and had with him Ens. Coyer, Lt(jg) Abell, and Ens. Pupillo. Lt. Haynes had the third division with Lt(jg) Tyner, Ens. James, and Ens. Darby. Lt(jg) Kirschke led the fourth division with Ens. Boyd, Lt(jg) Buckelow, and Ens. Massey; and Lt(jg) Parker had the fifth division with Lt(jg) Kerr, Lt(jg) Hughes, and Lt(jg) Russell. The attack was perfectly planned and executed. At 1045 the planes appeared over the carriers, all the divisions intact -- all were safely back!

The anti aircraft fire was just as bad, and the Japs had planes all over the sky, but our boys had learned from experience, and were just too damn good and wise for the unfortunate Japs.

The following was sent us: "Please convey to all hands in the Force my utmost admiration for their brilliant performance during their operations in the South Pacific. You have dealt severe blows to the enemy at Buka and Rabaul x Your first attack on Rabaul was another shot heard round the world. Your second equally effective, even though hampered by insufficient targets. I know you will carry out successfully your Central Pacific operations. Good hunting, and good luck. Halsey."

We returned to Espiritu on November 14th. Admiral Sherman gave the Task Force a party at the O Club, which turned out to be quite an affair. All the boys, even those who were not short snorters were getting signatures from Admirals Halsey, Fitch and Sherman. When that party was over, Lt. Cdr. Miller gave another cocktail party at Bomber 3 -- onuf said!

Crockett was dismissed from the Naval Base Hospital at Espiritu and returned to the Squadron on the 15th. Lt. Montgomery and Ens. Healy and Ens. Howard were detached from the squadron on the 16th, to report to Commander Fleet Air South Pacific.

On November 16th we left Espiritu Santo on another attack mission. We were to attack the Jap held island of Nauru, adjacent to the Gilbert Islands. The base was attacked on November 19, 1943, and the attack successfully carried out. Our boys had become most proficient in evading anti aircraft fire and strafing anything selected for them.

Claude Schmidt returned beaming all over the place; he had shot down a Jap Zero. He had really poured the lead into him, and enjoyed watching the Jap hit the water. Ens. McWilliams did not return with his division, and was believed lost, since Jap Zeros had jumped our boys and a first class dog fight ensued. However, it was not long before Mac was picked up on the radio, and shortly landed aboard. He was covered with grease from top to bottom, but had a big grin all over his face; he had a Zero to his credit also. All our planes were aboard, and the Japs were minus planes.

CONFIDENTIAL

Upon completion of this attack the following messages arrived: "From the Commander of the Task Force x Well Done to the Air Groups on today's strikes x This completes nine strikes by this Task Force in 19 days, which I believe is a record for carriers in this war x Again I say Well Done to this Force x "

On the evening of the attack, some Jap snoopers located our force and trailed us for quite some time, but would not close in. All hands were at General Quarters, and those on the flight deck watched the ships open fire on The Snooper. The fireworks would light up the area for miles. However it must have frightened the Nips, since they left and did not return.

Tarawa was being attacked and occupied by American Naval Forces. On November 23rd we met and escorted a large convoy headed toward Tarawa and then supplied the air coverage over the area.

November 25th was Thanksgiving. We were given a super lunch, turkey and all the trimmings, cake, ice cream, cigars and cigarettes; but it still would have been better were we at home. The occupation of Tarawa was successful, and on November 27th, at 0500, we received orders to perform all kinds of plane transfers. Saxation, our first class yeoman, who we discovered after the lapse of a year had been the checker champ of New York and is currently giving us checker lessons, earned the right to become a Chief today: he put out forty four sets of orders in fifty one minutes. We wonder if he derives his speed from the fact that he is a New York lawyer? And after all this speed and fuss, none of the orders were needed; - someone changed his mind fifty two minutes later.

What is to become of us? That remains to be seen. It looks as though we may head to some convenient port for a rest. Up to the present time we have crossed the Equator 36 times, and the International Date Line six times.

During the news broadcast later in the day the Chaplain read the following: "Heartiest congratulations on your success, and more power to you for the future. My warmest admiration to officers and men of all units, surface, ground, and air, taking part in this brilliant joint action. DeWitt Navy Staff College."

Saturday, November 27th. Claude Schmidt and his division ferried planes to another carrier. Upon landing he discovered that they intended to keep him for further operations. Upon making more inquiries, the more he was assured that he would not leave. Whereupon Claude asked permission to see Admiral Pownall. He is about as tall as Claude, so they had a heart to heart talk. Schmidt gave him all the details on Rabaul, and the 19 raids in eight days our boys had been on; after which the Admiral ordered him back to the PRINCETON with a recommendation that our boys had earned a rest. Claude asked the Admiral how the operations were proceeding, and he replied: "Fine, Fine, every Jap on the island has been killed."

Sunday, November 28th. Kirschke, Buckelew, and Hill ferried planes to the BELLEAU WOOD. Upon landing they were told that they would remain. Frantic calls for help availed them nothing, and the boys are still there. Three pilots from the LISCOMBE BAY came aboard. She had been hit by a torpedo and sunk.

Monday. Today is Sunday November 28th. Again having crossed the International Date Line. Word was sent us that our three pilots were transferred to a tanker and would either meet us or be taken to some port where we will go -- will they log the sack time! Ships from various forces have met and are refueling today. The forces around us would scare a Jap to death; it's the mightiest fleet in the world; secrecy prevents mentioning the number of carriers, battlewagons, cruisers, cans, etc., that are within seeing distance. It's really a magnificent sight, and one which makes one feel secure.

CONFIDENTIAL

November, 29th. Kirschke, Buckelow and Hill were transferred aboard today. We have been detached from our task force and ordered to proceed to Pearl Harbor, escorting returning ships. The convoy is to travel slowly, so that we shall not arrive until December 7th. The afternoons were spent playing volley ball, and one afternoon the Chaplain held a field meet on the flight deck, rope climbing, and line throwing. In a tug-o-war the Air Group enlisted men held their own, but were nosed out in the final tug.

On December 7th we arrived at Pearl. It seemed as though it took hours to get the O.K. to enter the harbor; finally the word was given, and as soon as we dropped anchor everyone was off for the rest home and various hotels.

The evening of the 8th the ship sent a representative to locate us and bring us tidings that we had to remove all our gear by 0700 the next morning, since the ship was leaving for the States, - minus the Air Group. What news!/@*?;/.

The next morning we were all down packing and packing in a mad rush, throwing things away. The ship's loud speaker was blaring forth for the squadrons to leave the ship immediately. Finally they tossed us off. There we sat on a stack of gear and listened to the heckling of the ship's crew as she pulled off for the States, - with Christmas around the corner!

For two days we remained around Honolulu, catching up on rest and social obligations that had been sadly neglected during our sojourn in the South Pacific. Leon Haynes was detached and found himself the quickest available transportation to San Diego, which had him home for Christmas.

We were finally ordered to depart for Puunene Naval Air Station, Maui, where we were to train during the absence of the PRINCETON. Hefler and Rickard were the first to set off, and had transportation, ready room, and rooming assignments all set when the rest of the squadron arrived.

All of our gear was placed on the SWAN, a minesweeper, and on arriving at Maui, to the disgust of all concerned, it was discovered that our gear had been ransacked and all our Christmas "spirits" removed. A hell of a fix we were in!

Lieutenant Commanders Fuhring and Curtis accompanied us to Maui.

Lt(jg) Syme having in his inimitable way made the correct connections in Honolulu, he and a small group were invited to spend Christmas at the Kukaiau Ranch, Nancy Russell's parents' place, on the big island of Hawaii. The balance of the Air Group were extended invitations to the Hinds Ranch, also located on Hawaii, next to the fabulous Parker Ranch.

Stories are still being retold about the various experiences enjoyed at these places. Louie Parent had a horse fall on his head; Hubbard surprised all at his prowess at Pheasant Hunting; Hefler was known as "the big bad wolf with a Dartmouth mind", while the same young lady, D. J. Gruin, referred to Korr as a "mass of tangled inhibitions". Kirschke met Lamie, and the boys found out what a rodeo and branding was like.

While this was going on the other half of the squadron was hard at work. Lt. Cdr. Curtis was working the boys on field carrier landings, night and day. On December 14th, two new Ensigns reported for duty, - Ensigns Hendrickson and Weickhardt; and on December 16th Ensigns Nicklin and Brugger reported for duty with the squadron. These boys needed field carrier landings, and gunnery, so were unable to rest, since much work had to be accomplished in a short time.

Christmas and New Years were uneventful. Some of the boys were away on the ranches, and those remaining scattered off to the Officers' Club or various homes in Lahaina and Kahuli.

- 14 -

CONFIDENTIAL

Ensign Parker reported on January 3, 1944. He had left San Francisco on the Clipper, New Years Day. We checked him out in an F6F as soon as possible, but due to his inexperience it was thought advisable to leave him ashore when we prepared to ship out.

Commander George Chafee, our former Air Group Commander, appeared and made preparations to take our planes aboard his carrier for a couple of days and qualify all hands. All the planes flew out on January 7th, and qualified without incident. Claude Schmidt was assigned a bunk in Sam Froelick's room. He was the same old Sam of Parris Island days.

The PRINCETON was back from the States, so on January 10th we embarked for a few days' cruise to qualify new pilots. Just as we were leaving Pearl Harbor our Chief Yeoman Saxstion opened what seemed like a routine envelope; but did it have a slow curve in it; -- Lt. Comdr. Miller was ordered detached and directed to report as Air Officer on a CVE! Wait until he flies aboard and gets that news!

The planes were to fly aboard. Ensign Eubank, flying a TDF, was the first to come aboard. As he approached and was allset to land, something happened which caused a terrible accident, and Ensign Eubank's death. The two passengers riding with him were rescued. It was our first fatal accident, and a very unfortunate one.

The next day, January 11th, Ensign Nicklin had a little bad luck coming aboard, and tore the tail off of his plane, but no one was injured; other than that everyone qualified without difficulty, and we returned to Pearl on the 13th.

A week was devoted to preparing the ship and squadron for the next combat mission. Planes were checked, new planes taken aboard, exchanges of enlisted personnel made. The foresighted brought aboard Coca cola, magazines and jars of candy. As to when we would be leaving no one knew, although our mission was surmised by everyone. Ensign Parker was temporarily transferred to ComAirPac on the 18th, since he was not considered qualified for carrier operations and combat as yet. This was a wise move, since he would not have been permitted to fly; as a result of which he would have lost all that time to practice.

At 1200 on January 19, 1944, we left our anchorage at Pearl Harbor for the Japanese held Marshall Islands. On leaving the harbor an Air Group meeting was held, and all were informed regarding our targets: Wotje, Maloelap, and Eniwetok.

Classes on plane and ship identification, and the Marshall Islands, were conducted by Lieutenants Hubbard and Hefler until January 27. During the first days out fighter director work was carried out by the carriers. On one particular day another carrier was given a "Well Done", while the Peerless P was conspicuously omitted. You can be sure that our gang were in there pitching from then on.

Two days later, while taking our planes aboard, we were missing a plane. After a frantic muster, it was discovered that Ensign Hahn was absent; when all of a sudden we discovered that he was trying to land on another carrier, -- by mistake of course.

D-Day was to be on 31 January 1944. On that particular day landings were to be made on Kwajalein Atoll and Majuro Atoll. However our attacks were to commence on the 29th.

On January 29th at 0555 our first strike against Wotje Island took off. Four divisions were on this attack, which was the first of three strikes for the day. Lt. Cdr. Miller's division consisting of McWilliams, Syms, and James was in the lead. Claude Schmidt with his division of Matlock, Aboll and Pupillo was the next off; followed by Korr's division of Boyd, Olin and Nicklin. The last division off was Crockett's, with Vadon, Tynor and Hendrickson.

- 15 -

CONFIDENTIAL

During the day combat air patrols were flown all day. Kirschke's division of Darby, Buckelew and Hahn, and Webb's division of Woickhardt, Hill and Muhlfeld were the ones who drew the assignment. There were three sorties against Wotje this first day, and four combat air patrols. The anti aircraft fire was not as intense as anticipated, and after the first sortie, was considerably less.

January 30, 1944, we were all awakened at 0400, battle breakfast of steak, eggs, fruit and coffee was served. The pilots were briefed on a new target, and the first attacks of the day against Wotje and Taroa were launched at 0545. Today our fighter planes, along with the strikes against the Japanese were conducting combat air patrols over the Jap airfield at Wotje, to make certain that no Nip planes took off or landed. Lt. Cdr. Miller's division of McWilliams, Sym and James; Kirschke's division of Darby, Buckelow and Nicklin; and Webb's division of Woickhardt, Hill and Muhlfeld were assigned the patrols over Wotje. They would patrol for three hours, and return to our carrier. However, just before leaving a few strafing runs against Nip installations were generally in order.

The strikes against Taroa were conducted by Crockett's division of Vaden, Tyner, and Hendrickson; and later Kirschke's division; when Schmidt's division of Matlock, Aboll and Pupillo, and Kerr's division of Boyd, Olin and Massey relieved the first patrols over the Jap airfield of Wotje. Throughout the day we had six patrols over the Nip base at Wotje, and four strikes against the enemy at Taroa. However it must be remembered that after each patrol the boys generally departed with a strafing run, so in all the Japs were kept quite busy.

The target at Taroa or Maloelap, also one of the Marshall group, was just south of Wotje, so we easily hit both bases simultaneously. Schmidt's division on its last patrol of the day went to Taroa and spotted for the cruisers that were bombarding the island. When that day was completed you can be certain that there were not too many lively Nips on that island.

D-Day was January 31, 1944. Our forces were landing at Majuro and Kwajalein Atolls. We continued our devastation of Wotje with strikes, patrols, and bombardment by cruisers. There were five patrols and three strikes over the island. During the last patrol, Lt. Cdr. Miller spotted for the cruisers that were bombarding, and from all reports the place was in shambles that evening. Today we had our first casualty of the operation. Lt(jg) Buckelew, while carrying out daring strafing runs against an enemy gun emplacement that he had spotted was struck by anti-aircraft fire which disabled his plane and forced him to make a water landing. Buck himself was not hit; he called Ensign Brugger, his wingman, and told him about his having to make the water landing. When the plane landed it disappeared immediately, and for some unknown reason Buck was unable to get out. Our planes circled for fifteen minutes, but without success.

This evening we received the following message: "Well Done x I have the best carrier pilots in the Navy.", signed, Admiral Ginder.

February 1. We retired to refuel. This gave the pilots an opportunity to catch up on some well earned rest.

February 2. We headed for Eniwetok Atoll, the western-most atoll in the Marshall Group. There we were to patrol and intercept any enemy planes trying to reinforce the Nip air bases in the Marshalls. Our forces had landed and the conquest was in the bag; but you can never tell, - the little Nips will try anything.

February 3. We attacked Engebi Island in Eniwetok Atoll. There were no enemy planes in the air, so a systematic destruction of their airfield was begun and carried on until February 6th. Sorties were conducted every day. The AA fire was reduced to nothing, and as a matter of fact the torpedo planes were taking passengers as observers towards the end; Hubbard, Hefler, and Hallowell taking trips and watching the bombs drop. They did admit that it was a hard trip just for a thirty-second look at the target.

- 16 -

CONFIDENTIAL.

At noon on the sixth we recovered our aircraft and left for Roi, our newly acquired base in the Kwajalein atoll.

From January 29th, until February 6th, we had carried out twelve strikes against the enemy and conducted ten combat air patrols over the enemy airfield which also included a strafing attack before leaving the target.

At about 0900 we arrived at Roi, which is on the northern end of the lagoon. From the distance we could see ships and ships in the lagoon. They were of all types and sizes. This lagoon is the largest in the world. It was an experience seeing it, and seeing all the ships we had there. As we entered we could see evidences of our landing forces in the various smaller islands in the entrance to the lagoon; tanks and landing boats littered the shores. You could see machine gun nests which were razed; some tanks were overturned, and marines were all over the place souvenir hunting.

The next day, Schmidt, Kerr, and Crockett were allowed to go to Roi and see the devastation. They came back with pockets packed with souvenirs and colossal stories. It seems the marines had cornered the market on Jap property and demanded terrific exchanges for a flag or sword. What they wanted above all was one of our .45 calibre revolvers. For that you would get a Jap sword. Next on their list was whiskey. For a bottle you'd get practically anything they had. Money meant nothing. By that time they had all of that that they wanted.

February 9th. We received a new operation plan. It was to occupy Eniwetok Atoll; so at 1400 we departed from Roi to carry out our orders. The Task Force was the same as we have had all along. Lt(jg) Kroeger and Ensign Cox and Lt(jg) Tyner were taken over to a ferry carrier, and will fly two TBFs and one F6F back to the PRINCETON. Ensign Boyd is still on another carrier. He will fly a Hellcat back to the PRINCETON tomorrow. He has been aboard that carrier since the 5th, when he bounced over the barrier on attempting a landing, and as he bounced over he gave it the gun and took off again. However, his tail hook was torn off by another plane's prop, as he took off, so he had to make a crash landing on the other carrier without a tail hook. That experience of Boyd's was really a thriller. So far it's tops, and we don't care to see any more like it, thank you.

Thursday, February 10th. We arrived at our assigned location off of Eniwetok Atoll, and launched our attacks beginning at 0900, with Lt. Cdr. Miller and Lt(jg) Webb's divisions going in first. Our next strike took off at 1115 with only Claude Schmidt's division going, and the third attack of the day taking off at 1315 with Kirschke's division following Lt. Cdr. Miller's division in for the attack. On this strike Kenyon decided to participate, so flew in with Lt(jg) Kroeger in a TBF. The anti aircraft fire was minimum and the place was still badly torn up from our previous visit.

Friday, February 11th. Still softening up Eniwetok Atoll for our contemplated landings. Engebi Island's airfield was bombed by our TBF's, and strafed by our Hellcats on two strikes. The place is in ruins, and no opposition is being encountered. Lt. Rickard rounded out the A-V(S) officers' trips by flying in on the first strike with Lt(jg) Spear.

We had another unfortunate accident today. Ensign Boyd on returning from the attack on Engebi, made a bad landing, struck the bridge, and went over the side. He was unable to get out of his plane.

Later this afternoon keep-away with the medicine ball was our form of exercise. Whoever is not in a standby condition generally gets up on the flight deck and limbers up, thereby staying in pretty fair condition.

February 12. Last night the Japs attacked Roi Island in Kwajalein Atoll. Our ship's operators picked their planes up, but General Quarters was not necessary. This morning Lt. Cdr. Miller, Lt(jg) Syme, Webb, and Coyer, and Lt. Schmidt's division of Abell, Tyner, and Ens. Weickhardt took off at 0700 and attacked Engebi. It was to be the last strike for the time being.

- 17 -

CONFIDENTIAL

On recovering our planes we left our intercept station and headed for Roi. Mail is expected, our first in a month. We wonder if it was one of the targets last night.

Tonight Dr. Fuhring broke out the "rations", and the boys are recollecting and comparing past raids.

Sunday, February 13, 1944. Today we returned to Roi, entered the lagoon at 1000, and immediately began refueling and taking aboard bombs. The Air Group was in condition 13, i.e., on thirty-minutes notice, so most of the boys caught up on sleep. Some took sun baths, and others tried their luck at fighting, but without much success. This afternoon the Catholic Chaplain from another carrier came aboard. Services were in memoriam of Jim Boyd. Later our exercises on the flight deck consisted of a little keep-away medicine ball, and at 1700 we weighed anchor and left the lagoon for the night.

Monday, February 14. We returned to Roi at 0900 and anchored in the lagoon for the day. Nothing was scheduled, so the boys spent the day sleeping and taking sun baths. As we left the lagoon for the night, one of our newest cruisers arrived and sent us word that she had mail for us. Consequently we can't wait to return to Roi in the morning and claim our long overdue mail.

Tuesday, February 15. We entered the lagoon again this morning, and anxiously awaited our mail. There were 339 sacks for the PRINCETON. Little by little it arrived, and as the squadron sacks came aboard they were immediately sent up to the office. The packages were in a terrible condition, and if they contained cakes or candy, it was worse. No first class mail arrived, which meant no letters! At 1425 we departed from Roi, and headed toward Eniwetok again, this time to capture the atoll.

Wednesday, February 16. Our attacks commenced early this morning, and continued throughout the day. Some anti aircraft was noticed, but it was spasmodic. The islands were well strafed and bombed, and are ready for the landings tomorrow. Ensign Cox of the TBF's was wounded in the neck in the first strike today.

Thursday, 17 February. Today is D-Day. Landings were made on two small islands adjoining Engebi, as our planes and ships bombed and bombarded the islands. Lt. Cdr. Miller was assigned the task of Air Coordinator with the ground forces. Landings were made according to schedule, and our transports entered the lagoon without difficulty. Ensign Pupillo on returning on the last hop of the day crashed into the barrier; no one was injured.

Friday, 18 February. Landings were made on Engebi itself today. Opposition seems to be of a minimum caliber. Our ships are now bombarding the rest of the islands in preparation to land on them. Ensign James crashed into the barrier today. It is beginning to look as though the boys are tiring.

Today, February 18, Eniwetok Island was captured by our forces. Lt. Cdr. Miller and Lt(jg) Webb were the air coordinators from our squadron who participated in the supervising of the landings; their flight lasted 5½ hours. It was the longest flight undertaken from the PRINCETON to date. Other divisions from the squadron, Lt(jg) Symo, Kerr, and Kirschke each leading one, participated in strafing the Nips after the landing forces had them cornered. The boys really enjoyed it today; there was AA fire, bombs falling, boats landing on the beaches and tanks roaming the island looking for Japs, - a Warner Brothers thriller could have done no better.

Sunday, February 20. The capture of Eniwetok was slower than expected; our forces were meeting with some resistance. During the day our six divisions each were given one combat air patrol over the atoll, and enjoyed watching the ground forces and tanks move in on the Nips. The transmissions between tanks were amusing, one particular tank complained that the rest which were supposed to be with him were gathering souvenirs. The tally from our other forces' raid on Truk was published today and enjoyed by all.

CONFIDENTIAL

Monday, and Tuesday, 21 and 22 February, were devoted to taking the remaining island on the atoll, Parry Island. Our boys were kept busy strafing Nip fox holes and snipers. Fuel was running low, so today, Wednesday, the 23rd, we refueled. Mail went off, but as yet none has made its appearance.

One year ago today, February 25, our ship was commissioned; Lt. Comdr. Miller and Lieut. Kenyon had attended the ceremonies. However, today we are a long way from Philadelphia here in the Marshall Islands, flying patrols over our latest conquest, Eniwetok Atoll, until the field is repaired and a squadron arrives to take over. Patrols have been cut down; we only had one flight today, which consisted of two divisions over the atoll.

February 26. Another day in the same area; more patrolling. We had expected to leave, but unforeseen circumstances made us remain. Today's schedule only called for one patrol over the atoll; the balance of the pilots stood by in a ready condition, and very bored with the whole situation. It's been six weeks that we have been without mail; one can well imagine our predicament, and there are no hopes of receiving any.

February 27th. Still on the same job. However today the Admiral allowed two planes to fly to Engebi and land. Hubbard returned with a TDF full of souvenirs, so tonight everyone is gathering something to take home.

February 28th. Today we were assigned the morning patrol. Lt. Cdr. Miller and his division led three other divisions off the deck. They came aboard at 1100, and the Task Force changed course, which heads us toward a harbor in the Marshalls. However, there we expect mail and provisions.

February 29th. After one patrol we departed for an atoll.

March 1. We dropped anchor at 1000 and immediately looked around for our long overdue mail. It soon came aboard, and all hands were swamped with forty-two days of mail.

March 2, 3, 4. All the mail was distributed at once, Ensign Parent and Nicklin being undisputed winners of the greatest loot, with forty letters each. We all took turns going to one of the small islands for a swim, and looking around for cats-eyes and various colored coral formations. We were probably the first white people to visit this little island, and honorably initiated it with a beer party. Some Navy nurses were located in a nearby island, but their doctor escorts upon seeing us immediately whisked them off. Kenyon, on returning to the ship, was sitting on the gunwale of the gig, all dressed, so Kirschke gave him a friendly tap, and over went Kenyon, clothes, coral and all.

March 8. At 0830 the ship weighed anchor. We are headed for Espiritu Santo, and as to what we will do after that is a great mystery. New planes were flown aboard by Lt(jg) Crockett, Olin, Tyner, and Ensign Nicklin.

March 9th. We crossed the equator for the 41st time, and conducted the ceremonies in accordance with the ancient tradition of the sea, Ensigns Hendrickson, Nicklin, Weickhardt and Brugger being the center of attraction. Hendrickson appeared as Alice in Wonderland, Nicklin as Charlie Chaplin, and the high chair pilot of the Navy, Weickhardt, as a beautiful hula dancer; and Brugger as one of our colored mess boys. King Neptune was Lt. Kelleher; the Queen, Lt. Whitney; the Royal Baby, Lt. Blackburn; Royal Judge, Lt. Cdr. Hatcher; Royal Prosecutor, Lt. Kenyon; Royal Barber, Captain Trumpeter, USMC; Royal Dentist, Lt(jg) Rapp; Davey Jones, Lt. Moiteret; and the Royal Doctor, Lt(jg) Schulman. Along with our pilots, the Executive Officer, Commander Murphy was the center of attraction; his most serious offense was impersonating a Naval Officer for 16 years and never crossed the line.

Today, March 10th, was omitted from our calendar; it is Saturday, March 11th. It was a quiet day, no flights were scheduled; so the boys devoted the day to sunbathing and sleeping.

CONFIDENTIAL

March 11th. Arrived at Espiritu Santo at 1520, and at 1525 we were all headed for the O Club. Two divisions flew ashore, and consequently got a half hour head start.

March 12th. Nothing doing; just recovering from last night. Lots of mail arrived.

March 16th. Lt. Cdr. Curtis is bouncing 12 new pilots just out of training. Attended LANGLEY party, which was A-1.

March 17th. Enlisted men sent aboard again; eight pilots still ashore; and we are on 6-hour notice.

March 19th. New pilots were being bounced in preparation for carrier qualification. Ens. Parker arrived from Pearl, having flown down to meet us.

March 20th. With various other ships giving parties, we decided to outdo them by sending out invitations to cocktails at the Officers' Club on San Juan Hill. We obtained the use of the LANGLEY orchestra for dancing, and took our small band to play for the dinner room which was beneath the bar and dancing floor. About 1700 while waiting for time to pass, at the club, the hospital ship, USS SOLACE, arrived in the harbor. Immediately Rickard and Hefler sent forth emissaries to obtain nurses for the party. When the party was finally under full swing, the committee of two had located and obtained between 35 and 40 nurses, between the hospital ship and various Army and Navy hospitals located in the near vicinity. Peterkin had obtained the use of nine vehicles with drivers, and Hubbard stationed himself at the door and greeted everyone from the Admiral to uninvited guests. The party was such a success, that instead of closing at 2200 as planned, it continued on until past 2300.

March 21st. The PRINCETON weighed anchor from Espiritu and cruised around the entrance to the harbor all day, during which time we qualified new pilots for ourselves and two other carriers.

Wednesday, March 22nd. Preparations were being made to get under way again; everyone was picking up necessary equipment, planes, and even clothing; since khakis could be purchased here. At 1600 we met our former dive bomber pilots who were returning from an Australian vacation, so a reunion and party was in order. Tolman, Maerki, Sullivan, Maloney, Tobey, and Hodden were all present. Of course the stories that developed were magnificent.

Today, the 23rd, at 0730, we left Espiritu for something big; everyone is guessing as to what it is, but no one is certain. This operation has been kept under cover better than average. Eight new pilots reported to us, all Ensigns, Parker, Supan, Hill, Munson, Blyth, Bledsoe, Waldron, and Phillian. Hefler and Hubbard immediately took them under their wing; and ground school was under way.

The following day, the 24th, lectures on Palau were given. It seems to be a good bet that we will strike there. However, Tally Ho Ack Ack, our Admiral Ginder's daily news report, did not give out any definite information, so it seems we will have to wait until our force is completely made up. The new pilots were given catapult instructions by Lieut. Elmo Runyan, and then taken up on the flight deck and taxied on the catapult to show them how it's done. The doctors issued first aid kits and gave them their first aid lectures tonite.

Today, 12 fighters carried out practice interceptions on planes from accompanying carriers; also pilots were given recognition instructions.

The 26th, we spent refueling our Task Force. There was an early morning anti submarine search, and a combat air patrol. They were landed by 1000 when the tanker came alongside. Here we are refueling at a spot that a few months back was controlled by the enemy, and we would not have dreamt of entering. Truk is only a stones throw away from us, but here we are.

CONFIDENTIAL

March 26. Our forces have been organized; the operations plans have come aboard, and we are headed for Palau and Yap. When you get on the flight deck and look around, one has a sense of security, since the greatest fleet in the world is before your eyes, and it's headed toward giving the Japs hell. A Jap snooper came in close today, within thirty miles, then left for home. It's doubtful if we will get in undetected, so the next two days will be looked forward to with interest. The pilots took it easy today, most of them sleeping or taking sun baths. At 1600 we had athletics on the flight deck, played keep-away with the medicine ball in the warm sun. Presently we were on the Equator. This is crossing number 42 for us, headed west. Consequently the heat is something to write home about. Ensign Weickhardt's new ship's orchestra entertained the crew on the flight deck. This evening it was a beautiful sunset. Too bad no girls were around to round out the evening.

Wednesday, March 29th. Was a quiet day until noon, when one of the carrier C.A.P. spotted a Betty coming in low and finished it off. About five o'clock the boys picked up a couple more Japs, and ended their flight; this was followed by the "H" carrier planes who downed another. Right after dark, the Nips came in full force, tracers were lighting the sky, and soon one Betty blew up right off our starboard quarter. This was immediately followed with our guns getting a Nip off of our stern, causing beautiful explosions and fires. Immediately after the second one, a third came over our bow, strafed our flight deck, and you can be sure all hands hit the deck. Hubbard, Rickard and Kenyon practically dug a hole falling so hard. The Nips kept coming in and the other ships were giving them warm receptions. All the pilots were ordered to bed, since tomorrow will be a hard day.

March 30th. Today is D-Day. We attacked Palau at 0630. Lt. Cdr. Miller took off and led Fighting Squadron 23 on the fighter sweep to clear the air of Jap planes. Ens. McWilliams, Lt(jg) Syme, and Ens. James were in his division. Lt. Schmidt led the second division with Matlock, Abell, and Hill. Lt(jg) Korr led the third division in with Ens. Vaden, Lt(jg) Olin and Ens. Hendricks. On arriving at the target a few Zeros were encountered, and in quick order two were shot down by Miller and McWilliams. The airfield was then thoroughly strafed. Attacks were carried out all day long without further incident, with the exception of Lt(jg) Webb, whose motor cut out and he made a water landing next to a destroyer. At 8:00 P.M. when all planes were aboard and darkness had set in, the Nips again showed up to attack us with low flying torpedo planes. Ships opened fire from all directions, and tracers were going in all directions. This lasted a few hours, and finally those that were left decided to go home.

March 31st. The second day of attack on Palau, March 31. The fighter sweep took off at 0730 with Lt. Cdr. Miller, McWilliams, Syme, and James. Schmidt led the second division with Matlock, Abell, and Hill; Les Korr the third with Muhlfeld, Olin and Hendrickson. The fireworks began early; on the way in Syme spotted a Betty and with a beautiful run shot it down. On arriving at the target, Zeros all over the sky greeted our boys. Olin and Hendrickson had to return with motor trouble; but the rest of the boys waded in with guns blazing and carried on dog fights for an hour without stopping. Schmidt's division waded in and in a few minutes had shot down eight Zeros. Abell after shooting down one, returned to base with Les Korr who had engine trouble. Les already had shot down two however. After shooting down a Zero, Lt. Cdr. Miller and Ensign McWilliams strafed the airfield. Lt. Schmidt after getting two, stuck around with Ensign Hill who shot down three. Ens. Matlock with one to his credit. Likewise for Ens. James and Lt(jg) Muhlfeld.

On returning to base Claude discovered that Muhlfeld was badly wounded and also that their gas was dangerously low; so after frantic calls, landed on the nearest base.

CONFIDENTIAL

During all this melee, Lt(jg) Kirschke with his division of Lt(jg) Darby, Lt(jg) Massey, and Ensign Brugger were sent out on combat air patrol to intercept an approaching torpedo plane. The boys located the Jap, and in quick order shot it down. When all our planes were aboard and a count taken, it was discovered that Jimmie Syme was missing. Some believe that they saw him parachute, so searches are being made to try and locate him.

In the afternoon attack our group escorted our torpedo bombers to the target. Mr. Miller spotted a Zero and shot him down. Kirschke, Darby, Massey and Brugger; and Crockett's division of Vadon, Tyner and Weickhardt flew in also and strafed all installations.

Later in the afternoon Lt(jg) Korr led his division into Palau to search for Syme, but without success. Ensign James returned to our carrier, and brought word that Lt(jg) Muhlfeld was all right, despite severe wounds. Muhlfeld and James each shot down a Zero, which made our day's total 15 Jap planes. For the first time in three nights we were not under attack. Consequently all hands got a well earned sleep.

The score is as follows:

March 30		March 31	
Miller	1	Schmidt	2
McWilliams	1	Matlock	1
	2	Abell	1
		Hill	3
		McWilliams	1
		Kirschke's Div.	1
		Syme	1 Betty
		Korr	2
		Miller	1
		James	1
		Muhlfeld	1
			15

April 1, 1944. At 0730 three of our divisions took off on the fighter sweep over Woleai, just east of Palau, and west of Truk. They were Lt.Cdr. Miller's division, Kirschke's, and Crockett's divisions. On the way unidentified planes were encountered, which threw our planes off course, and they never reached the target. The balance of today's attacks on Woleai were cancelled, so combat air patrols were flown. Despite distance and war, a dispatch arrived detaching Lt. Cdr. Miller; he has avoided reporting to the CVE for three months; the question is, can he put this one off?

April 2. This was a day of rest; the ship took on fuel, and Joe Webb was returned to us from the destroyer that picked him up. Our combat air patrol took off for a short hop.

April 3. Lt. Comdr. Ralph Fuoss received orders today designating him Commanding Officer of Fighting Squadron 23, and orders came designating Lt. Cdr. Hatcher as Air Group Commander. The question remains whether Lt. Cdr. Miller will remain until Ralph is qualified, which may mean a few more weeks' delay, and maybe another operation. Tally Ho Ack Ack announced today that we are headed for our usual port in the Marshall Islands, and should arrive at the end of the week. Good News; it may mean mail for us. There was only one flight today, an early C.A.P. Lt. Comdr. Miller and Lt(jg) Coyer took Ensigns Parker and Blyth with them for a little experience.

April 4. This was all sleep and no work. It poured rain all day, so even the sun baths were curtailed. We again crossed and re-crossed the Equator, making our total equal 44 crossings.

- 22 -

CONFIDENTIAL

April 5. Rain all day; all flights cancelled.

Today is Holy Wednesday, April 5, again. We are headed toward the Marshalls, and have picked up the day we lost on going to Espiritu. Tomorrow we are due to arrive, so will be anticipating overdue mail.

April 6. The following message was received from the Task Group Commander: For Air Group and Squadron Commanders x I sincerely appreciate the cooperation and support given me by your commands during the operations now terminated x It will be a pleasure to serve with you on any and all future operations x signed, Ginder.

April 7th. Mail was delivered last night. Consequently today everyone was answering letters. Some of the boys went ashore and enjoyed a few beers under the palm trees. Muhlfold was transferred to the USS RELIEF this afternoon; we should be able to pick him up at Pearl later, when we get there.

April 8th. Four new pilots reported to us today; Lt. Tripp, and Ensigns Sprinkle, Farnsworth, and Schollenberg. Everyone is taking things leisurely and doing a lot of sleeping.

April 9th. Easter Sunday. Sunrise services were held on the flight deck at 0630; then at 0800 Catholic mass was celebrated in the hangar deck. Later in the day most of the boys went to the beach for a swim and a drink of beer.

On Monday an Air Group outing was arranged, so that at 0900 all started to go ashore and set up an O Club in a vacant Quonset hut, on one of the islands. A ball game between the married and unmarried officers ended in the fifth inning, with half the married ones leaving the game due to exhaustion, but with them leading. By 1300 we had consumed our supply of liquor. However other air groups arrived with their beverages just in time, so that the Bar continued to serve, and everyone had more than enough. Some had cameras; when a picture was to be taken of someone, before it was snapped, everyone had posed and gotten his face into the group. The party broke up around 1700 with everyone feeling their way through the coconut trees and helping each other out of the island jungle.

The next day was a quiet day after the outing; some made an appearance, and some did not.

April 13th. Preparations were being made in order to get under way. Lt. Cdr. Miller, Crockett, McWilliams and Tynor went ashore at 0630 in order to fly new planes aboard. The ship was under way at 1200. From the flight deck we watched the world's greatest fleet steam out of the lagoon; it was a magnificent sight watching each type of ship steam out in single file. We are headed south, and will take part in the biggest operations yet carried out in the Pacific; it will mean the end of the Jap in a certain area. The operations plan was being carefully studied, and lectures being prepared for the pilots. As the ship weighed anchor, great quantities of mail were delivered, so that everyone was in a happy frame of mind.

Friday, April 14th. One combat air patrol took off for a routine flight. When the boys landed they provided everyone with excitement. The first one aboard, John Hill, hit the barrier. Then came Parker, and practically repeated the story. Sprinkle followed, and blew out a tire. Lack of wind across the deck was the main trouble. Lectures on New Guinea are being given to all the pilots, along with the plans for the coming landing operations, which are to be of gigantic size. Our task group, of which Admiral Black Jack Reeves is in command, is composed of numerous types of ships, and large enough to handle any situation that the Japs may wish to throw against us.

CONFIDENTIAL

There was no yesterday, Saturday, 15th of April. It was omitted, and today is Sunday, the 16th, due to the fact that we are again headed West, and therefore are in East Longitude time again.

Surprise gunnery and bombing flights were ordered today by the Admiral, which gave the pilots an opportunity to get in form again. Due to the unexpected flights, all ground school classes were cancelled. Athletics were conducted on the flight deck; calisthenics; then keep-away with the medicine ball.

Monday, April 17th. Last night we crossed the equator for the 45th time. A combat air patrol was flown, and gunnery flights were scheduled. The weather has been perfect, so everyone is acquiring a sun tan.

April 18th. Today was Group Commander day. Each group commander from the various squadrons called on each other, and made final plans for the attacks on New Guinea. Lectures on the targets, and plan of attack were held, so all the pilots are familiar with the whole plan by now.

Wednesday, April 19th. Our radar operators picked up a strange plane about 0300 this morning, which sent all hands to their battle stations, and started an active day. At 0600 a tanker came alongside and refueled us. It was done in record time, since the Task Force had to be refueled today. Los Korr, Weickhardt, Olin, and Blyth took off for a routine combat air patrol. They were catapulted, since there was no wind. However, it was not long before a snooper was picked up, and the boys took after him. As soon as the Jap twin-engine torpedo plane was sighted, he was a dead Jap, and at 1315 he splashed.

We are still a couple of days from our target, but those Nips are persistent guys, so we are expecting more before arriving. Tonight's message from Admiral Reeves: From 58.3 to Princeton: Congratulations.

20th. Last night we re-crossed the Equator for the 46th time, and remained north of it all day. Since yesterday's shooting down of the Jap plane, all the boys are anxious to get in the air and do a little shooting themselves. Two divisions drew patrols today, but no Nips showed up to accommodate them. The high light of the day was a submarine contact inside our screen that sent all hands to their battle stations, and set all the ships zig-zagging frantically; but nothing turned up.

Final lectures on tomorrow's targets were conducted, so all is ready for the attack. Tonight we changed our course, and are headed South, crossing the Equator for the 47th time.

April 21st. D-1 Day. Our squadron was assigned three strikes over the airdromes, Hollandia, Cyclops and Sentani. The first strike, consisting of Lt. Cdr. Miller's and Lt(jg) Korr's divisions took off at 0815, and raked all Jap planes on the runways that could be located through the mass of clouds that covered the fields. Schmidt's and Crockett's divisions were the next to visit the enemy, and carried on with the devastation. While they were coming aboard, the forward elevator broke, with Olin on it. No crack-ups. But the third strike had to be cancelled, which was unfortunate, since a few Jap planes were attempting to escape, and were beautiful targets for our patrolling fighters from a sister carrier. The troop transports are due to arrive tonight, and the landings will be carried on in the morning.

- 24 -

CONFIDENTIAL

D-Day, April 22nd, was uneventful, so far as our expectations were concerned. We sent combat air patrols in over the landing forces, but they were not called on to help in any way whatever. The Japs evidentally moved into the mountains, and will venture forth later. When the planes were returning to base, the weather closed in, and it began to pour. Lieut. Comdr. Miller, Claude Schmidt and Les Kerr were in it, and had a time going through black clouds and with practically a zero ceiling. Our troops landed according to schedule, and were busy building roads as our boys left their patrol sector. Our sector was over Tanahmera Bay, where some of the landings were carried out; the other half of the landings taking place in Humboldt Bay, near the Town of Hollandia.

The 23rd was a quiet, uneventful day. It consisted of routine patrols over our task force and our landing forces. The weather would close in intermittently, which would give the pilots a scare, but the base was always located and all landed safely.

The following day began with an early flight over the landing forces. Jap planes would appear, but leave when our fighters took after them. During the afternoon our boys were called on to strafe ahead of our troops. The Japs had built obstacles along the road, so they were thoroughly strafed. Our planes landed after sundown; it was even necessary for the Signal Officer to use the lighted wands. Just as the boys landed, the Japs appeared over the force, so all hands proceeded to General Quarters. The night fighters shot one down, but the rest of the Japs proceeded on into Hollandia to bomb the landing forces.

April 24th was refueling day for the task group. While the tanker was alongside the balance of the task force was within sight; it was the first time in a few days that we could see them. A Jap bomber came too close, and one of our sister carriers shot him down in a hurry. There were four survivors, who were picked up and delivered to the Admiral. Whether we will stick around or leave is the $64.00 question; everyone is guessing whether we will return to our usual port to go on a raid on the way back. The pilots are all for a direct trip to Pearl. The four pilots we received just before leaving this time, - Tripp, Sprinkle, Farnsworth and Schellenberg, - were permanently transferred to us today.

Not since the Baker Island days has there been more excitement and enthusiasm than today, April 26th, 1944. Lieut.(jg) Webb, Ens. Bledsoe, Ens. J.R. Hill and Ensign Parker took off on a routine combat air patrol at 0610. Lieut.(jg) Tyner's division was also catapulted at the same time, and for the same purpose. Neither Joe Webb or Bob Tyner had at that time shot down any Japs; consequently both boys were hoping for some unsuspecting snooper to appear. It was not long before one did show up; he was near Webb's division. Joe was in luck, and on locating his victim, sent him splashing into the blue Pacific, each of the four boys in the division getting one or more runs on the Nip, so that they each received credit for the kill. All during this time Tyner's division was evidently over the ship, hoping for another Jap to appear. As luck would have it, another one did show up, but he was 20 miles nearer to Webb's division, who were consequently sent out for the intercept. They chased this fellow for a good 70 miles before they finally caught him. It was a new Jap twin-engine fighter, and had the speed, but not enough; since on being overtaken the boys went to work on him, and sent him into the drink.

Having finished up this second Jap, the pilots found themselves a good 100 miles away from their base, and practically out of gas. On hearing of their predicament, Captain Buracker immediately requested permission from the Admiral to be detached from the task group and speed towards our pilots, so as to cut down their distance and take them safely aboard. Permission was granted, so Captain Buracker had them pour the coal on the engines. This consideration won the admiration of the Air Group for the Captain; he really produced when our boys needed help. When the ship met the pilots, Ensign Parker's gas gauge indicated empty. However the ship was already into the wind, and all Parker had to do was head straight in, and with Curtis handling the flags he made a beautiful approach and landing. The other three followed him in, without wave-offs or nervous landings. When the boys were safely aboard, the entire ship roared with three lusty cheers.

- 25 -

CONFIDENTIAL

April 26th (continued).

It looked as though Fighting 23 started something, since in the afternoon the Japs sent in three more snoopers, and each of them went forth to meet his ancestors. We did not get these three, since as luck would have it some other air group had the patrols.

No one mentioned about going home today; everyone wants to get into the air and pick up a Jap or two! This evening the following messages were received:

> TO YOU AND YOUR TASK FORCE, CONGRATULATIONS ON ANOTHER JOB WELL DONE - NIMITZ.

> From CTF 58, to PRINCETON:
> WELL DONE. MITSCHER.

> From CTG 58.3 to PRINCETON:
> GOOD WORK X YOUR BOYS ARE RIGHT ON THE JOB. REEVES.

> From: ComDesDiv 100:
> IF I AM PERMITTED TO SAY QUOTE VERY NICELY DONE UNQUOTE.

> From: INGERSOLL, destroyer:
> THE PLEASURE IS OURS X IT GIVES US A CHANCE TO FEEL WE ARE DOING SOMETHING.

April 27, 1944. Yesterday was a day no one mentioned about going home. However, today a new low has been reached, and a pall has been draped over the squadron. An operation order has just been brought aboard ordering a two-day attack on Truk! It has knocked the boys back on their heels, since everyone was practically packed and on their way home for a few days' leave. However the Jap has to be defeated and the complete destruction of Truk is one step further in reaching our goal; so, Japs beware of Fighting TWENTY THREE, the boys are really hot under the collar this time!

After last night's shock of the contemplated attack on Truk, the boys today are resigned to it, and are gathering all the available information obtainable on the target. The forecastle talk has turned to the humorous side, and now it will be a sensational surprise if we are ever relieved.

April 29th, was devoted to last minute lectures and preparations for tomorrow's attack on Truk. The pilots checked their planes thoroughly and are ready for the Japs. A wonderful surprise greeted us today; we received mail, and we are only 300 miles from Truk! It seems a certain battlewagon joined us, and was thoughtful enough to bring our mail along. We say, Well Done.

April 29th. D-Day; our attacks on Truk took off according to schedule, and the great Jap fortress is being reduced to bubble. Two divisions of fighters went in on the first attack. Lt. Cdr. Miller led the group and had McWilliams, Coyer and James in his division. While over the target a Jap fighter closed and was another dead Jap when Miller and McWilliams boresighted the Nip. Kirschke led his division of Darby, Massey and Brugger in on the first attack also. Big John's division is famous for its desire and aptitude in giving ships and boats hell in strafing runs. The boys really wrapped it up today, and despite severe anti aircraft fire and lurking zeros, they gave the Japs hell.

During this first strike Schmidt's and Kerr's divisions drew combat air patrols. Claud's division was sent out to intercept an unidentified plane, and before he realized it, he was in the middle of Truk and A.A. bursting all around him. This certainly was not his job, so he quickly left that particular spot.

The second strike was composed of Lt. Cdr. Miller, Ens. McWilliams, Lt. Tripp, and Ens. James; also of Lt(jg) Crockett's division of Ens. Vaden, Lt(jg) Tynor and Ens. Hendrickson. The aerial opposition had dwindled considerably, and no Jap planes were to be seen airborne, so the grounded planes were the main objective for the boys.

CONFIDENTIAL

April 29th (continued):
The third strike was led by Lieut. Schmidt and his division of Ensign Matlock, Lt(jg) Abell, and Ens. R. T. Hill, along with Lt(jg) Kerr's division of Ens. Weickhardt and Ens. Blyth. When all had landed everyone was in a happy frame of mind, since all were safe. Break out the rations, Doc.!

Sunday, April 30th. The second continuous day that we are attacking Truk. The same schedule was carried on with the Jap fortress receiving one blow after another. The place is in shambles and good targets are difficult to locate. In the midst of all this activity Lieut. Kenyon received orders to report to N. A. S., Bunker Hill, Indiana. About all that can be said about the place is that he may be lucky to have his family with him if a room is to be found.

May 1st, 1944. Word was received that our ship is ordered back to Pearl along with a couple of others, which news was greeted with smiles and great expectations that upon arriving there we will be sent to the States.

May 2nd was another quiet day. Vice Admiral Mitscher sent out the following:
ONCE AGAIN IT HAS BEEN MY PLEASURE TO SERVE WITH THE FINEST ASSEMBLY OF MEN AND SHIPS IN THE HISTORY OF THE UNIVERSE X MY PRIDE IN THEM IS UNBOUNDED X THIS TIME OUR WAY HAS BEEN LONG AND OUR DUTIES TIRESOME X THE LONGING FOR ENGAGEMENTS WITH THE ENEMY FLEET FORCES WAS NOT ACCOMPLISHED DUE TO THEIR TIMIDITY WE CANNOT GUARANTEE A FIGHT EVERY TIME WE GO TO SEA BUT WE CAN ASSURE OURSELVES AND OUR PEOPLE AT HOME THAT WE WILL BE IN THERE HITTING WHEN THE TIME DOES COME ."

May 4th. We entered our usual port at 1000 and immediately speculated on how long we would stay before shoving off for Pearl and points East. Air Group and squadron pictures were taken next to the bridge, and all the Jap flags indicating the squadron's success in the past year. Lieut. Perkins reported aboard; it took him two months to locate and catch up to us.

May 5th was a quiet day; spent the day turning in ship's gear that had been checked out to us. The Langley Air Group gave us a party, a farewell token, and as expected, it turned out to be quite an affair. Everyone came aboard soaking wet, and cheered up the movie audience. The ship is packed with passengers, so anchors aweigh!

Saturday, the 6th, saw us leave our anchorage in the Marshalls, and head toward Pearl Harbor. We weighed anchor at 0900, with everyone in a happy frame of mind, since we were headed in the right direction. We are due to arrive the 11th, and look forward to a short visit there before leaving for California.

So, for the nonce, ends the War Diary of Fighting 23.

Our schedule to date has been as follows:

    May 28, 1943 - sailed from Hampton Roads, Norfolk.

    July 3, - Returned - 36 days at sea (Trinidad)

    July 21, - Sailed - from Philadelphia Navy Yard.

    August 9, - Pearl. 19 days at sea (Panama)
                        16 days ashore (Barbers Point).

    August 25, - Sailed.

    September 23 - Returned. 29 days at sea (Baker-Tarawa)
                              18 days ashore (Ford Island).

    October 11th - Sailed.

    December 7th - Returned. 57 days at sea (Buka-Bonis, in northern
                              Solomons; Rabaul; Espiritu Santo;
                              Nauru, and capture of Tarawa).
                              34 days ashore (Puunene Air Station, Maui).

    January 10th - Sailed.

    January 13th - Returned. Pearl. (qualified new pilots).
                              3 days at sea.
                              6 days aboard ship at Pearl.

    January 19th - Sailed. Capture of Marshall Islands; Majuro;
                              Espiritu Santo; raid on Palau and Woleai;
                              capture of Hollandia; Raid on Truk.

    May 11th, 1944-Returned. Pearl. 113 days at sea.

        Since May 28, 1943, we have been at sea - 257 days.

        Since May 28, 1943, we have been ashore - 92 days.

AIR GROUP TWENTY THREE STATISTICS

41 enemy planes destroyed in aerial combat (4 by VT-23)
3 enemy planes probably destroyed in aerial combat.
11 enemy planes damaged in aerial combat.
1 enemy plane shot down by ship's gun fire.
11 enemy planes destroyed on the ground.
4 enemy planes probably destroyed on the ground.
11 enemy planes damaged on the ground.
2 enemy heavy cruisers torpedoed.
1 enemy destroyer torpedoed.
1 AK destroyed
1 PT boat set on fire.
6 medium AK thoroughly strafed
2 small AK thoroughly strafed.
1 minesweeper thoroughly strafed.
3 large motor launches strafed.
4 barges thoroughly strafed.
18 boats thoroughly strafed.
62 raids.

9,028.51 combat hours flown.

Ship Statistics.

597,640 pounds of bombs dropped, including 14 torpedoes.
661,710 rounds of ammunition expended by aircraft.
4,867 carrier landings - average interval 40 seconds.
1,386 catapult launchings - average interval 55 seconds.
22 barrier and deck crashes.
 (a) 8 major overhaul.
 (b) 2 minor overhaul.
 (c) 2 complete losses.
844,108 gallons of aviation gasoline consumed.
13,990 gallons of motor oil consumed.
80,962 miles travelled by the ship.
8,241,483 gallons of fuel oil consumed by the ship.

Summary of Strikes:

Makin - 1
Tarawa - 1
Buka - 2
Bonis - 2
Rabaul - 1 (5 Nov 1943)
Rabaul - 1 (11 Nov 1943)
Nauru - 3
Wotje - 16 (9 were CAP over Wotje)
Taroa - 4 (1 was CAP over Taroa)
Eniwetok- 27 (13 were CAP over Eniwetok)
Palau - 4
Hollandia- 9 (7 were CAP over Hollandia)
Truk - 5
 76
 7 (CAP over task force resulting in action)
Total - 83

CONFIDENTIAL

Strikes per pilot

Pilot	Strikes	CAP over enemy territory
Miller, H. L., Lt. Cdr.	26	16 CAP; 3 Air Coordinator
Schmidt, C.C., Lieut. 124507	21	15
Crockett, S.K., Lt(jg) Stanley 5-01-43	12	10
Kerr, L.H., Lt(jg)	14	10
Abell, J.K., Lt(jg)	20	16
Kirschke, W.J., Lt(jg)	15	9 (took pictures 16 times)
Tynor, R.S., Lt(jg)	13	13
Olin, D.H., Lt(jg)	10	10
Webb, J.H., Lt(jg)	13	10 CAP; 2 Air Coordinator.
Syme, J.W., Lt(jg)	17	13
Massey, D.E., Lt(jg) -156706 1-01-44	12 Eugene	11
Coyer, F., Jr., Lt(jg) 158105 1-01-44	15	13
Darby, G.J., Lt(jg) 156972 3-01-44	10	10
Muhlfeld, F.B., Lt(jg) 156761 3-01-44	8 Bearss	11
Pupillo, C.S., Lt(jg)	12	4
Vaden, F.W., Ens. 251392 5-01-44	12 William	11
Hill, J.R., Ens. 263766 5-01-44	12 Roland	11
Matlock, G.J., Ens. 63544 5-01-44	10 Joseph	17
McWilliams, L.F., Ens. 263508 5-01-44	18 Francis	16
James F., Ens. 263532 5-01-44	18	18
Hendrickson, H.E., Ens.	14	11
Brugger, L.O., Ens. 283044 6-16-43	7 OTIS	8
Nicklin, T., Ens. 283077 6-16-43	3	9
Juickhardt, C.E., Ens.	8	9
Hill, R.T., Ens.	2	4
Blyth, R.I., Ens.	2	13
Tripp, D.K., Lieut.	1	2
Sprinkle, C.I., Ens.	0	2
Bledsoe, I.T., Ens.	0	0
Parker, W.E., Ens.	0	0
	325	291

5 Air coordinator
16 photographic missions.

Talk by Commander Henry L. Miller, Commander, Carrier Air Group SIX at Propeller Club Luncheon 21 June 1944.

Gentlemen, the first part of my story sounds like the Mutual Admiration Society of Navy and Merchant Marine getting together for a lengthy pat on the back. Nevertheless those of us who have been out that way seeing the supplies pile in, have taken off our hats to you people who build those ships for the Navy and you who operate those ships to get the men and materials to us. We know that the Armed Forces have taken most of the help and realize the shipping industry is operating on a shoe string, that is why we in the Navy just wonder how you do it.

Mr Wheeler suggested that I talk on some war experiences in those battles in the Pacific, so I'll go ahead with a few until I see someone throw in the towel.

My first job in the Big Time was pretty easy. Back in February of '42 I received the assignment of training General Doolittles' pilots to take off from a carrier to hit Tokyo. It was thrilling work for me because up to that part of the war, I was instructor at the Naval Air Station, Pensacola, Florida and I at least felt that with this assignment I was finally getting into some contact with war. After a free ride on the Hornet to the jumping off spot for the Bombers, I returned to the U.S.A. and in August got orders to a Fighter Squadron as Squadron Commander. Our assignment was aboard the new navy cruiser hull carrier. After training like a bunch of <u>beavers</u> for several months during which time I got to be Group Commander in addition to my Squadron Commanders job, we headed for the Pacific and the war with the Japs. We weren't long in getting started. While other carriers were hitting Marcus Island, we covered a landing force that built an air strip on Baker Island, after which we hit Tarawa and

Makin. From there, we started to play the South Pacific circuit where the going was really tough. After four (4) strikes on Bougainville, to keep those airfields neutralized while our forces made landings at Empress Augusta Bay, Admiral Halsey ordered us on an all out strike against the strongest spot in the South Pacific, Rabaul. The Japs had a strong cruiser and destroyer force there just ready to come down and knock off our small force at Empress Augusta Bay. We with a big carrier, killed that deal by sinking or seriously damaging eight (8) cruisers and two (2) destroyers in Rabaul Harbor. That strike was pretty rugged. Everything in the Pacific after that was anti-climax. The A.A. was so intense that it seemed as tho one could step out of his plane and walk down from 20,000 feet to the ground. In addition, there were 75 - 100 Jap fighters in the air, of which our task group shot down about twenty-five (25). One of my pilots protected the Group Commander of the big carrier. He shot down one (1) Jap fighter and came back with 288 bullet holes in his plane. The Hellcat looked like a sieve. They even shot the wrist watch off his wrist and the throttle out of his hand. He was ready to go in to battle again about ten (10) days later. We hit Rabaul again about a week later, then started for Nauru Island which we beat up pretty badly while the other carriers were hitting Tarawa. From Nauru, we proceeded to Tarawa where we helped out while the landing forces were taking that island. When that job was in the bag, we proceeded to Pearl Harbor at which place the pilots got some much needed rest before going on the Marshalls Operation. Civilization really looked good to us for a change, plus fresh vegetables, a can of beer, and those wonderful island steaks. The people in the islands were very generous in their hospitality and did much in providing a home-away-from-home for the pilots over Xmas.

In January, we hit the Marshalls with the whole works. Our assignment was the islands of Wotje, and Taroa. In three (3) days of bombing and strafing, those islands looked pretty moth eaten and the Japs took an awful pasting. It looked pretty easy, so off we went to the Northwest part and started in on Eniwetok where after bombing the place to pieces, we supported the landings. When the air strip was smoothed over at Eniwetok, some of us were given the opportunity to fly in and land and see the damage that we had done. One and one half (1½) hours on that island and our hearts went out to the Army, Navy and the Marines who had to live on the place. It was full of holes from bombardment, full of dead Japs, and full of just plain dirt. I didn't feel clean for a week.

Our next operation was close ahead. We joined up with the rest of the Carrier Navy, the BB, CAs, and DDs and proceeded to find out what the Japs had at Palau about 500 miles from the Phillippines. The U.S. Navy that we saw was really an impressive sight. There were ships as far as the eye could see. The day before we got in there, the Japs picked us up and of course sent quite a few torpedoes plane attacks against us that nite. Well, they never got back to tell the folks about what they saw because our fighters and ships gun fire knocked them all down. Our task force got quite a few ships, shore installations, and about 90 Jap planes on that operation. On the way back, we made raids on Yap and Woleai islands, left our calling cards, and returned to our base.

Hollandia was next on the list. We worked with General McArthur in bombing the spot and supporting the landings. The hardest part of that work was the weath It seems as tho there are always a maze of thunder storms around there and one just has to get by them some way. At times it is nip and tuck but fortunately we didn't lose any planes on that account. With the greater part of the Navy down in the Southwest Pacific it seemed to be a pretty good idea to give Truk a jolt as we went by. So on 29 and 30 April, we spent quite a few hours dropping bombs, strafing ground installations, and shooting down planes at that Jap stronghold. It looked pretty sick when we left. Every island in that atoll that had anything of value on it was bombed. On the second day, all the planes were given the big island of Dublon at Truk for a target, that spot was really plastered. We had cleaned out all the planes in the air and on the ground the previous day, so there was no air opposition the next day.

Truk was the last job for our Air Group. After 9½ months of combat, we returned to the states for some rest, then to reform and go out again. I was given a bigger Air Group, and at present we are in a training status trying to get to the point of being a hot outfit before going out to the Big Time.

Our Air Group was together for 18½ months. During that period, we lived, and fought together most of the time. An outfit like that really gets pretty close, in a way, just as close as any family. When the time comes for breaking up and going back for a rest, one certainly hates to do the parting. We had a fine bunch of boys who got along together beautifully. If we lost one after all that we had been thru, it was pretty hard to take. As a comparison, a husband sees his family after the days work is done. We were together for 18½ months almost every day, all day.

The war game always has its amusing side. One squadron in the South Pacific had a young pilot, who was trying to make good, going down to Guadalcanal for some supplies so they told him to try and bring back some beer. This youngster put about four (4) cases of canned beer in the wings of his plane just aft of the ammunition boxes and proceeded to return to his base. On the way, he figured that a strafing run on this Jap island would finish up a good day so down he went. The pilot realized the plane was hit after he pulled out of his strafing run and had a hard time sitting it down at his home base. However, with the whole squadron waiting for the beer, he felt quite the hero until they opened up the wing and found that a 90 millimeter shell from the AA had gone thru the four (4) cases of beer.

On one job where we were supporting the landings on an island, we listened in on the tank circuit. The lead tank called another and said "Hey Joe, I've got all the Japs pushed back on this corner, how's to tell the other tanks to come up here and give me a hand". Joe called back and said "I'll be right there but those other guys are all down in the south end hunting souvenirs". The great American boy

One of our really crack Group Commanders who is just now coming back for a rest got so enthused over an attack that he forgot to use his bean for a couple of minutes. The following conversation tells the story. Lets call the characters Singing Sam and Barry.

"Barry this is Singing Sam, go ahead" — No answer.

"Barry this is Singing Sam, answer me" — No answer.

Very indignant now —

"Barry, this is Singing Sam, when I call you, answer me" — Still no answer

a long pause, then "Barry, this is Singing Sam, if you don't hear me, turn on your radio"!

If the ships are fortunate in dropping the hook at the right base, one can usually find enuff nurses for a dance. Just before we hit Palau, we were at one of those bases and the boys were making up for lost time. Two carriers had a party then came out turn. Our pilots wanted to have the best one that was ever put on, so for three (3) days, they went tearing around the countryside bartering real eggs and real round potatoes, no foolin', for dates with the nurses. It was pretty tough going because the nurses at this base had lots of Army, Navy and Marines who

ISBN 978-3-11-075130-7
e-ISBN (PDF) 978-3-11-075132-1
e-ISBN (EPUB) 978-3-11-075150-5
DOI https://doi.org/10.1515/9783110751321

Dieses Werk ist lizenziert unter einer Creative Commons Namensnennung - Nicht-kommerziell - Keine Bearbeitung 4.0 International Lizenz. Weitere Informationen finden Sie unter https://creativecommons.org/licenses/by-nc-nd/4.0/.

Library of Congress Control Number: 2022932168

Bibliografische Information der Deutschen Nationalbibliothek
Die Deutsche Nationalbibliothek verzeichnet diese Publikation in der Deutschen Nationalbibliografie; detaillierte bibliografische Daten sind im Internet über http://dnb.dnb.de abrufbar.

© 2022 Ottmar Ette, publiziert von Walter de Gruyter GmbH, Berlin/Boston
Dieses Buch ist als Open-Access-Publikation verfügbar über www.degruyter.com.

Coverabbildung: John Everett Millais: Ophelia, circa 1851. Öl auf Leinwand. London: Tate. Quelle: Wikimedia Commons: gemeinfrei. https://commons.wikimedia.org/wiki/File: John_Everett_Millais_-_Ophelia_-_Google_Art_Project.jpg
Satz: Integra Software Services Pvt. Ltd.
Druck und Bindung: CPI books GmbH, Leck

www.degruyter.com

Vorwort

Vorlesungen und Forschungen stehen in engem wechselseitigen Durchdringungsverhältnis: Was die Forschungen an Ergebnissen zeitigen, fließt direkt in die Vorlesungen ein; und in den Vorlesungen wird das ausgetestet, was als Ergebnis der Forschung publiziert und in die wissenschaftliche Zirkulation gegeben werden kann. Für die Studierenden in den Vorlesungen ist es wichtig, sozusagen an der Bugwelle der Forschung teilzuhaben und durch eigene Anregungen diese Forschungen, ja selbst die Richtung dieser Forschungen verändern zu können. Das große Interesse der Studierenden an existenziellen Lebensfragen hat die Richtung meiner Forschungen stets beflügelt. Auf diese Weise bilden Vorlesungen die Bühne für Forschungen, die im Werden sind; sie ermöglichen eine erste Rückmeldung, wie Forschungsrichtungen ‚ankommen' bei denen, die im Labor der Lehrveranstaltungen maßgeblich zur Einheit von Forschung und Lehre beitragen: also bei den Studierenden. Ihnen sei an dieser Stelle für unendlich viele Fragen und Anregungen Dank gesagt!

In keiner meiner Vorlesungen dürfte das Wechselverhältnis zwischen Forschung und Vorlesung – auch in der Verbindung mit Seminaren und Kolloquia – intensiver gewesen sein als bei den Vorlesungen über Geburt, Leben, Sterben und Tod. Die Wissenschaft von den Literaturen der Welt – und auch die Romanistik in ihrer Gesamtheit – muss sich schon aus Freude an der literarischen Kunst mit existenziellen Grundfragen und Grundbegriffen beschäftigen. Denn genau dies tun die Literaturen der Welt. Es gibt folglich Fragestellungen, die vom Objekt der Forschung her direkt vorgegeben sind – und dazu gehören die Lebensfragen.

Aber nicht allein die Literaturen der Welt und das Interesse der Studierenden geben diese Zielstellung und diese Fragehorizonte vor: Es sind auch die Philologien, die hier bewusst in der Mehrzahl genannt seien. Denn in der Geschichte und Tradition abendländischer Philologie sind Grundfragen des Lebens ebenso präsent wie in Tradition und Geschichte nicht-abendländischer Philologien wie etwa der chinesischen. Wenn wir die unterschiedlichsten Eigenlogiken der Literaturen der Welt berücksichtigen wollen, so sollten wir dies zunehmend auch auf der Ebene philologischer Grundeinstellungen tun. Die mit diesem neuen, sechsten Band der Reihe „Aula" vorgelegten Vorlesungen versuchen, transareal eine Erweiterung der auf die Romanistik bezogenen und beziehbaren Objekt-Areas ebenso vorzunehmen wie nach Fragestellungen zu suchen, welche nicht nur der Geschichte der abendländischen Philologie gerecht werden.

∂ Open Access. © 2022 Ottmar Ette, publiziert von De Gruyter. Dieses Werk ist lizenziert unter einer Creative Commons Namensnennung - Nicht-kommerziell - Keine Bearbeitung 4.0 International Lizenz.
https://doi.org/10.1515/9783110751321-202

Wie stets wurden die Texte der Vorlesung vor dem wöchentlichen Halten der Vorlesung erarbeitet und nach den entsprechenden Sitzungen wiederum überarbeitet. Dabei folgte der Verfasser jener Arbeitsweise, die bislang bei all seinen Vorlesungsbänden zur Anwendung kam. Für die schriftliche Endredaktion der unterschiedlichen Bände wurden alle Skripte noch einmal grundlegend ausgestaltet und selbstverständlich an den jeweiligen Grundfragen überprüft und ausgerichtet. Die zwischen Forschungen und Vorlesungen entstehende Vernetzung ist offenkundig; sie geht im Sinne der Studierenden und der zu erfüllenden Curricula zugleich weit über die thematischen Ausrichtungen meiner Forschungspublikationen hinaus.

Mit der Veröffentlichung der drei Bände *Von den historischen Avantgarden bis nach der Postmoderne. Potsdamer Vorlesungen zu den Hauptwerken der romanischen Literaturen des 20. und 21. Jahrhunderts*, *Romantik zwischen zwei Welten. Potsdamer Vorlesungen zu den Hauptwerken der romanischen Literaturen der Welt im 19. Jahrhundert* sowie *Aufklärung zwischen zwei Welten. Potsdamer Vorlesungen zu den Hauptwerken der romanischen Literaturen des 18. Jahrhundert* ist die Reihe der literarhistorischen Vorlesungen in dem Sinne abgeschlossen, dass in diesen Bänden zum Ausdruck kommt, was der Verfasser zu diesen literaturgeschichtlichen Fragestellungen zu sagen hat. Dass sie keine verkappten Literaturgeschichten darstellen, besagen bereits die Titel dieser Bände. Dass sie zugleich eine transareale Neuorientierung der Romanistik intendieren, braucht an dieser Stelle nicht nochmals wiederholt zu werden: Es handelt sich um Bände, die meinen Überlegungen zur Romanistik als einer Archipel-Wissenschaft entspringen.

Doch nicht allein die literarhistorischen, sondern auch die thematischen Bände sind transarchipelisch und stets aus der Bewegung aufgebaut. Dies gilt für den ersten Band der Reihe „Aula", der sich vordringlich dem Verhältnis von Reisen und Schreiben wie in einer Art Grundlagenbuch widmete, wie für den zweiten Band, der die Beziehung zwischen Lieben und Lesen untersuchte. Mit dem sechsten Band kehren die Vorlesungen wieder zur thematischen Ausrichtung zurück, so auch der Titel des vorliegenden Bandes: *Geburt Leben Sterben Tod. Potsdamer Vorlesungen über das Lebenswissen in den romanischen Literaturen der Welt*. Ein freiheitsbasiertes, polylogisches Denken in transarealen Zusammenhängen war bei einem gewissen Mut zur Lücke auch bei dieser themenorientierten Vorlesung das Ziel.

Inmitten der Vorbereitungen seines eigenen brillanten Habilitationsverfahrens gilt Markus Alexander Lenz mein herzlicher und freundschaftlicher Dank für die wie immer stets umsichtige und zielführende redaktionelle Bearbeitung, für kluge Ideen und viele anregende Gespräche, die wir am Rande der Vorlesungen führten. Wenn in nicht allzu ferner Zukunft einmal die Arbeit an diesen Vorlesungen zu Ende gegangen sein wird, werde ich unsere anregenden, nicht selten lustigen Gespräche, in denen ein Wort das andere gab und wir immer wieder neue Horizonte für die Forschung erörterten, sehr vermissen. Für den vorliegenden Band hat Markus überdies die Illustrationen besorgt, wofür ich ihm ebenfalls sehr dankbar bin. Mein Dank gilt des weiteren Ulrike Krauss, die sich von Beginn an beim Verlag Walter de Gruyter für die einzelnen Bände und die Gesamtidee der Reihe „Aula" eingesetzt hat, sowie Gabrielle Cornefert, die auch diesen Band verlagsseitig und gemeinsam mit zahlreichen Mitwirkenden wieder bestens betreute. Meiner Frau Doris gebührt mein Dank für den initialen Anstoß, die Manuskripte meiner Vorlesungen in Buchform zu veröffentlichen, und für die liebevollen Ermutigungen, das Vorhaben der Reihe über die Jahre weiterzuführen.

Ottmar Ette
Potsdam, 28. April 2022

were more or less permanent settlers on this island. Party day came around and only about 12 of the pilots had dates. Nevertheless, they went ahead with the arrangements. Down-stairs of this so called club was fixed up with the food (a buffet supper), soft lites, sweet music (from a makeshift quartet who were pretty good), and all sorts of nite club effects. Up-stairs, they had the big orchestra, which was borrowed, the bar, dancing, tables, and even a photographer. Everything was all set but the gal situation, when lo and behold, two hours before the Big Event a hospital ship steamed into the harbor. Our boys were out there in boats before they anchored and when the orchestra played its opening number, in marched about 25 brand new fresh caught nurses with our pilots just beaming behind them. The other two Group Commanders turned around, looked at me and said "O.K. Miller, you win".

Thank you gentlemen for your kind attention, it was certainly a pleasure to be here. —

www.ingramcontent.com/pod-product-compliance
Lightning Source LLC
Chambersburg PA
CBHW080621170426
43209CB00007B/1485